D0554482

A LAND GONE

LONESOME

OTHER BOOKS BY DAN O'NEILL

The Firecracker Boys

The Last Giant of Beringia:
The Mystery of the Bering Land Bridge

A LAND GONE
LONESOME

An Inland Voyage
Along the Yukon River

DAN O'NEILL

COUNTERPOINT
A MEMBER OF THE PERSEUS BOOKS GROUP
NEW YORK

Portions of this book are based on the essay "Coming Out of the Country" published in *Under Northern Lights: Writers and Artists View the Alaskan Landscape,* University of Washington Press, 2000.

Copyright © 2006 by Dan O'Neill
Published by Counterpoint,
A Member of the Perseus Books Group

All rights reserved. Printed in the United States of America. No part of this book may be reproduced in any manner whatsoever without written permission except in the case of brief quotations embodied in critical articles and reviews. For information, address Counterpoint, 387 Park Avenue South, New York, NY 10016-8810.

Counterpoint books are available at special discounts for bulk purchases in the United States by corporations, institutions, and other organizations. For more information, please contact the Special Markets Department at the Perseus Books Group, 11 Cambridge Center, Cambridge MA 02142, or call (617) 252-5298 or (800) 255-1514, or e-mail special.markets@perseusbooks.com.

DESIGNED BY JEFF WILLIAMS

Library of Congress Cataloging-in-Publication Data

O'Neill, Dan (Daniel T.)
   A land gone lonesome : an inland voyage along the Yukon River / Dan O'Neill.
     p. cm.
   Includes index.
   ISBN-13: 978-1-58243-344-8 (hardcover : alk. paper)
   ISBN-10: 1-58243-344-5 (hardcover : alk. paper)
   1. O'Neill, Dan (Daniel T.)—Travel—Yukon River (Yukon and Alaska) 2. Yukon River (Yukon and Alaska)—Description and travel. 3. Canoes and canoeing—Yukon River (Yukon and Alaska) I. Title.
F912.Y9O64 2006
917.98'6—dc22
2006007323

10 9 8 7 6 5 4 3 2

For Kyle

HEADINGS IN
GEOGRAPHIC ORDER

Dawson City, Yukon Territory, 1

Moosehide, 9

Chandindu River, 17

Fifteenmile River, 23

Halfway House, 25

Cassiar Creek, 27

Hammer Bar/Sunset Creek, 30

Fortymile River and Forty Mile, 31

Coal Creek, 40

Old Man and Old Woman Rocks, 41

Mel's Camp, 42

Stan Zuray, 46

Bill Fliris/*Ichthyophonus Hoferi*, 49

Dozen Islands, 53

Fanning Creek, 54

Poppy Creek, 55

Robert Cameron's Cabin, 57

Bio Camp, 58

The Border, 59

Steve Ulvi and Lynette Roberts, 60

Eagle, 65

Seymour Able, 69

Calico Bluff, 80

Seventymile River, 81

Seventymile City and Star City, 86

Tatonduk River, Heinie Miller, 86

Dick Cook, 89

Wood Islands, 121

Montauk Bluff, 123

Pollack Joe, 126

Nation River/Dave Evans, 129

Nation City, 140

Taylor's Place, 141

Ivy City, 142

Rock Creek, 143

Glenn Creek, 147

Seymour's Old Camp, 148

The Steam Tractor, 151

George Beck's Cabin at
    Washington Creek, 152

Washington Creek Roadhouse,
    152

Charley's Village, 154

Sarge Waller's Cabin, 155

Ricketts's Cabin, 156

Biederman's, 157

Kandik Trappers, 162

Randy Brown, 165

Dirty Fred's Cabin, 173

Mail Trail Way Station, 175

Crazy Man Island, 176

Ed Gelvin's A-Frame, 178

Charley River/Charlie Kidd, 180

Ames Cabin, 183

Sam Creek/Carolyn Kelly, 189

Slaven's Roadhouse, Coal Creek,
    195

Coal Creek Dredge and Camp,
    197

Woodchopper Roadhouse, 200

Woodchopper Creek/Joe Vogler,
    201

Eureka Creek/The Other
    Fortymile, 213

Falcons and Jaguars, 220

Shahnyaati', 228

Into Circle City, 230

Afterword, 238

Index, 245

Acknowledgments, 243

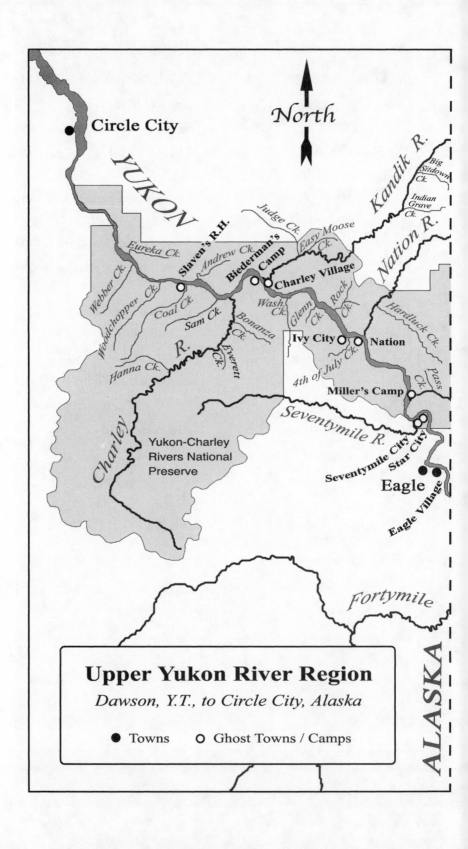

Circle City

YUKON

Judge Ck.

Eureka Ck.
Slaven's R.H.
Andrew Ck.
Biederman's Camp
Easy Moose Ck.
Charley Village

Webber Ck.

Woodchopper Ck.

Coal Ck.

Sam Ck.

R.

Wash. Ck.

Glenn Ck.

Rock Ck.

Ivy City

Nation

Hanna Ck.

Bonanza Ck.

Everett Ck.

4th of July Ck.

Kandik R.

Big Sitdown Ck.

Indian Grave Ck.

Nation R.

Hardluck Ck.

Miller's Camp

Charley

Yukon-Charley
Rivers National
Preserve

Seventymile R.

pass Ck.

Seventymile City
Star City

Eagle

Eagle Village

Fortymile

ALASKA

Upper Yukon River Region

Dawson, Y.T., to Circle City, Alaska

● Towns   ○ Ghost Towns / Camps

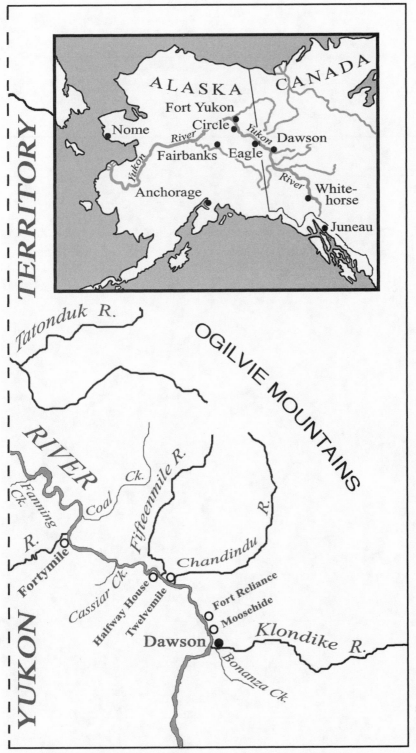

TERRITORY

ALASKA CANADA

Fort Yukon
Nome   Circle   Yukon   Dawson
River
Fairbanks   Eagle

Anchorage   River   Whitehorse

Juneau

Tatonduk R.

OGILVIE MOUNTAINS

RIVER

Coal Ck.

Fanning Ck.

R.

Fortymile   Fifteenmile R.

Chandindu R.

Cassiar Ck.

Halfway House   Twelvemile   Fort Reliance

Moosehide

Dawson   Klondike R.

Bonanza Ck.

YUKON

O'Neill

A LAND GONE
LONESOME

Dawson City, Yukon Territory

It is a fine Saturday morning in mid-August. I am hammering in my boat stake among a row of riverboats at the Dawson City beach on the Yukon River. Whack. Whack. Whack. Suddenly something large and very near me moves. It had been lying so inert in the bottom of an open skiff next to my canoe that I hadn't seen it. It is a wild thing with matted black fur. Irritated now, it props itself up, half in and half out of a canvas tarp that contains in its folds remnant pools of last night's rain. It—he—is pale to the point of bloodless. Through his beard, parched-looking lips suggest cotton-mouthed dehydration. The morning light is not welcome either. Only one eye is cracked a slit, just enough for him to determine the source of his torment. For a moment, I hold the ax head suspended. He stares. He does not speak, but I hear him wondering if it is absolutely necessary for me to be here, pounding that goddamned stake through his brain. I take it as a wordless "Welcome to Dawson." Nodding to the town greeter, I give the stake one last skull-cracking wallop and leave him soaking in remnant pools of last night's partying.

The discovery that launched the Klondike gold rush came on August 16, 1896. That day, Discovery Day, is a holiday in Canada's Yukon Territory. Coincidentally, today is August 16, and as I stroll into Dawson, the Discovery Day parade rolls through the center of town. At the head is a detachment of the Royal Canadian Mounted Police (RCMP). A half dozen scarlet-jacketed Mounties march in step behind a handsome, square-jawed officer riding a glossy, black, prancing horse. Cameras snap as the troop files past the still-operating hundred-year-old post office, with its door set into a turret in the corner of the building. Past Diamond Tooth Gertie's, where Dawson's signature cancan girls perform nightly. Past the restored three-story Palace Grand Theatre, built in 1899 by an old Indian fighter who entertained patrons by shooting glass balls from between his wife's thumb and index finger. Next, the silver-haired members of the Yukon Order of Pioneers proceed in quaint and stately grace in vintage automobiles, like an old photo colorized and come to life. A flatbed truck serves as a mobile stage for Barnacle Bob Hilliard, the local piano player, an important personage in a gold camp of any era. He is hunched over the keyboard, clawing out ragtime, his face hidden by a mass of tangled hair that bounces emphatically in time. Making sure no one is sucked into a time warp, a file of decibel-dueling muscle trucks brings up the rear. They hang back and rev their unmuffled engines until we spectators have to cover our ears. When their attention spans catch up with them, they pop clutches and lurch back into position. The parade is a little gold rush river of humanity, every character a nugget tumbling by.

Not just on parade day, Dawson is colored by the gaudy circumstances of its birth, comfortable in its skin, happily marketing itself as a raucous frontier town. Walking its streets is like walking through the set of a beer commercial, running now for a hundred years. Here at Second and Queen is the false-fronted Downtown Hotel, home of the "World-famous Sourtoe Cocktail," a tourist favorite. Dawsonites say that during the 1920s, when Alaska was suffering under Prohibition, a pair of local bootleggers named Louie and Otto Liken made a run with their dog team across the border. Deliberately, they mushed into a blizzard, bad weather being in a smuggler's favor. But on this trip they broke through some ice, and Louie soaked one of his feet. There was no time to stop and build a fire because the boys suspected the Mounties were, so to say, dogging their trail. When they finally did stop, Louie's big toe was frozen solid. There was nothing to do but to take the toe off before gangrene set in. Fortunately, the boys were traveling with the surgical essentials: a sharp ax and a sled-load of painkiller.

Half a century later, Captain Dick Stevenson (who has written up this bit of history) was cleaning out the old cabin of the long-gone

Liken brothers when he found the toe preserved in a masonry jar under the floorboards. Stevenson, a former wolf poisoner for the department of game, had turned to trapping tourists. He operated a little tour boat, an imitation of a stern-wheeler. Perhaps it was a happy convergence of these two professions, poisoner and tourist host, that led Stevenson to invent the Sourtoe Cocktail. The directions were simple: drop the toe into a beer glass, fill it with champagne, then "drink it fast, or drink it slow, but the lips have gotta touch the toe."

In "The Ballad of the Ice-Worm Cocktail," gold rush poet Robert Service sketched the boys gulling a newcomer into downing a repulsive worm, which by poem's end turns out to be colored spaghetti. The current Dawsonites have gone Service one better, as the toe is not a fake. It resides at the Sourdough Saloon in the Downtown Hotel. So far, 18,000 people have earned a certificate of membership in the Sourtoe Club, including British Columbia prime minister Gordon Campbell. Of course, among 18,000 rowdies there are going to be a few swallowers. The first was a placer miner named Garry Younger who, in 1980, was shooting for the Sourtoe record. As Younger tossed down his thirteenth toe champagne, his chair fell over backward, and with a gulp the toe was gone. Had it been recovered when Younger passed it, the original Louie Liken toe might still be in use. But a replacement was sent in by a Mrs. Lawrence of Fort Saskatchewan, who'd had it amputated because of a corn. For a while, her toe resided in a jar of salt at the Eldorado Hotel, but it disappeared during renovations. Toe Three was a more traditionally obtained part, having come from a trapper in Faro who lost it to frostbite. Lost to the cold, and lost again to a thieving soldier who set it up as an attraction in a tavern in London, Ontario. The military helped to track down and return the toe in 1983, but it made its final journey soon thereafter when it followed a shot of booze down the gullet of a baseball player from Inuvik. Toe Four had a longer run but met with foul play while on tour at Watson Lake. A Texas big game hunter took it home and refused to give it up until the Watson Lake police asked the Yank how he'd like to face extradition proceedings for transporting human body parts across an international border. Toes Five and Six came as a set from a Yukon old-timer too modest to have his philanthropy recognized. Three women drove all the way from Sudbury, Ontario, to deliver Toe Seven, donated by a diabetic who'd read about Dawson's cultural traditions in the newspaper. The latest toe came from someone who no longer mows the lawn in sandals.

IT IS LIKELY THAT The Pit was the town greeter's undoing. The Pit is the "Beer Parlour" in the Westminster Hotel, which was established in 1898. It's a half-a-block's-worth of false-fronted buildings in the middle of town, all tarted up in pink and purple and strung with Christmas lights, several of which work. Everyone calls it The Pit, even the Parks Canada people at the visitors' center. In its fundamentals, a night at The Pit is not so unlike a night in this same bar during the gold rush. I imagine the atmosphere was the same then as now: charged with a heavy layer of smoke, clothes reeking with sweat and creosote from leaky stove pipes, a volatility fed by testosterone and jangly music. One night a friend of mine saw a scuffle break out over a provocatively dressed inflatable doll. I guess there weren't many other women in the bar at the time, and the doll had attracted two patrons, one staggering through a two-step with her, the other trying more and more insistently to cut in. Push came to shove, but not much more. The last time I was there, the prettiest girl in the place was dressed in Carhart coveralls with tire tread marks running diagonally across the front. I wondered if she'd peeled the clothes off an accident victim, like a thrifty trapper might skin a roadkill. People say The Pit's regular band, the Pointer Brothers, has a bar tab so enormous that the group has become essentially indentured servants, having to work for years into the future without compensation to square up on the bill.

The Pit is also a venue where Elvis Presley once headlined. That's not Elvis Aaron Presley from Tupelo, Mississippi, but Elvis Aaron Presley from Tagish, Yukon Territory. Tagish Elvis. Before the aliens visited, he was known as Gilbert Nelles. Visited, yes, but he insists he was *not* abducted, according to a story in the *Yukon News* by Karan Smith. Rather, a passing UFO bathed him in a harmonic beam of light that suffused his soul with the "conscious awareness" of the rocker, who was then thirteen years dead. That night, the Ghost of Elvis Past appeared in a maroon suit studded with rhinestones. In the morning, Nelles sang a few tunes and decided that he was, essentially, the Elvis Channel. He dyed his hair black and staked out large sections of his cheeks as reserves for sideburns. Later, he legally changed his name to Elvis Aaron Presley and acquired a pink Cadillac, which he adorned with plastic cherubs.

Elvis's career was taking off like a starship, what with gigs in clubs like The Pit and appearances in homemade music videos, when disaster struck. An argument with a neighbor in Tagish resulted in a visit from an RCMP officer who recommended a psychological evaluation. That was defamation, said Elvis, and he sued the Mounties for ten million dollars. It was "The King versus the Queen," as the *Yukon News* had it. And the trial, coming at the end of a long winter, did not disappoint entertainment-starved Yukoners. It was a little like *A Miracle on 34th Street,* with Elvis trying to prove he was *the* Elvis. For a while, Elvis seemed to enjoy the proceedings. He represented himself, showing up at court in a white jumpsuit with multicolored sequins and an embroidered eagle and bear on the back. He brought as exhibits 439 documents about flying saucers, videotapes of his performances, and surveys he'd conducted himself. Several exchanges between Elvis and his fellow officers of the court are possibly among the more memorable in the annals of Yukon jurisprudence. When at one point Elvis referred to the government's distinguished attorney, a Mr. Willis, as his "colleague," Willis leapt to his feet in protest, "I am *not* his colleague!"

Things got worse when Elvis tried to introduce hearsay evidence, specifically a list of people he'd contacted who thought, yes, Elvis did seem a bit odd. This proved *his*, not the government's, point, he figured, because if folks thought Elvis odd, it must be because of the government's campaign of character assassination. The judge, Lucien Beaulieu, attempted to explain the concept of hearsay. He asked Elvis to imagine his honor running around Whitehorse shouting, "I am an egg! I am a hard-boiled egg!" Now, he asked, "Would that prove I am an egg?" Elvis replied evenly, "I am going to have to ask you to step down from this case," and he began to pack up his papers. Judge Beaulieu warned him that leaving the proceedings would mean an end to the lawsuit. "No," said the King to his court, "It is the end of you, your honor. I have dismissed you." With that, Elvis left the building.

DOWNTOWN DAWSON, with its parade and with its tourists—wide as Winnebagos and just as difficult to pass on the narrow wooden sidewalks—can be wearying. You feel vaguely ill, like after a day at the carnival—too much confected sugar and manufactured fun. The river is the antidote, but before pointing myself toward the beach, I head over to Klondike Kate's for a feed. On my way out, I pay with an American twenty-dollar bill and, with the good exchange rate, receive a Canadian twenty in change. "It's like eating for free," I tell the cashier. "No," she says, dropping some coins on top of the twenty, "It's like we paid you to eat."

Dawson's boats could be plotted along the same entropic arc as its people. Just below on the far bank is a steamboat graveyard, where the *Julia B*'s 159-foot deck undulates like a sinusoidal curve, its massive hull relaxing into the contours of the ground beneath it. If you poke around in the brush over there, you can find seven boats, their great paddle wheels looming up amid the leafy willows and alders, boilers and stacks rusting, graying boards peeling away from cabins and decks. During the 1898 stampede, sixty of these wood-fired stern-wheelers worked the Yukon. They carried an amazing assortment of goods: the necessities for extracting gold and sustaining the miners (bacon and beans, hand tools and dynamite), alongside the super-fluities that gold could buy (evening gowns and canned oysters, vin-tage wine and crystal glasses). Tough men—some from the Mississippi, some sea captains—captained the boats, reading the shifting channels of the silty water, dodging the hidden snags and bars. For nearly ninety years, from 1867 to 1955, the great wooden boats were the apotheosis of technical and commercial accomplishment on the Yukon.

Tied up at the Dawson dock today is a cartoon version of a steam-boat, a burlesque of the glory days, with a bright red paddle wheel ready to churn for the tourist dollar. Opposite this lies a flat-bottomed, plywood riverboat, its owner aiming for a down-market niche in the tour-boat game: an overstuffed chair perches in the bow, a bench seat from a pickup truck faces sideways out over the gunwale. Finally, off by itself is an authentic re-creation, if that's not an oxymoron. It is a sailing dory constructed the way Klondike stampeders might have done on the shore of Lake Bennett in 1898. Her hull is of whipsawn spruce planks dripping with tar. The boom is a forked birch tree, its crotch riding a spruce-pole mast. For the cabin, what else? A white canvas wall tent.

I spin my canoe around and step into the stern, shoving off. I had forgotten to notice if the town greeter had left his post, but it is too late to see now. The river sweeps along at five to eight miles per hour, and Dawson unzooms behind me. My own vessel is a nineteen-foot canoe, a square-stern Grumman Freighter. It was shiny silver when I bought it used in Fairbanks twenty-odd years ago, but I've painted it a light, flat green. It has a thirty-nine-inch beam and will haul up to eleven hundred pounds. That is, it will haul two guys, gas, grub, camping gear, and a cut-up moose. Mounted on a lift is a fifteen-horse Evinrude outboard motor that I bought new in 1982. The canoe can do about fifteen miles an hour downstream on the Yukon, ten miles per hour upstream. It is the pace of a Sunday drive in the country in the days of the Model T. It's slow enough that you can feel where you are—you aren't sealed up inside a streamlined bubble, like in a modern car or inside the cab of a riverboat, streaking through the country faster than you can properly take things in.

WHO WAS THE FIRST TO DISCOVER the gold that launched the Klondike gold rush and built Dawson? The answer may depend on your loyalties, or how much of a social lesson you want your history to teach. The Canadians say it was a Canadian; the Americans say it was an American; the Indians say it was an Indian; and a female Indian said it was a female Indian, namely herself. Robert Henderson, the Canadian, did find decent pay (at a not-too-shabby eight cents to the pan) on a creek he named Gold Bottom, a tributary of the Klondike River. But it was George Washington Carmack, the American (obviously), who, after one pan yielded an unheard-of four dollars, filed the discovery claim on Rabbit Creek. Carmack wasn't the first person to spot the gold, however, according to Carmack's Indian sidekicks who had been packers on the Chilkoot Trail. Skookum Jim Mason and Tagish Charley say the white man was snoozing under a birch tree when Jim noticed gold in the creek. Last, Carmack's Indian wife Kate ended her days (after Carmack abandoned her for a white woman) claiming that it was she who found the gold and showed the others.

Robert Henderson knew Carmack wasn't much of a prospector. He knew that the American had sunk a few shafts up in the Fortymile River country but that he preferred the life of the Indian. Carmack did a little fishing, cut a little wood, but clearly was not one of the driven souls working himself into an early grave, hoping to strike it rich. Still, Henderson abided by the code of the prospector and made a point of stopping at Carmack's camp at the mouth of the Klondike in the summer of 1896 to pass the word that decent pay could be found on Gold Bottom Creek. Carmack was only mildly interested. After a bit, he and his friends decided to scout for timber that they might raft up and float down to the sawmill at Fortymile.

If Carmack, the white man, romanticized Indian ways, Skookum Jim was moved by modernity. Money appealed to him. He might have fit in well with such ambitious men as Robert Henderson, but Henderson's dismissive attitude toward the Native people had been apparent from their first meeting. In any event, Carmack, Skookum Jim, and Tagish Charley eventually hiked over the hill above Rabbit Creek, off the Klondike River, to visit Henderson and check out his diggings on Gold Bottom. Henderson was optimistic about the area and encouraged Carmack to prospect Rabbit Creek. He made a point of asking Carmack to come back and let him know if he found good color, even offering to pay Carmack for his trouble. Shortly after they left Henderson busting his hump for pennies, Carmack (or was it Jim or Kate?) discovered gold by the spoonful in Rabbit Creek. Then, for one reason or another, Carmack and his party decided not to walk back the few miles to let Henderson in on the news.

Utterly unaware of the discovery, Henderson toiled away the rest of the summer. He figured he was doing pretty well when he came onto ground producing thirty-five cents to the pan. Meanwhile, Carmack had gone down to Forty Mile* and tilted a shotgun shell casing full of nuggets onto the bar at Bill McPhee's saloon. In no time, men were flooding in from all over the district to Rabbit Creek, and a town— Dawson—was springing up just a few miles away, at the confluence of the Klondike and Yukon rivers. Eventually, a prospector wandered over the hill, and Henderson learned that Rabbit Creek was now called Bonanza Creek; that it was already staked for fourteen miles; and that Bonanza and its feeder pup, Eldorado Creek, were the richest placer gold streams in the world.

---

*The town is called Forty Mile; the river, Fortymile.

One can imagine Robert Henderson aiming a scorching string of hat-stomping profanities at George Carmack that day. It is said, however, that he simply dropped his shovel and walked to the creek bank, where he sat speechless.

Moosehide

On the right bank a couple of miles below Dawson, I see a pretty little church with a bell tower sitting amongst a few cabins on a grassy hillside. This is the Indian village of Moosehide. No people live here, though it is still used periodically as a "culture camp," where Indian traditions are celebrated and passed on. By the fall of 1896, stampeders were filling up Dawson and sprawling into the Tr'ondek Gwech'in village, which was located just across the Tr'ondek River (the Stone-for-Driving-in-Fish-Trap-Poles River). The Gwech'in came to the Tr'ondek River every summer to fish the salmon runs, pounding sticks into the riverbed to make a weir and trap. The newcomers didn't just appropriate the Indians' name for the river, modifying it to "Klondike," they muscled in on the village site, successfully pressuring every one of the Indians to sell. The Gwech'in attempted to relocate across the Klondike on the Dawson side, but the Mounties claimed forty acres there and did not want Indians as neighbors. With most of the rest of the land having been bought up by speculators, the Indians found themselves dispossessed on their traditional ground. Tens of thousands of newcomers poured into the Gwech'in territory. The strain on food sources alone was terrific. In one account, a Native hunting party "killed in all about eighty moose and sixty-five caribou, much of which they sold to the miners in Dawson."

There were five or six hundred tents at the mouth of the Klondike in the early summer of 1897 when Frederick Fairweather Flewelling struck a deal with the RCMP on the Natives' behalf. Flewelling, an Anglican missionary, bought forty acres at Moosehide, the nearest unclaimed land. He constructed mission buildings, then gave the remainder of the land to the Tr'ondek Gwech'in. St. Barnabas Church went up in 1908, but with a glittering boomtown just two miles away, Native souls were inevitably sucked into a vortex of music halls and saloons packed with gamblers, lawyers, newspapermen, and other sharps and scammers.

By 1923, Native dancing during Christmas celebrations at Moose-hide occurred "only as an exhibition during an evening of modern entertainment," according to the *Dawson Weekly*. Jobs lured some of the people away. Disease ravaged the holdouts, as diphtheria and influenza epidemics took hold in the isolated community. One observer in 1922 noted that the village was seldom free of sickness and that mothers had more children in the graveyards than at home. The population of Moosehide dwindled until, by 1957, it became too expensive to maintain the virtually empty school. As a pamphlet published by the Dawson Indian Band put it, when the last of the Moosehide people moved back to Dawson, "integration of the two groups was complete."

WITH NO ONE AROUND, I tie up the canoe at a new-looking dock probably built to accommodate a tour boat and climb the hill for a peek inside St. Barnabas Church. Beyond the unlocked door, I find a lovely old space suffused with a rosy light from the stained-glass windows. On the walls, cream-colored paint tops off a wainscoting that has darkened nearly to black, the two tones suggesting the strata of a glass of Guinness. The wood floor has buckled in waves so that the pews and rails are cocked this way and that. An old barrel stove stands stolid as a boar, smitten and turned to steel. It reminds me that I do not wish to tempt a vengeful God, and I let my trespassing self out. Out, and at the same time into another holy space. The great slab of liquid slides by below me. Silent. Luminous. At water level, it is big. From the hill, it is monstrous. In a minute, I will be borne by it down another sort of aisle, into another sort of mythic realm.

WHERE DOES IT ALL BEGIN? There isn't much agreement. And it isn't a simple question. At its headwaters, the Yukon's tributaries finger out dendritically, tapping lakes scattered over the high country of northern British Columbia, in back of Southeast Alaska's Coast Mountains. How to decide which stream should be designated the main trunk and which the feeders? Should it be the branch that would yield the greatest total length for the river, regardless of flow volume? Or the one that drains the greatest area? Or maybe the one that best aligns itself with the Yukon's general geographic trend? Or the stream that begins farthest to the south? Or the one that drops from the highest elevation? The hydrologist, the geographer, the mapmaker, each may have his preference.

If it were up to me, I think I'd work my way upstream from what is incontestably the main stem and turn up every fork that spills the most water annually. I reckon that takes me up a little unnamed creek that terminates at the face of the Llewellyn Glacier, on the east side of the Coast Mountains. And then into it. The glacier, I would conclude, is water after all. A stream of sorts. Its water is colder than the rest of the river's, but not much colder. If frozen, the glacier is still flowing, slowly, downhill and so behaves in this respect like a river. Glacial ice is something like its pellucid cousin, glass. Glass does not have a crystalline structure, as nearly all solids do. Of the two, glass and ice, glass is more like a liquid. Water molecules do form a crystalline structure when they freeze, but molecules deep in a glacier nonetheless warp and creep past one another in response to pressure from the weight above. Glaciers don't just lurch down the mountainside like a skidding block. The ice flows over itself, like a super-viscous liquid. In a sense, glaciers are the stained-glass windows of mountain cathedrals: not quite liquid, not quite solid; not quite wall, not quite sky. I like the idea that the Yukon descends from this borderland between earth and heaven, between science and myth.

THE REMARKABLE THING is that the Yukon launches its journey just over the hill from the object of every river's desire: the sea. Fifteen or twenty miles away, the river is near enough to smell the salt. But it is nonetheless drawn inland, the first voyageur to push through this wild country, two thousand miles to the Bering Sea coast. And like the later trekkers, it packs its load. The White River, so named because it transports a light-colored volcanic ash and silt, rolls down from the vast snowfields of the Wrangell–St. Elias Mountains and joins the big river above Dawson. There, the relatively clear Yukon becomes a pearly gray and stays that color for the rest of its length. The Tanana River, which is somewhat wetter than a horizontal mudslide, delivers twice as much silty sediment from the rock-grinding glaciers plastered onto the north side of the Alaska Range. Each summer, these two rivers haul about eighty million tons of mountain down to the main conveyor belt, which dumps most of it into the sea. Only one percent of the land drained by the Yukon River is permanently covered in ice, but it is enough to cloud the river for about fourteen hundred miles of its length. Except when we can't see it. From October to April, freezing temperatures shut down the glaciers' silty outwash, and the Yukon runs clear under its frozen surface.

Within a seventy-five mile stretch above Dawson, the White, the Stewart, the Sixtymile, the Indian, and the Klondike all join. The Yukon swells to tremendous proportions, over a mile wide in spots. It can be terrifying just to look at the thing. This river doesn't roll or tumble or dance. It slides like slurry down the chute of a concrete truck. It foments surging boils and sucks itself into whirlpools. It is ponderous, inexorable, and silent, except for the hiss of grinding silt. Robert Service, the Klondike poet, got at it in a poem called "The Woodcutter":

> *By day it's a ruthless monster, a callous insatiable thing,*
> *with oily bubble and eddy, with sudden swirling of breast.*
> *. . . it cries for human tribute.*

The Yukon River drains about a third of a million square miles. Along its upper reaches, it receives the output of drainages that each could hold states. The Teslin drains a land area the size of Massachusetts and Connecticut combined. The Pelly and the Stewart each contribute the runoff from drainages the size of Vermont and New Hampshire. The White adds a Maryland and a New Jersey's worth. Downstream, where the Yukon arches its back across central Alaska, it collects its three largest rivers, the Porcupine, Tanana, and Koyukuk, picking up drainages the size of Pennsylvania, Ohio, and Maine, respectively. With a little jigsawing, the drainage basin of the Yukon River could contain all of Texas and California, the largest of the contiguous states, or sixteen of the little ones.

Between Dawson and Circle, the Yukon alternately pinches and bulges, mostly between about three-tenths and half of a mile wide. In some places the river splits around groups of islands and dilates into an aneurysm a mile and a half across. At Circle, the hills recede, and the channels of the Yukon spraddle like a fat woman's legs released from their stockings. The Yukon Flats. Three miles from bank to bank. Not for another two hundred miles do the hills finally manage to gather the river back into a distinct channel. Water sliding past Circle has more than a thousand miles to go to the sea, but only six hundred feet of elevation from which to fall, which means that for the last half of its length, the Yukon drops only 6.8 inches per mile. One third of all flowing water in Alaska ends up in the Yukon. And a fifth of the river's volume is brought to it by the Tanana, which presents its tribute at the geographic center of the state. In this way, the Yukon River discharges twelve million cubic feet of water and a hundred tons of silt each minute into the Bering Sea.

Vast, grassy lowlands containing many divergent, sluggish, and meandering channels conceal the Yukon's mouth. From a boat on the river, it is nearly impossible to see which way the main channel goes. The shoreline all around appears like a pencil line drawn horizontally across the middle of a blank sheet of paper. The hills are too far away to offer any reference. From a ship offshore, there is even less, visually, to suggest that you are alongside one of the great rivers of the world. Besides the low relief of the land, the Yukon's channels empty into the sea at many different points along an arc of coastline about eighty miles broad.

MOOSEHIDE, if not exactly a suburb of Dawson—it isn't road-connected—is nonetheless on the outskirts of town. But from here a traveler breaks free of Dawson's orbit and launches into an immense wild land. There is no town, no phone, no link to the rest of the world until Eagle, one hundred four miles away. But for me it will be a stroll in the park compared to the treks of the early explorers. Russian traders in the west of Alaska, both south and north of the Yukon's mouth, and English traders in the east, each had heard Native stories of a great river that lay between the two powers' territories. But it took an ambitious Russian named Aleksey Ivanov to finally locate the Kwikhpak (big river), as the coastal Eskimos called it. Sometime in the early 1790s, in midwinter, Ivanov's Native-led party set out from Iliamna Lake at the northern base of the Alaska Peninsula. He skied north until he hit the broad river and returned at Easter, probably covering six hundred miles or more altogether. A better-documented "discovery" resulted from an expedition organized by Baron Ferdinand von Wrangel, governor of Russian America. In 1833, he sent Andrei Glazunov, an Eskimo-speaking Russian creole, overland in winter from Saint Michael Redoubt on Norton Sound. Glazunov reached the Yukon where the Anvik River joins it, three hundred miles from the Yukon's mouth.

But the Arctic explorer and historian Vilhjalmur Stefansson is inclined to credit the discovery (by white men, anyway) to one who didn't so much behold the river as infer it. "To discover a river as large as the Yukon, it is not necessary to see it," Stefansson writes. Navigators can detect the presence of a great river while still well out to sea, even before sighting land. The tremendous volume of water delivered by such a river may freshen the sea detectably before land is visible from a ship's bridge. And the sediment, too, is carried far offshore, creating shoals that large ships must look out for. "A passing ship, then, becomes aware of such a river without seeing it, through the immemorial custom of navigators, particularly exploring navigators, of guarding against the unexpected grounding of their ships by the twin methods of sounding for depth and tasting the water for saltiness." Captain James Cook (according to H. H. Bancroft, according to Stefansson) suspected the presence of a great river in the fall of 1778, as he proceeded southward along the Alaska coast. But he didn't see it.

After Ivanov's and Glazunov's reports, the Russians began ascending the river in summer. In 1838, Vassili Malakof reached Nulato, nearly five hundred miles from the Yukon's mouth. Four years later, L. A. Zagoskin explored as far as the Rapids, more than seven hundred river miles from the coast. At this same time, a Scotsman named Robert Campbell in the employ of the Hudson's Bay Company punched west from Canada. Campbell for years had hoped to find a river-and-portage route to the Pacific. In 1840, he and his party paddled up a branch of the Liard River in Yukon Territory, hiked over a pass that he correctly suspected was the Continental Divide, "descended the west slope of the Rocky Mountains, and on the second day . . . had the satisfaction of seeing from a high bank a large river in the distance flowing North-West." He named it the Pelly, and though no one knew it at the time, the river is one of the Yukon's principal sources. Campbell had discovered an inland approach to the Yukon river system, but neither he nor his Hudson's Bay superiors knew where the Pelly went. At various times, traders suspected it drained into in the North Pacific near Juneau as did the Taku River, or into the

Arctic Ocean as did the recently discovered Colville River, or into the Bering Sea as did the Kwikhpak, the Great River of the Russians.

Meanwhile, to the north, another Hudson's Bay officer called John Bell (also a Scotsman) crossed the mountains from the Mackenzie River in 1845 (some accounts give 1844 or 1846), ascending first the Peel, then the later-named Bell River, built canoes from birch bark that he'd packed in, and floated down the Porcupine River to where it entered a river big enough to rival the Mackenzie. Approximating the Gwech'in Indian word for it, *Yu-kun-ah,* Bell wrote its name as "Youcon." Yet another Hudson's Bay Company Scotsman, Alexander Murray, built a fort at the confluence of the Porcupine and the Yukon in 1847: Fort Youcon. Not until 1851 did Robert Campbell, floating in a canoe from the Pelly, confirm that his original conjecture was correct: the Pelly, which he had discovered far to the south; Bell's Youcon, at the mouth of the Porcupine; and the Russian's Kwikhpak, which emptied into the Bering Sea, were all the same river.

NOT SURPRISINGLY, the Yukon was the last major river system in North America to be discovered, explored, and settled by outsiders. The river's mouth is elusive. Its interior regions are nearly inaccessible, with the highest mountains on the continent walling it off from the sea. The climate is harsh in winter, and the river is thousands of miles distant from supply centers on the West Coast. For many of the same reasons, the Yukon River drainage is hardly settled now. Discounting two densely populated pinpoints within the Yukon basin—Whitehorse (23,000) and Fairbanks (84,000)—there are only 19,000 people living in an area the size of Pakistan. To compare densities, one might imagine decreeing land reform for the 141 million Pakistanis and dividing that country up equally among them. Each would own a plot of ground the size of a football field, counting the end zones and sidelines. Doing the same for the bush residents of the Yukon basin would give every man, woman, and child a spread of about seventeen square miles. Between Dawson and the next village downriver—Eagle, one hundred six miles away—only one person lives year-round.

THE AIR IS COOL AND NICE. No need for a jacket. Across the channel from Moosehide and up against the left bank is Sister Island. A clearing on the north end of it marks where the Sisters of St. Ann once operated a farm to provision their hospital in Dawson. Beyond it looms Dog Island, tapered at each end and proportioned like the issue of a husky who is getting a fair bit of meat in his diet. Mike Rourke in his *Yukon River* says the island was used to isolate cases of smallpox. The steamer *Whitehorse* sat in quarantine here for seventeen days in the summer of 1902. Spiral-bound Rourke is one of my guides. His book offers good line drawings of the river channels and does a better job with bars and cut banks than do the national geologic surveys. Also included are bits of history and rough photocopies of archival photographs. I keep it in a clear plastic bag under a bungee cord on top of my gear.

THERE IS LITTLE TO SIGNIFY THE SITE of long-gone Fort Reliance, three miles below Moosehide on the right bank, where the temperature was once authoritatively recorded by the U.S. Geological Survey at eighty degrees below zero. In 1874, on this spot across the river from a Han Indian village known as Nuklako, Jack McQuestin and eventually his partners Al Mayo and Arthur Harper ran a trading post, exchanging trade goods for furs. They had situated themselves just six miles from the richest gold-bearing creeks in the world, but it would be twenty-two years before that became known, and by then they would have moved. The first on the scene, the strike would never make them rich.

After twelve years in the relatively stable business of fur trading with the Indians, the custom shifted to supplying the increasing number of miners in the country. When the Stewart River produced a modest strike, nuggets replaced furs as the currency of the region. With that shift came the imperative to relocate to wherever the diggings showed promise and the miners had aggregated. The traders must have felt they had become as erratic and stampede-prone as the prospectors who chased hunches all over the country. In 1886, McQuestin, Mayo, and Harper abandoned Fort Reliance and rebuilt at Stewart River, seventy-odd miles upstream. But that same year, news arrived that prospectors had found coarse gold on the Fortymile River. Once again, McQuestin and his partners abandoned their post and rebuilt, now at the mouth of the Fortymile, one hundred twenty miles downstream. Then a strike at Birch Creek in the early 1890s prompted McQuestin to build at Circle City, two hundred four miles below the Fortymile.

Finally, at the end of the decade, the traders rushed two hundred fifty-five miles back upstream to build at Dawson, nearly to the spot where they'd started twenty-two years earlier. Notwithstanding all this itiner-ating, the three merchants were a steadying influence. They promoted a systematic exploration of the country's mineral potential. They were unfailingly willing to outfit the miners on credit, supplying the bacon and beans, the picks, shovels, and pans. And as the resident old-timers of the Yukon, they dispensed tips, advice, and encouragement. They didn't make the big strike, but they made it possible.

The buildings of Fort Reliance are gone. They do not exist even as a burial mound of rotted logs under a blanket of moss. They were cre-mated in the boilers of steamboats—atomized and mingled with the at-mosphere. Another account says some of the logs were used by Indians to make a raft to carry them to Fortymile. But what does endure is the reputation of the three traders who started here at this site. Mc-Questin, Harper, and Mayo, with their blend of toughness, optimism, and generosity, are remembered as the gold standard of the pioneer spirit. And Fort Reliance contributes another benchmark, too. It is Mile 0 of the upper Yukon River. Twelvemile River, Fifteenmile River, and Fortymile River are so named because of their estimated distance downstream from this spot. And the scale goes in the other direction, too, accounting for the Sixtymile River upstream.

Chandindu River

I've heard there is a fish weir a little over a mile up the Chandindu River, so I swing the canoe into the beach below its mouth. The Chandindu joins the Yukon on the right bank about nineteen miles be-low Dawson and roughly twelve miles below Fort Reliance (hence, its other name, Twelvemile River). In 1883, military explorer Lt. Freder-ick Schwatka named the river Chandindu after an Indian word, the meaning of which he did not record. I want to see the weir and the bi-ological investigations going on there, but I am a little nervous. I am not sure if this is the place where Richard Smith and Faye Chamberlain were attacked by a huge grizzly bear a few years ago. I don't have my handgun along because of Canada's strict laws against them. And I hadn't wanted to pay the fifty dollars for a permit to bring a rifle. I de-cide to walk up the trail with my Hudson's Bay ax. That way, I'm thinking, if a grizzly bear charges me, I can knock myself on the head. But just then I see a riverboat streak around the bend and pull into the cobbley beach. It is Tommy Taylor, a Native man of about 65, his two adult sons Mike and John, their nephew Clinton, and a couple others from Dawson. They say they are going up to relieve the crew at the weir. Tommy decides to wait in the boat, and I join this two-rifle escort.

John is no sooner up the bank than he stops abruptly. He says he heard an animal chomping its teeth off to our left. Mike levers a shell into the chamber of his rifle. John does the same. We stand still and stare hard into the willows and fireweed but see nothing. Mike motions for Clinton and me to go ahead of him, putting the guns at the head and rear of our column. We move quickly and quietly up the trail single file, all eyes left. But as soon as we move, a low throbbing sound fills the woods. For a moment, I think it is the *Yukon Queen,* the tourist boat that now runs between Eagle and Dawson. But it is too early in the day for the *Queen*. It is obvious this rumble comes from a bear, warning us. We walk ahead, but with frequent looks rearward. The bear does not charge, and we do not see it. Not far along, we side-step a pile of bear shit, pink and tan and studded with cranberries. It's big enough to fill a shovel and soft to the press of my boot. No accident, I think, that he placed his calling card in the middle of the humans' trail.

Clinton is a pleasant, chubby kid about twelve years old, and brisk walking appeals to him less than enjoying the scenery at a leisurely pace. As he lags behind, Mike and I stop to let him catch up. The rest of the party continues on, stopping periodically to wait for us. Thus we advance like one of those spring-bodied dachshunds on wheels, with the head of our troop stretching us apart until our elastic limits are reached and tension pulls our hindquarters back into position. Perhaps in his thirties, Mike is slim and tan and engaging. A model of avuncular kindness. Stopping often for Clinton creates a certain level of unease, but Mike never utters a syllable of admonishment to his nephew.

Eventually we reach a clearing in the spruce forest hard by the tumbling Chandindu. The well-ordered camp consists of a little log cabin and several ten-by-twelve wall tents stretched over wood frames with plywood floors. As we step over an electrified wire, a very pretty young woman named Catherine greets us. The electric fence is in response to a recent—and uneventful—visit from a bear, and it might deter one who is merely curious. Catherine seems to be in her twenties. In order, one notices striking green eyes, a ponytail, a gray sweater, and carpenter jeans. She seems to smile a lot. Mike smiles a lot too. I suspect that they are happy to see each other, and I move off to check out the weir noisily straining the river.

The Indians used to hammer sapling stakes into the river bottom a hundred years ago at the mouth of the Klondike. Now they work in steel. Tripods made of four-inch channel iron (steel members, U-shaped in cross section) sit in the stream, ten feet apart. Rails of the same iron connect the tripods, and pipes of heavy-gauge electrical conduit are attached to the rails, like pickets in a fence, except that they lean downstream at about a forty-five-degree angle. The river threads between the pipes, but the migrating salmon cannot. Against the near shore, a gap in the weir allows the milling fish to penetrate the fence and enter a "live box." From a tree platform above the box, a worker can look down on the fish. If he is merely counting, he can pull a rope to open a door, and the fish swim through. This year, besides counting, the crew is doing a biopsy procedure to procure a DNA sample of the Chandindu chinooks. They scoop each king out of the box and with a punch tool remove a small plug of tissue from the tough gill plate.

The program began four years ago, Mike says, a partnership between the Tr'ondek Gwech'in and the Yukon River Commercial Fishing Association. The idea was to count the fish, take tissue and scale samples, determine genetic differences between early and late run spawners, and then look at the feasibility of restoring salmon stocks on the Chandindu. Of principal interest are Chinook salmon, or "kings," as the Americans say. The run has not been impressive in recent years. Mike thinks this year's king run is about done, as the count is falling off and the frontrunners of the fall chum salmon run are showing up. The crew has counted only one hundred twenty-five kings so far. Four years ago there were two hundred. But some recent evidence suggests the count may not be highly accurate. Twenty kings that spawned upstream and then died (as they normally do) later washed up on the weir. When the crew looked at these fish, they found that only three had been biopsied. In other words, seventeen of a random sample of twenty had made it past the weir uncounted. Mike thinks the problem can be traced to a fire that burned on the Chandindu three summers ago. Since then, heavy rains bring flash floods. The water level rises against the weir until the salmon can jump over it. Many fish probably make it past undetected, he says.

There has been a mix-up, and Catherine is not scheduled to be relieved for another day. Mike decides to stay over and return with her tomorrow. I walk out with Clinton and his uncle John and a couple of the relieved crew heading up to Dawson for R&R. John, who carries the rifle, does not frequently wait for his straggling nephew. He is less easygoing than Mike, more inclined toward tough love. "Hurry up there, Chubs." And, "That bear will think you're a big round berry." And, "Let's go. TODAY!" Later, when he himself is probably tiring: "Young fellow like you should be carrying the rifle for your uncle."

Neither Mike nor John knew where, exactly, their father Tommy was born, except to say, "Somewhere around here." So when I reach the boat, I ask him. "Right there," says Tommy, nodding to the willowy bank where the bear had snapped and growled. I look where he indicates, but all I see is the bones of a pole-framed greenhouse where bits of tattered Visqueen (polyethylene sheeting) flutter like Tibetan prayer flags. In the late 1930s, when Tommy became its newest resident, there was a small community here. "We had a row of cabins down there," he says. Apparently this settlement, known as Twelve-Mile, began in 1896 when some of the displaced Han Indians moved here from the mouth of the Klondike. At one time, there may have been more than ten families at this place, which the Han called *Tthedëk*. Over the years most of the people moved up to Dawson. In 1957, a flood destroyed the remaining houses.

Tommy comes here often in the summer, returning like the salmon to the natal ground they share. Waiting for his sons, he pokes around among his memories. He notices things. One day he noticed that the *Yukon Queen* had no sooner cleared the upriver bend, a good four miles away, when seagulls seemed to appear from out of nowhere and gather at the mouth of the Chandindu. It happened every time the big boat steamed by. If he stays out of sight, Tommy says, the boat won't slow down but will roar through, and a good-sized wave will curl up and splash down on the stony beach below the mouth. Heaved up too and stranded among the rocks will be the little salmon fry that inhabit the shallows. Twice each day, the *Queen* sets this banquet table for the gulls. And if the salmon run is faltering, as it seems to be, Tommy figures this can't help. One survey estimates the *Queen* strands between thirteen and fourteen thousand fry each season. Of course every fry doesn't normally live to become an adult fish. The typical mortality rate for fry may be as high as ninety-nine percent. Still, this loss is on top of that natural mortality.

As an afterthought, John asks his father if anything came out of the woods.

"Oh yeah. A little bear."

"Black?" I ask.

"Yeah."

I am glad to hear it was a little blackie because it is time to camp, and I'd rather not share the area with a grizzly bear. After I shove the Taylors' boat off, I motor up to a little island above the mouth of the Chandindu. It has a nice long sandy point on the downstream end, and the upriver breeze should keep the bugs in the brush. It is a perfect campsite, with a patch of dry sand just big enough for the tent, surrounded by damp sand that won't blow around if the wind kicks up. Where the island proper begins, there's a fast-eroding bank, and there a little copse of alder has keeled over onto the beach. With the roots dangling in air, the wood has dried to snap-offable perfection. I'll have a good campfire.

Along the beach on river left, twelve feet up from the waterline, I see a tiny brown object. It looks like an amulet made of sand. A little washing reveals a miniature salmon, two inches long, perfectly formed with bright silver sides. It's about the right size to have leapt off the label of a can. In fifty feet of beach, I find four of his mates. I can imagine the *Queen* sweeping through, brushing these lesser mortals aside. There is a little scarp, maybe a foot high, cut into the sand well up from the water's edge. It appears the boat's wake is cutting down the sandy point along this line, tossing the fry up on the beach and under-cutting the alders where the bank is steeper.

Of course, we all make a wake, I'm thinking, as I break off a few alder sticks. I guess the important thing is: how big a one, and to what purpose?

I've had no lunch, and suddenly I am aware that I am hungry. The camp goes up quickly, and soon I have a fire snapping under a cast-iron frying pan. A small cutting board takes up no room on the side of the grub box, and I make a lot of use of it, now whacking up a couple spuds from a big bag of precooked ones. Into the pan with them, along with a splattering shot of squeeze-bottle margarine. I draw a nice sizzle from a couple handfuls of chopped onions and set on the grill a few links of my own homemade moose sausage, redolent of sage and boosted with pork fat. I want them to char a bit and pick up some of that lovely alder smoke before I add them to the pan. The rising aroma is almost a cruelty when I am in this state. But I am reassured by the size of the pile. It looks enough for two and wants to spill over the sides when I give it a stir.

I am one of those people upon whom hunger leaps out of the shadows like a mugger. I am all right one minute, and then it's on me, riding my back hard. I am so hungry that I am angry. My brain fogs. The absolute best I can do is just be silent. When, irritatingly, people speak to me, I reply with an economy of speech that my wife, my mother-in-law, and certain friends and co-workers identify instantly. Cars are pulled over. Meetings are interrupted. Sandwiches are produced and pressed upon me. The effect is like that of filling the empty tank of a sputtering engine. I come right back up to the proper RPM. Tonight, I survive the crisis. Half a pound into the tucker, I know I'll be all right and try to slow myself. But I cannot. I dig my spoon into the mound like an excavator. I try to talk myself down: you can stop gobbling; you can stop hunching your shoulders like a hoarder. The pan is empty and my bowl is scraped clean before any effect has registered. I know I just need to wait. Soon a rusty switch in my stomach will finally trip and flash the "full" signal to my brain. I'll be all right.

As satiety sets in, relaxation settles over me like a surging wave. I am suffused with both by the time I turn to dessert: a cup of coffee and a slab of Irish soda bread, raisin-studded and generously buttered. It's been a generous day. There is time now to linger in my chair and watch the sky and the water experiment with colors.

After a bit, I take care of the dishes and pack the grub box and galley gear back into the canoe. Finally, dessert's dessert: a ration of ardent spirits and a good long stare at the fire.

As the gloaming advances, clouds move in from the west. Before dinner, a T-shirt was perfect. But the breeze keeps rising in stages, and the temperature dips with the sun. A flannel shirt keeps things perfect. A little later, I add a nylon windbreaker. Pretty soon my hood is up, and one hand is jammed in a pocket. Only the hand that holds the cup is on the cool side of perfection. I am inclined to see it as a little tax on the whiskey. Not burdensome. Happy to pay.

I am captivated by the living painting before me. As the sun goes down, the sky first ambers, then concentrates into an intense, blazing orange. Below, the river plays out, shining like a satin ribbon unreeling. It absolutely glows. It is as if it has absorbed light all day and now begins to fluoresce. What a crazy blue. It's like the blue of the noon sky but mixed with mercury and electrified. A color intrinsically agreeable to the human heart, and the more exquisite for being the chromatic opposite of the neon-orange sky. Sometimes when my concentration wanders, the scene slips into two dimensions. A composition blocked into thirds. Across the middle, a black band—the hills—without depth or texture. A jagged black crack between the two luminous regions, sky and water. An allegory of night: the dark between the day that's done and the day that's coming.

The crack widens, and I fall into it.

All night, the breeze holds steady. All night, the tent walls pulse, and a half-dozen zipper pulls tinkle like a carillon of tiny bells.

Fifteenmile River

It's a warm, blue-sky day. There is just the odd friendly looking cloud here and there. Puffs of white that boost the blue and tweak the composition to please a painter's eye. T-shirt weather. Even my life vest is too warm. A mild upriver breeze tousles the leaves of the aspen, and they shiver their silvery undersides, flashing gray-green-gray-green, a thousand flashes a second. Trembling. Shuddering. Quivering. Quaking aspen. *Populus tremuloides*. The most widely distributed tree in North America. The only tree in these woods you will also find in Mexico. Fast-growing and short-lived, it's kind of the reckless teenager of tree society.

Just around a broad bend and three miles below the Chandindu, the Fifteenmile River emerges almost undetectably from the Ogilvie Mountains and seeps into the north-flowing Yukon. Today it does, anyway. But if the rocks hereabouts could talk, they might tell a different story. For Allejandra Duk-Rodkin, who is a Chilean-born, Russian-educated Canadian geologist—and who is, perforce, good with languages—the rocks do talk. They say that millions of years ago the Yukon flowed the other way. For two million years, it flowed south into the Gulf of Alaska, probably debouching somewhere northwest of Juneau. And the headwaters of the paleo-Yukon, according to Duk-Rodkin, was this unprepossessing little stream opposite me. Upriver from this point, prior to about three million years ago, the Fifteenmile River *was* the Yukon.

I met Duk-Rodkin once in Fairbanks, along with fellow Canadian geologist Rene Barendregt. Duk-Rodkin is an energetic and voluble middle-aged woman with short black hair and bright, dark eyes that shine when she is having fun. For her, revealing the solutions to geologic puzzles is clearly fun. In 1996 and 1997, she says, she and colleagues followed a hunch and went searching up the Fifteenmile for old gravelly terraces—floodplains, essentially, of the ancient Yukon River. Most of Duk-Rodkin's searching took place from her office, as she is more an expert interpreter of aerial photographs than a field geologist. Perhaps because terrace remnants present a hilly topography today—having been weathered, eroded, and covered with wind-blown silt for millions of years—other investigators had not found them. But using aerial photos first, and a helicopter second, she tested the most terrace-like features in the hills here and found what she was looking for: old river terraces stepping down the Fifteenmile River and away to the south—that is, *up* the main channel of the Yukon River. The farther south she found them, the lower were the terraces' elevations (from six hundred seventy meters high at the mouth of the Fifteenmile, to four hundred sixty meters at the mouth of the Stewart River), proving, Duk-Rodkin says, that the Yukon once flowed the other way.

Where the Indian River joins the Yukon, she also found bits of argillite, a form of shale found in the Ogilvie Mountains, north of Dawson. But the Indian River joins the Yukon south of the Ogilvies, putting the found argillite *up*stream from its source. Upstream today, but downstream eons ago when the Yukon transported it. Yet another clue came from a core drilled into the Yukon Flats, a ten-thousand-square-mile catchment below Circle where an ancient lake once existed. Here sediments consisted of silt and clay until about three million years ago, when gravels appear. It marks a change from lake to river.

A RIVER IS MATHEMATICS come alive. Liquid logic. A vector plotting the sum and total of all the forces acting on the surface of the earth—insolation and gravity, tectonics and topography, climate and vegetation. One of the amazing things about a river, says Duk-Rodkin's colleague Barendregt, is that it responds to external stimuli like a sentient thing. If the main channel drops, the side tributaries cut their way down to it, reestablishing equilibrium. If the main channel is high, the side creeks accrete, or fill in sediment until the levels are in balance again. So, when a glacier in the late Pliocene (between 2.9 and 2.6 million years ago) pushed its way out of these mountains and across the south-flowing Yukon, damming it, the river backed up, hunted for a chink, and wiggled through. Like many a subsequent renegade, it escaped to the north.

This glacier came down the valley of the Fifteenmile River. And when the dammed water spilled out to the northwest, it carved a canyon. The deepening channel established a new, north-flowing drainage that survived the melting of the ice dam. These high hills I see on either side of the Yukon, stretching away downriver from the Fifteenmile toward Alaska, are the now-rounded walls of that canyon. "The most incredible thing is that the Yukon River is incised in the northern part of the Dawson Range," says Duk-Rodkin. The Tintina Trench nearby to the east would have been a more logical channel for the river, as it was lower and made of softer material. But because it was filled with ice, the river couldn't follow the Trench, she says. The Yukon ambled north and, like a runaway hopping a freight, jumped aboard the Kwikhpak, as paleogeographers now call the ancient river. They rolled all the way to the Bering Sea. Meanwhile, tectonic forces lifted up what is now the Wrangell–St. Elias Mountains, cutting off the old southern exit and tilting the Canadian portion of the Yukon until it spilled into Alaska. Voila: the modern river.

Halfway House

Twenty-six miles below Dawson, on the left side, a high grassy bank is growing up in brush. On this site Percy DeWolfe built his Halfway House. An archival photo in Rourke's book shows a trim cabin, with Percy standing on the porch alongside three of his smiling girls in identical starched white jumpers. Another photo taken by Rourke, perhaps in the mid-1980s, shows it cockeyed, with the roof caved in. Today it is a pile of boards in an open grave, the remains of the structure having collapsed into the cellar hole.

DeWolfe and a partner built the place in 1901 as a base for their fishing, woodcutting, and freighting operations. He may have grown hay, too. In the 1920s and 1930s, he ran a fur farming business. But mainly, Percy DeWolfe carried the mail. From 1915 to 1950, the "Iron Man of the Yukon" ran his route between Dawson and Eagle. Besides a team of big, 100-pound huskies, he kept two horses to pull sleds. In the course of thirty-five years on the trail between Dawson and Eagle, DeWolfe drowned five pairs of horses. Running on the frozen Yukon River, the horses sometimes broke through the ice and perished, but each time Percy managed to escape with his own life and walk to the next cabin. Once he saw three horses and a sled get sucked under the ice and swallowed up by the Yukon. Still, he managed to save not only himself but also the mail. He walked into Dawson. It wasn't a much safer proposition during the boating season, especially because he would push the seasonal limits. One year, in mid-October, with the river building up ice along the shore, he flipped his canoe and lost the mail near this spot. The shore-fast ice prevented him from climbing out, and he only just managed to do so before the near-freezing water sapped his strength. After a while, Percy made the summer mail runs in thirty-foot boats with twenty-five-horsepower marine motors. But one fall, as he was trying to squeeze one more run out of the season, the river clogged up with ice. He had to abandon his boat at Fanning Creek and make his way upriver on foot. When he reached the bluff just below Forty Mile, he traversed the icy face of it in stocking feet so he wouldn't slip. But he did slip and fell a hundred feet. "Dazed but no bones broken," says one account. When the sternwheelers took over summer mail service, DeWolfe continued to use his boats for freighting and hauling passengers. But in 1951, when he was seventy-four, the airplane—air mail—put an end to DeWolfe's career as a mail carrier. He died the same year.

Still today you will hear people in Eagle say, "When Percy carried the mail, it took four days from Dawson to Eagle, regardless of the weather. Now it takes twice as long." Eagle is just one hundred miles away to the northwest, but the Canadian and U.S. postal services will send a letter mailed between the two points an extra three thousand miles on a great tour of the Pacific Northwest. First, it will head off in a direction exactly opposite to its destination, fourteen hundred miles via Whitehorse and Vancouver to Seattle. Then it will turn around and head back north, fifteen hundred miles via Anchorage to Fairbanks, before finally traveling east two hundred fifty miles to Eagle. Of course, the letter sits for a bit in each of the five intermediate cities en route. As a test, before I left Dawson I sent a postcard to a friend in Eagle. Ten days. It is a marvel and a measure of how far we've come that the technological innovations of airplanes, computers, and mechanical sorting devices—not to mention the developments in "human resource management," like team-building exercises and motivation seminars—have resulted in a mail service two-and-a-half-times slower than that delivered by Percy DeWolfe one hundred years earlier by dog team.

Cassiar Creek

No boat is tied up where Cassiar Creek spills musically into the Yukon, and where Quebec native Cor Guimond built a home in 1976. It was named in the 1880s by miners who had worked the Cassiar District in the Stikine River country of British Columbia. No one ever found gold in paying quantities here, though the valley was once the focus of a stampede. It seems a Dawson miner known as Nigger Jim, who was actually a white man, set out for this creek in the middle of the night, in the middle of winter, in the middle of a cold snap that bottomed out at sixty degrees below zero. Jim had made a fortune on the Klondike, so rumors began to fly when he started acting as if he'd tumbled onto a strike. Quietly, people got their gear in order. It was about eleven o'clock on the night of January 10, 1899, when Jim put down his glass at the Aurora Saloon, climbed on his dogsled, and pointed the team downriver.

Fifty sleds followed him into the night, with more on foot behind. Jim led all on an anything-but-merry, hundred-mile chase, first to Cassiar Creek and then up the valley and over the hills to a most unlikely spot where he staked a claim. Only when the exhausted stampeders had staked claims and returned to Dawson did the word go around that the whole thing was a hoax. Meanwhile, several men suffered severe frostbite, one losing both feet. Some say Jim had bought a map from an old sourdough. Others figure it was his way of commenting on Dawson's susceptibility to rumor. Quite likely it was the sort of perversity that sometimes stands in for humor when it's sixty below and dark and nothing much else is going on.

CASSIAR CREEK has not proved to be the end of the rainbow for Cor Guimond, either. I have missed him this trip, as I missed him the last time. But I talked to him once on the phone. After finishing college with a degree in agriculture and mining technology, he came out to the Yukon. But he came to trap. His uncles were trappers. They had taught him the craft from the age of five, as soon as he was big enough to set a small trap. When he arrived in the Dawson area in 1974, he discovered his other great passion, dog mushing. The two activities fit well together and suggested a third: fishing to feed the dogs. Guimond established a fish camp here at Cassiar Creek and liked the place so much he spent most of twenty years here, full time.

But in Canada, the government tightly regulates who can trap. The rules allow trapping only by a registered concessionaire or by his assistant. Each concessionaire is given the exclusive use of an area, and he can renew his concession for life for about ten dollars a year. Some do that, even if they do not trap seriously. Guimond worked on various lines in the area as an assistant trapper, but when a concession opened up, the game warden, with whom Cor did not see eye to eye, passed him over. Eventually, he was able to buy a trapline above Dawson at the Sixtymile River. Upriver, the country is better for trapping with a dog team because the terrain is less steep and has more trails. Cassiar Creek remained a better base for his fishing operations, though, because there are more good eddies and fishwheel sites around here than upriver. So Guimond and his new wife Agata have been hauling their household and twenty dogs back and forth seasonally by boat. The dogs are so used to the drill that Agata can turn them all loose, and they will run down the bank and jump into the boat, where Cor clips them into place on short chains. But with ten years of disastrous fish runs, some summers Cor did not make the trip. Today a piece of plywood propped up on the bank reads "For Sale."

THERE ARE THREE good-sized and nicely built log cabins here. One has a loft and a covered porch with burled spruce columns. A note posted there invites travelers to stay in the last cabin. It's too early for me to stop, but I partake of the place. There is a blue bench positioned so that its occupant can take in the view and catch the sun, which is just what I do. Someone has tacked a plywood heart on the bench. Blue birdhouses for the swallows sway atop high spruce poles. Cassiar Creek gurgles behind the harmonic shushing of birch leaves tossing in the breeze. Rose hips, ripe and heavy, bend their stems and bob in the sun. But for all its lovely serenity, the place has a melancholic air. You feel a void at the stomach. The three cabins here, but they are as forsaken as the tumbled-in ruins of Percy DeWolfe's Halfway House. There's a story behind the joyful little heart on this bench. But a visitor can only wonder what it might be.

I REMEMBER GUIMOND sitting one winter's night at the table at Slaven's Roadhouse—one hundred sixty-odd miles downriver—when he came through on the Yukon Quest Sled Dog Race. He is a solid man, not tall, with fingers thick as sausages. He had a creased, stubbled face that showed some mileage. Not highway miles, either. Not even gravel road miles, but trail miles. I guess I noted the fingers and face because that was all the flesh that could be seen. He must have sat for an hour eating at the table, but he did not remove his big green parka with its glossy wolverine ruff, nor his beaver hat and headlamp. He just sat hunched over a bowl of moose stew in the lantern light, his back to the woodstove. In its essentials, the scene was not different from a thousand other nights that the roadhouse had seen. Roadhouses were built all along the trail system, usually a day's journey apart. They offered a bunk for two dollars and wild game stew for another two dollars. Guimond could have been a mail carrier or a trapper or a missionary, stopping to give his dogs a rest on a cold night, to crumble a little hardtack into a bowl of Frank Slaven's slumgullion, to listen to the gossip of who was where on the trail.

Looking at Guimond from the back dispelled the illusion. Across the table from him sat a brace of intently focused Quest paparazzi who had flown in to cover the race, landing in a bush plane on skis on the river ice out front. There were two photographers (one Swiss, one American) and a two-man Japanese film crew. The photographers were each peering through a camera while holding aloft a flash apparatus. From his shoulder, the video cameraman aimed what looked like an electronic bazooka while his soundman pointed a long tubular microphone. Six wicked-looking black instruments pointed at a man who'd just stepped out of the nineteenth century. When the Canadian spoke, which was almost not at all, it was to the Swiss in French.

He can't really afford it, as he has no sponsor, but Cor plans to run the Yukon Quest again in 2006. The Quest is billed as "The Toughest Sled Dog Race in the World," and that is probably the truth. It borrows its route from many historic gold rush and mail trails, one thousand miles between Fairbanks, Alaska, and Whitehorse, Yukon Territory, with the two towns alternating as hosts for the start and finish. Several rules make the Quest very different from the more famous Iditarod Sled Dog Race, which runs eleven hundred miles from Anchorage to Nome. A musher may start the Quest with a maximum of fourteen dogs (compared to sixteen in the Iditarod) and must finish with at least eight (compared to a minimum of five in the Iditarod). Consequently, an Iditarod musher can burn through better than two-thirds of his dog team, while the Quest musher must keep the majority of his starting team healthy enough to finish. In addition, the Quest has half the number of checkpoints, meaning that the distances between them are about twice as far on average. One stretch between two Quest checkpoints is more than two hundred miles long. This means that more dog feed and camping gear must be hauled, which in turn means the loads are heavier, the sleds stouter, and the pace slower. All this makes for a race that is harder on the musher but results in more humane treatment of the dogs. Cor has run the Quest six times, finishing as high as fourth. Agata ran the race in 2004 and placed seventeenth as a rookie.

Another dog race goes through Guimond's front yard as well: the Percy DeWolfe Memorial Mail Race. Run since 1977, it follows the Yukon from Dawson to Eagle and back, with a brief six-hour mandatory layover in Eagle. The winner covers two hundred ten miles in less than a day's running time. Guimond is always a threat to win this race. He might have done so the year he finished second by two minutes had he not used a big, seventy-pound Quest sled.

Hammer Bar/Sunset Creek

Gray clouds slink in over the hills from every direction, it seems, but are never quite upon me. It is as if I am towing a small high-pressure zone down the river, a spotlight of sunlight tracking my shuffle across the stage. Nine miles below Cassiar Creek on the right bank I see the mouth of Sunset Creek opposite a low mud island called Hammer Bar on my map. I land below and bust through the willows until I hit a trail and soon find a tiny log cabin. Inside, it's little bigger than a king-size bed: about six feet wide by eight feet long, maybe six feet tall at the ridge. Plucked out of these woods and set down in a suburban back yard, it would be instantly recognizable as a playhouse. But this diminutive structure does not humor some precious notion. Here, it addresses a few common imperatives of the North. Limited money. Limited time. Short logs are easier to handle. A small space is easier to heat. And when the temperature hits 50 or 60 degrees below zero, that means something. As a stopover on such a night, it is a sanctuary.

Fortymile River and Forty Mile

A few minutes later, rounding a bend that takes me from heading slightly south of west to heading slightly east of north, I see a pointy hill centered in the notch of a valley. Frederick Schwatka noted it in 1883 as marking the mouth of the largest Yukon River tributary for several hundred miles. The local Natives called it the "Zit-zen-duk," which anglicized is the lovely and assonant "Creek of Leaves." But tin-eared Schwatka, the first man to explore the Yukon River from headwaters to mouth, and who renamed practically everything he encountered along the way, replaced the Athabascan name with "Cone Hill River." Happily, it didn't stick. The early miners called it the Fortymile in consequence of its approximate distance below Fort Reliance.

The town of Forty Mile, on the left bank just above the mouth of the Fortymile River, is a genuine ghost town. Log buildings with doors and windows agape line a riverbank now choked with willows. There's a two-story Mounties' barracks and a log cabin Anglican church. A huge, high-ceilinged shop is still fairly plumb and level, but people with more interest in lumber than history are deconstructing it in stages. Someone has chainsawed out every other collar tie, the horizontal board that makes a rigid triangle of a pair of rafters and keeps the nongabled walls from collapsing outward. And they've removed the siding to the point where the walls will go one day when there's a snow load on the roof and the wind kicks up.

Oddly, there is an excellent barrel stove with stout legs and a welded cooktop sitting unmolested here. Odder still, it's hooked up to a stovepipe. There are four stumps set around it, as if the boys from the shop still settle here for their lunch break, to light their pipes and swap a few lies. But it's a curious installation because the entire near side of the building consists of bare studs sheathed with nothing but the great beyond.

The Fortymile River owes its place in history to the fact that the first coarse gold in the Yukon watershed was found here in 1886. Miners didn't want to fool with gold dust when they could find the stuff that "rattles in the pan," as they said. The find launched the first Yukon stampede; established the Yukon as a major mining district; and built this town, the first in the upper Yukon. It all started when Howard Franklin and his partner Harry Madison lined their boat up the Fortymile at the suggestion of the trader Arthur Harper. On the evening of September 7, 1886, Franklin was off by himself when he pulled a shovelful of gravel out of a crevasse in exposed bedrock along the river's edge. Panning this, he found about half an ounce of coarse gold. The code of the prospector required he pass the word, so in October, Franklin and Madison poled their boat one hundred miles upstream to tell the boys at Stewart River. The hundred or so miners digging thereabouts were averaging eight hundred dollars a year, which was considered good pay. Notwithstanding, the news of coarse gold on the Fortymile substantially emptied the Stewart River creeks.

The traders Jack McQuestin and Arthur Harper had just that summer abandoned Fort Reliance and built their new trading post at the mouth of the Stewart, sixty miles farther upriver. For the second time in a year, they shrugged, abandoned their buildings, and followed on the heels of the fickle miners, this time to rebuild at Forty Mile. It turned out that the early Fortymile miners would average eight hundred dollars a year, the same as they had been making at Stewart River.

It was here on the Fortymile that a man named Fred Hutchinson developed the technique of sinking a shaft during the winter. He started by building a fire on the ground big enough to burn all night. In morning he shoveled away the ashes and what dirt had thawed, then built a new fire in the depression. He continued that way, deepening the shaft in stages, day by day. Before that, the miners used to let the summer sun do the work, scraping away the few inches that thawed each day. But it might take the better part of a summer to reach bedrock and the gold-bearing gravels that lay just on top of it. And it meant the men were idle over the long winter. Occasionally, a hole would collect water due to subsurface aquifers. By morning, the upper several inches of this water would have frozen in the cold air. Hutchinson found that he could use his ax to chip away at the layer of ice, being careful not to punch through to the liquid water below. If he broke through, his hole would fill up again with water, back to the top of ice. But if he was careful and stopped short of chipping all the way through the ice, then the next day the ice would have frozen deeper, and he could chip down a bit more, again stopping before breaking through to water. In this way, he could force the freezing deeper and deeper, until he got past the aquifer. Then he could continue to burn his way down to bedrock.

Apparently, the prospectors ribbed Hutchinson as he toiled away during the winter of 1887 on Franklin Gulch. But his shaft kept getting deeper. And he noticed that he didn't need to shore up the hole with timbers as the miners did in summer. The below-freezing temperatures kept the permafrost walls rock-hard and stable. Fortunately, bedrock is not very deep in Fortymile country. Once he reached it, Hutchinson began to "drift" laterally, hauling the excavated gravel up to the surface in the usual way, with a bucket and windlass. But without water to sluice it, he simply heaped up the gravel in a dump pile where it froze hard. Each day, or a few times a day, he would take samples from the face of his tunnel. He would pan these samples with a little water inside his cabin, and in this way he could keep track of the pay and adjust his drift to follow a streak. Hutchinson stockpiled the gold-bearing gravels in a separate area from the barren overburden. By spring, when the other miners were just starting their shafts, he had a sizable pile of gravel ready to sluice and a lot of converts to his innovative methods.

With regular steamboat service in the summers, the settlement at the mouth of the Fortymile River grew to more than three hundred inhabitants. There were ninety log cabins; half a dozen saloons, restaurants, and hotels; a library; and even an opera house (however, of this establishment one writer notes that "the entertainment provided by the camp's hurdy-gurdy girls was something other than its name suggested"). The town was well within Canadian territory—forty-five

Yukon River miles inside the border—but it was an American town. The flagpoles flew the American flag. American steamboats brought supplies from American ports and took out mail bearing American stamps. There was no formal law, no sheriff, no top-down administration of justice until the North West Mounted Police arrived in 1894, just two years before everyone abandoned Forty Mile and stampeded to the Klondike.

What kept the community functioning was a sort of code. Pierre Berton, a Canadian chronicler of the gold rush who grew up in Dawson and whose father came over the Chilkoot Pass in 1898, writes about it in his book *The Klondike Fever.* Forty Mile thrived on an unwritten law grounded in "a curious mixture of communism and anarchy," he says.

> By the peculiar etiquette of the mining camp, a man who bought a drink bought for everyone in sight, though such a round might cost a hundred dollars; while a teetotaler who refused a drink offered a deadly insult—unless he accepted a fifty-cent cigar in its place. Hooch, like everything else, was paid for in gold dust, and the prospector who flung his poke upon the bar always performed the elaborate gesture of turning his back while the amount was weighed out, since to watch this ritual was to impugn the honesty of the bartender.

A true-blue sourdough was open and trusting and generous. He never locked his cabin. It was understood that any traveler could enter an empty cabin, eat, and spend the night. The only expectation was that he should make sure that he left tinder and kindling and wood, ready to light, so a man in trouble might save himself. (The hands refuse to function when they are very cold, and it can be difficult to grasp a hatchet— let alone to pluck and strike a match.) If a prospector had a bit of luck, he told one and all the location of good ground. A group of early miners wintering on an island at the mouth of the Fortymile elected to stake claims of only 300 feet, instead of the 1,500 feet permitted, so as to allow room for latecomers. Another magnanimous practice on Forty Mile allowed prospectors who had not found enough pay on their claims by the first of August to dig on someone else's paying claim until they took out enough gold to buy their next year's outfit. And a prospector never speculated in food, but sold a needy man food at cost.

Occasionally, selfish or lazy or misanthropic men ignored these conventions. A couple hundred miles downriver, in the Circle mining district, Deadwood Creek was known as Hog-Um Creek because of the greedy way that early arrivals staked it all. And a miner's meeting once convened in Circle City at the Pioneer Saloon when a black prostitute brought suit against a white miner for failing to pay her for boarding his dog team. The jury deliberated in the saloon's storeroom, where they, as the foreman later wrote, "drunk at least two gallons of the very best and all staggered out to report." Not only did they throw out the case and fine the woman court costs, but they had arranged for the dog team to be taken from her property while the trial was going on. Finding the team gone, the woman refused to pay the judgment. In response, the jury moved to sell her house, intending to "spend it all with her." Eventually, "wiser heads stopped this idea," said the foreman, but the woman was essentially forced out of town.

In its heyday, Forty Mile was home to a population that may have reached a seasonal peak of 1,000. But it emptied almost totally in less than three days in August 1896 as the miners rushed to the Klondike. Some, finding the good ground on the Klondike already taken up, returned. But Dawson City overshadowed Forty Mile thereafter. Ten years after the Klondike strike, the town limped along, sustaining a two-man RCMP detachment, a store, a roadhouse, the customs house, and the Anglican church. The police and the missionaries finally left in the 1930s. Bill Coulter, an old French Canadian miner and trapper who hung on after everyone else pulled out, was Forty Mile's last resident. In 1958, he sent a little raft down the Yukon with a note saying he guessed he was about done in. An Eagle resident found the note, and Coulter spent his final few weeks looked after by the nuns in the Dawson hospital.

PERHAPS, THOUGH, Coulter is not Forty Mile's last resident. In a clearing, I see a little cabin, the fixed-up former store, where folks named Sebastian and Shelly sometimes stay. I gather they are informal caretakers, that they live here in winter but work up in Dawson during the summer. They come by to keep an eye on things and to beat back the brush so the floaters can see something of the buildings. Their cabin is open, and a note invites travelers to come in, sign the ledger, make tea, spend the night. I'm tempted to do that, actually. It's looking like rain, and this snug little cabin—with its checked tablecloth, oil lamp, and quilty bunk—is damned inviting. But I can't bring myself to intrude on this couple's homey nest. I wish they had been around today, though. Then I could have met one hundred percent of Forty Mile's population and fifty percent of the winter population of the entire Yukon River drainage for a hundred miles between Dawson and Eagle. I should meet the rest of the population downriver.

Before I get back to my canoe, I hear her eerie thrumming, hear it for a good while before I see the upriver-bound *Yukon Queen*. She cruises by with her sleek, swept-back lines reminiscent of absolutely nothing associated with this country. I'm not sure how defensible my reaction is. Would I rather see steam-fired sternwheelers out in the channel? Hell, yes. And the denuded hillsides that were the consequence of their operation? Well, no. Still, the *Queen* seems to push its way into quiet company, like a noisy tourist charging up the aisle in an old cathedral where local people come to pray. I linger out of sight in the willows until she passes. I just don't care to be a prop in anyone's tableau. I've seen the *Queen*'s brochure: "Wave to rugged homesteaders as you pass their stakes." (A wave in another sense is what people on the river get, as the boat's wake rolls dangerously toward them and tears up fishing gear.) "Today the river is a magnet for those who love wild, untamed scenery virtually untouched by the hand of man." Without irony, the advertisement invites you, at one hundred and ten U.S. dollars each way, to streak through the "untouched" country in custom-upholstered reclining chairs, behind oversized viewing windows, on a four-million-dollar, one-hundred-four-passenger, high-speed catamaran sightseeing vessel with full-service galley, snack bar, captain's lounge, and gift shop.

But then, I must acknowledge that the slow, stately, and steam-powered sternwheelers were in some instances as palatial as the grand packets of the Mississippi. With observation salons and plush dining rooms outfitted with chandeliers and Persian rugs, the boats must have been mighty luxurious in their day.

One pull, and the old Evinrude starts and gurgles. I poke up the Fortymile a little, just to have a look at it, then swing around and slip out into the Yukon, chugging down a northeast reach.

THIRTEEN MILES BELOW Forty Mile, Night Island looms aptly, offering four-star luxury: a sandy point on the downriver end, graciously littered with driftwood, and an upriver breeze dialed for bug control. To a mammoth bowl of Zatarain's New Orleans Style Red Beans and Rice I add a couple of juicy moose links, nicely blackened over the fire, then cut up and mixed into the pot. For several days my dinners will center on sausage. This is partly due to the obvious ascendancy of this food, but also because, without refrigeration, one eats the fresh meat first until it is gone. For dessert: boiled coffee and a couple trick-or-treat–sized chocolate bars. At times like this, when things are perfect, especially if we are sprawled in the dirt somewhere, a friend of mine will say, "Oh, I feel sorry for the rich people tonight." Finishing up a little after 11:00, I manage to get the camp squared away while dancing between the first few rain drops that descend from ranks of dark clouds now marching in over the western hills—great gray troops scattering silver coins to us street urchins below. As I duck into the dry, snug tent, I find that tonight I feel sorry for all the salad people. It doesn't seem fair. Me with a three-pound bolus of honest chow radiating well-being within me; they, making do with a meal of leaves. We must do something nice for the salad people, I resolve, next chance we get.

IN THE MORNING it is still raining when I wake up, so I lie abed thinking about the old-time sourdough and his code—his honesty and generosity and communal spirit. I'm thinking about when I first came to Alaska thirty-three years ago and stopped in Ketchikan and saw the people's easy way with money. I was staying on a small boat with a fellow I met on the ferry, a welder named Pat Haley, and an Indian kid whose name I forget. One day the three of us went off to buy showers. We stopped at a little store to pick up some things like soap and toothpaste, and whoever reached the counter first paid for everything. I tried to give him my share, but he waved it away. Then the other fellow bought the showers and likewise wouldn't accept my money. I wasn't at all used to this, and I began to feel like a freeloader. I was accustomed to trading rounds in bars, but apparently the Alaskans handled all transactions this way and couldn't be bothered with keeping accounts.

I remember something like the same thing going on during the pipeline days in Fairbanks in the mid-1970s, when the big construction boom hit, and a table full of total strangers would buy drinks for your table too. Of course, in those days everybody was awash in money. Now, the only vestige of this brotherhood I notice is that people who have been here a while will almost always stop when it's cold out and they see a vehicle by the side of the road. The old-timers will roll down their windows and say, "Have you got everything you need?" The young ones will say, "I've got a cell phone. . . . "

But the big Klondike gold rush of 1898 must have radically changed the ethos of the pre-Klondike Yukon miner. Maybe 30,000 stampeders, ninety percent of them Americans, poured into the country in one of the more singular instances of mass hysteria in human history. If the experience at Forty Mile was illustrative of the brotherhood and the general competence of the old-time prospectors, the Dawson scene was a monument to foolishness and cupidity. For one thing, hordes of the stampeders were wholly ignorant of the rigors—and the dangers—they faced. Tappan Adney joined them as a special correspondent for *Harper's Weekly*. Adney, an American with considerable experience in the woods of New Brunswick, landed in Dyea with packhorses, climbed the Chilkoot Trail, built a boat at Lake Lindeman, spent the winter of 1897–1898 in Dawson, and altogether was sixteen months in residence along the stampeders' trail. His book, *The Klondike Stampede,* is a thoroughgoing, almost anthropological, firsthand account of the madness. He writes that a certain "man of means as well as leisure," who was not a trader, had brought along a case of thirty-two pairs of moccasins, a case of pipes, a case of shoes, two Irish setters, a bull pup, and a lawn-tennis set. The stampeders came from their desks and counters, he said, and were unaccustomed to hard labor. They were all armed. A horse packer told Adney, "There are more inexperienced men to the square foot than in any place I have ever been to . . . they will be shooting themselves." No one could be trusted. "We have already learned to place no reliance on any person's word," wrote Adney. "Everyone seems to have lost his head and cannot observe or state facts." A mining engineer said, "I have never seen men behave as they do here. They have no more idea of what they are doing than the horse has."

One conversation Adney memorialized seems emblematic of Dawson at the height of the Klondike stampede:

Among the throng there was none who interested me more than a tall figure I used to see from day to day. He wore a pair of deer-skin pants fringed on the outer seam, a loose blue-flannel shirt, belted in, and a wide-brimmed gray hat, from beneath which locks as soft as a girl's straggled to his shoulders ... [He] began talking to Mr. Hannon. The conversation proceeded for a while, touching matters of general interest. At length, and there was note of sadness in his voice, he looked squarely in Mr. Hannon's eyes and he said, "You don't remember me?" "No, I can't say that I do," replied Mr. Hannon. "Why don't you know me? I'm the barber, across from your place in Seattle."

Pierre Berton offers another glimpse of the town filling up with stampeders in the spring of 1898: "Day after day for more than a month the international parade of boats continued. ... They brought sundowners, shantymen, sodbusters and shellbacks, bucka-roos, Gaels, Kanakas, Afrikanders, and Suvanese. They brought wife-beaters, lady-killers, cuckolded husbands, disbarred lawyers, dance-hall beauties, escaped convicts, remittance men, card sharps, *Hausfraus,* Salvation Army lasses, ex-buffalo-hunters, scullions, sur-geons, ecclesiastics, gun-fighters, sob sisters, soldiers of fortune and Oxford dons."

Forty Mile was none of that. And though overgrown and falling down and hauled off and eroded away, it remains like a lesson un-learned. It hopes to remind us that years before the big Klondike strike, the country had been opened up by a hardy and competent class of pioneers who installed riverboat service, trading posts, roadhouses, mail delivery, law officers, and missionaries; that the early camps were less gaudy and rip-roaring than the Dawson scene, and far less popu-lated with greenhorn stampeders; and that the whole society was sup-ported by an ethical structure, a sourdough code that valued honesty, openness, generosity, and vigor. So what, I wonder, does it mean that Forty Mile lies amoldering, and the side creeks along the Yukon are empty, while Dawson survives, serving up cultural false fronts for the tourist trade, like its celebrated cancan dancers, who were never part of Dawson's nightlife until the idea occurred to tourism promoters in the 1960s.

Coal Creek

Last night I motored past Coal Creek, five miles below Forty Mile, where Tim Gerberding and James Bouton had a camp some years ago. No one is there now, but I met Gerberding once in Dawson. In 1972, he and Bouton partnered up and established home cabins near Coal Creek. Tim, a native of Wisconsin, came to the Yukon in 1971 after finishing college in New Mexico. He spent seventy dollars building his cabin. Somehow, the partners ended up with the best fishing site for hundreds of miles around. Their eddy at Cliff Creek is said to be more than a hundred feet deep, and they hauled out fish by the thousands. Some people call the road to the mouth of the Fortymile River the "Tim and James Road" because it seems to have been built largely to accommodate all the fish they produced. Tim married, had children, and when his kids became school-aged, he and his family moved to Dawson. He went to work as executive director for the Tr'ondek Gwech'in Tribe in Dawson. James moved to Dawson as well.

Not quite a century before Tim and James showed up, prospectors had located coal seams twelve miles up the creek. Construction of a mining operation began around the turn of the nineteenth century, and a coal-fired power plant operating on the creek supplied electricity to the Klondike gold dredges via thirty-five miles of power line. The mine also served the sternwheelers via a narrow-gauge railway that hauled coal down Coal Creek to the Yukon. A ton of coal brought six dollars at the creek mouth, ten dollars in Dawson. Construction of a hydro-electric powerhouse just outside Dawson on the Klondike River around 1910 put the coal-fired plant out of business.

A HUNDRED YEARS AGO, thousands of people bustled along this river. Today, it is a ghost river connecting ghost towns. Dawson is a tiny remnant of the glory days when twenty-five or thirty thousand people resided there or on the nearby creeks. Moosehide is abandoned. Fort Reliance has disappeared. Gone are the Indian camps of Nuklako and Twelvemile Village. Forty Mile is a ghost town. On the American side, the town of Seventymile is no more; Nation City is gone; Star City, Ivy City, Independence, Coal Creek, all gone. Just the road-connected towns of Eagle and Circle survive. Circle's population is ninety-nine. Eagle is home to 129, while sixty-eight Han Indians live just up the road in Eagle Village, formerly known as Klat-ol-klin or David's Village.

Outside of these settlements, though, the people who lived out along the river are gone too. In the old days there were prospectors, trappers, freighters, mail carriers, and woodcutters. They all died off or moved away as the mines played out and the steamboats quit. To some extent, their places were taken up by young people in the 1960s, 1970s, and early 1980s who were interested in living beyond the towns, in the simple and old-time way. Now that cohort has dwindled to just about zero. In the ninety-three miles between Dawson and the U.S. border, there is only one full-time resident. Upriver from Dawson, it is the same story. Torrie Hunter of Yukon's Department of Environment started working along the river in 1982. At that time, he says, perhaps a dozen households lived on the river above Dawson and below Fort Selkirk, a distance of one hundred seventy miles. Now there is only one full-time resident. It puts me in mind of something the Irish playwright J. M. Synge heard from a peasant in the west of Ireland a century ago, after English repression and famine forced a great diaspora: "Now all this country is gone lonesome and bewildered, and there's no man knows what ails it."

Old Man and Old Woman Rocks

The morning's rain has freshened the air and lent a bit of sparkle to the world. Motoring along in shirtsleeves, it seems like I can actually *taste* the air on my skin, like I'm drinking it through my bare arms, breathing it through my pores and picking up something of its spruce-strained, river-moistened flavor. Motorcycle riders know what I'm talking about. It's like you need the weather—breeze, drizzle, sunshine, snowflakes—to be on your skin, or you don't feel like you're breathing.

Just below my Night Island camp is "a remarkable-looking rock," according to Schwatka, "standing conspicuously in a flat level bottom of the river on the eastern side, and very prominent in its isolation." He named it, possibly with tongue in cheek, for a French geographer called Roquette. Once again, the miners ignored Schwatka's fusty appellation, preferring instead a translation of the Indian name, Old Woman Rock. Its counterpart on the left bank is called Old Man

Rock. According to legend, a long-suffering old boy finally hauled off and walloped his nagging wife, who fetched up out in the flats. Then, to ensure his peace, he diverted the Yukon to flow between them.

I SEE A RUST-COLORED SPOT in a scree slope on the left bank and know it for the site where a giant beaver was killed. That's what I heard in Dawson last spring from Louise Profeit LeBlanc, a tall, striking-looking First Nations woman from the Yukon Heritage Branch. She told several stories of Traveler (also known as Tu-cha-cho-ki, Sol-gee, and Beaverman), a hero who roamed the country in ancient times. One of his great deeds was to kill a giant beaver. Still today, says LeBlanc, when the old people see a brown spot of earth in a cut bank, they may say, "That's where a giant beaver was killed." Of course, cultural myths have all sorts of value and importance apart from the conveyance of empirical truths. But this story got me thinking about the fact that, during the Pleistocene, there *were* giant beavers in this country. *Castoroides ohioensis* was the size of a black bear, measuring eight feet in length and weighing more than four hundred pounds. Was it possible that this oral history account dated back that far, that there was an aspect of the traditional story that was literal scientific fact? I asked two anthropologists, Craig Mishler and Bill Simeone, who said they didn't doubt for a minute that the story might date to the Pleistocene, that it transmitted a fact ten thousand years old. Louise LeBlanc says there is even a Native story to explain the downsizing of the giant animals who roamed this unglaciated refugium during the Ice Age. Traveler killed the animals' parents and told the young animals, "That's as big as you are going to be."

Mel's Camp

From a long way off, I can see a bright yellow riverboat just below Sharp Cape on the right bank. It has taken seventy miles of river travel below Dawson, but it looks like I am finally to encounter a resident human being. I know that the yellow boat belongs to Mel Besharah and that this is his fish camp. There is a commercial fishing opening right now, and as I get closer, I can see Mel's net in the water in the eddy in front of his camp. I pull in above the net, and he comes down the cobbley beach to see who the heck I am. He is rugged-looking in a way that suggests a big man, and it takes a while to realize he is not above average in height or weight. He looks like he might have been a middle linebacker in high school who leaned-out after a couple of decades picking fish nets and trapping behind a dog team. He has dark brown hair that is beyond curly. It springs from his tanned face, thicker than sheepskin, upwelling in rosettes, like the boils in the Yukon. The bottom half of his head is covered with a curly brown beard that he keeps trimmed, making it easier to tell which side is up.

Mel says he was just about to knock off and fishes a couple of beers out of the ice in his fish tote and rolls a smoke. He says he came to the Yukon as a "white, suburban kid from Ottawa." I ask about fishing. "I can't stand not fishing when there's an opening," he says. Apparently he's one of the lucky ones. With the fish runs declining in recent years, and the Alaskans taking the bulk of the run, people have had to look for regular jobs in town. So now, even when there's an opening and the fish are in the river, the fishermen can't get away from their jobs. "I work in construction with an old friend of mine," says Mel with a chuckle, "and he's well aware that if he tells me I can't go fishing, then I'll quit."

"When I moved out here, there was probably a dozen different households along the river between Eagle and Dawson, year-round. Now there are three." One neither traps nor fishes. The other fishes only. And though Mel is counting himself as one of the three, he does split his time on the river with time in town, where his family stays. He's in town most of the summer, working at his construction job. In winter he traps the Fortymile country, but he spends some time in Dawson during that season too. It used to be that when Mel drove his dog team up to town, he could stop in at a number of places for a cup of tea and a warm-up. But these days there is nobody at all between the Fortymile and Dawson. "Now it's a long, cold, lonely stretch in December, I'll tell you that much."

The reasons for the declining human population involve more than declining fish populations. "Canada is just in the throes of putting our Native land claims together," he says. "And the Natives are sewing up large blocks of land and basically cutting the white man out. So unless you had a claim—if you're white—to live in this region, I'd say before 1990, in that area, then you're pretty much excluded." In the mid-1970s, when Mel arrived, it was possible to stake a small homesite and secure title to it. "Young people now—and I've met a few—that would like to move out into the bush and try the subsistence lifestyle, it's simply out of the question. There's not a chance in hell they can do it."

The land claims agreement includes race-based regulations with regard to trapping as well. The government has assigned seventy percent of all trapping concessions to the local Native tribal entities. At the same time, and for reasons of their own, the Native people have been voting with their feet: for years they have moved steadily away from trapping and fishing and dog teams and toward the amenities of town life. Notwithstanding, the treaty mandates that when concessionaires wish to sell out, the local Native tribe is given the right of first refusal until such time as seventy percent of the concessions are held by Native people. In the Dawson area, the Tr'ondek Gwech'in tribal entity exercises these options whenever they are presented. Then the tribe tries to recruit one of its members to take the trapline. "All these traplines have been allocated to the Natives, but they don't want them," says Mel. Even with this regulation in place, Native-held traplines still amount to less than fifty percent. "So any white guy who wants to come in and wants to go fishing or trapping—forget it. It's simply not available."

Meanwhile, there are white assistant trappers who would like to acquire their own concessions, according to Torrie Hunter of the Yukon Department of Environment. But, he says, there are ways to skirt the regulation. Canadians have an impressive knack for "stick handling" around dicey problems. A white concession-holder can't sell his trapline to another white—say, his assistant—but he can sell him a partnership in the business. Then, if (when) the senior partner decides to retire, the junior partner can buy out the senior partner. Basically, instead of a single-installment deal, it's done in two installments. The law arches its eyebrow at the practice from one side of its face, and it winks from the other side. Everybody who sees trapping as culturally important in these Northern outposts agrees that it's better to have trappers trapping than to let the practice disappear. If there isn't sufficient Native interest, it's better that the openings are filled with white trappers than that they go unfilled.

Lately, the fishing allocation is goofier still. A couple years ago, anticipating a low king salmon run and the likely closing of the commercial fishery, the fisheries agency asked the Natives to cut back on their fishing, while it paid other local commercial fishermen to fish. Then it gave the catch to the Native people. As part of the deal, the fishermen agreed to take Native kids along to teach them about salmon fishing. And again, everybody was happy.

Still, Mel thinks it's too bad that the river people are disappearing. "People who are out there doing this kind of thing like what I'm doing, I think you've got to have people like that in society, just as a counterpoint." But, as new people are blocked by government regulations, and with attrition of the established folk, their numbers approach zero. "We're all getting older. And, you know, it's a tough life. I've been pretty lucky to maintain my health. One of the guys got MS. Another fellow blew his back out. And some of them got married and had kids, and, you know, the bush life is not really suitable to some people in that—you can only do that kind of thing so long."

It strikes Mel as a little strange that as well-meaning city folks work overtime devising regulations to reestablish Native subsistence lifeways, nonnative subsistence traditions are barely noticed. "Well, you know, I trap along here," he says, waving his hand across the landscape to the south. "And so I see a lot of the country that people don't see because I get back across those flats. And there's trails back in there. There's old cabins back there. In untold numbers. I mean, they're all over the place. And there is a history back there that most people don't really know about." Mel has spoken with some emotion, and a sheepish look comes across his face, as if he's suddenly found himself on someone else's trapline. "OK. That's enough," he says, having reached his limit with my interview questions. "Time for more beer."

FISH. SALMON. It is the most important animal in the Yukon River country. "Crucial to life on the river," Mel had said. For a decade it seemed to be disappearing. Now it seems to be rebounding. King salmon (chinooks) are the cash crop, sold for human consumption. The smaller chum salmon are fuel. They're like torpedoes of gasoline that motor themselves upriver each summer and fall to be gathered, stored, and later poured into the traditional conveyance of choice: dogs. Of all the animals utilized in a subsistence economy since time beyond memory, the salmon is the most important. It is an enormous quantity of biomass that annually delivers itself from the ocean to the interior regions. It can be counted on to be in predicted places at predicted times, year after year. It can be preserved relatively easily by simple drying in the open air. It is lightweight when dried and makes a highly portable, high-protein, hydratable food, perfect for traveling. Salmon permit dog teams, and dog teams permit general transportation and freighting, which greatly enhances a trapper's range. Trapping success means cash, and cash buys what the country does not produce. So fish means flour and sugar and tea, kerosene and .30-.06 shells, and a flight to town to see the dentist.

Stan Zuray

A few hundred miles downriver, a fellow named Stan Zuray is working on the problem of assessing the strength of the Yukon salmon run. He is a fisherman, compact and rugged, with hair pulled back into a ponytail that, via the inevitable alchemy, is turning from straw to silver. His face is exactly as weather-beaten as you would expect after thirty years in the Alaska bush. Around the village of Tanana, Stan is known as a smart and tough trapper, fisherman, dog driver, and mechanic. He ran the Iditarod sled dog race about twenty years ago, and not until 2005 had anyone before or after placed higher on their first attempt (except when the race was brand new, of course). People say that he could have had eighth place instead of ninth, but he had been running with Don Honea, the veteran Native dog driver from Ruby, and Stan was content to have the elder cross the line first.

Stan likes working on mechanical things, and he shows so much flare for modifying and streamlining that he is as much inventor as mechanic. The fishwheel is one machine Stan has refined. It is a traditional device that has been catching fish on Interior Alaskan rivers for a century or so. Imagine a sort of waterwheel that turns on an axle mounted on a floating raft. Two opposing baskets pass through the water in a downstream direction, scooping up the migrating salmon swimming upstream. Also radiating from the axle are two paddles, located between the baskets such that they catch the current and keep the wheel turning during the moment when neither basket is in the water. When everything is working properly, it's a brilliant contraption, constantly rotating, gently intercepting fish. As the basket rises in its rotation, the fish slide into a box beside the raft. And all without human effort. Theoretically. In practice, however, there's a lot to do besides collecting the fish from the box and processing them. Driftwood can pile up and even jam the wheel. And the baskets need constant adjustment as the river level changes. When the river drops, they have to be raised relative to the raft so that they don't hit the bottom but continue to sweep *near* the bottom, where the kings like to swim. If a basket hits bottom and stops, it might back up enough current to break the whole thing apart.

Stan changed the way the baskets are raised and lowered, and his method has been adopted by others all up and down the river for a hundred miles and more. But for all his mechanical wizardry, there was one machine that Stan never had much to do with. The computer. In fact, he had never even used a typewriter until the fall of 1999 when he pecked out a letter concerning trapping regulations on an old manual typewriter. He barely had time to gloat over his mastery of this nineteenth-century technology when the twenty-first century dawned, and a U.S. Fish and Wildlife Service biologist named, coincidentally enough, Underwood, (the manufacturer of the first typewriter) dragged him the rest of the way through the keyboard barrier. Stan had been running his fishwheel for the agency and had designed a 12-volt video recording system that spared the fish a lot of trauma. At the end of the season, Tevis Underwood asked Stan to put his innovative ideas down on paper for the Fish and Wildlife Service. He handed Stan a laptop computer with five hours of battery life, saying, "It's your report. Go do it." Stanley's composition began with his name and address. Five hours later, when the battery ran out, he had added the word "Introduction."

After a recharge, Stan managed to string a few sentences together. But there was one feature of the laptop that he found particularly irritating. It seemed only to be able to type capital letters. Except if he held down the shift key when, paradoxically, it produced a lowercase letter. It seemed completely backward, but what did he know. He plunked away for two hours, his left index finger continuously mashing down the shift key, while his right index finger hunted and pecked. Unless, of course, he needed a capital letter. Then he'd let go of the shift key, just for that one stroke. Finally, he decided there just had to be a better way, so he called up Bill Fliris, who probably knew more about computers than anyone in Tanana. Fliris wasn't home, so Stan started to explain the problem to Bill's young son Jesse. Before he got very far, the kid spoke two unfamiliar but exceedingly useful syllables: "caps lock."

Stan wrote about how he'd modified his fishwheel for the Fish and Wildlife Service. Underwood had begun to notice that tagged fish tended to fare less well than untagged fish. Survival rates declined if the salmon were held in a "live box," which is a partly submerged wooden pen on the side of the fishwheel (the holding box used by fishermen is not submerged, and the fish die there). Typically, biologists check a wheel a couple of times a day and release the fish once they have been counted or measured or tagged. But in the process, the fish get battered about a fair bit. First, they flop around in the basket when they are caught. Sliding fast down the chute, they slam hard into a crowded live box. Then they mill about for hours, periodically trying to leap over the walls, but mostly smashing their heads on the boards or landing on their bellies on the top of the wall. Last, they are scooped out with a dip net and thrash violently while the worker wrestles the fish into position to tag or weigh it before finally pitching it into the river.

To eliminate much of this abuse, Underwood and Stan considered how a fishwheel might be modified with new, fish-friendly features and with electronics. Instead of wire mesh for the baskets, Stan installed springy plastic webbing. He built a slippery white plastic chute that schusses the fish straight back into the river. Zweeeee-kerplunk. As the fish zoom down the chute, they crash through a lightweight, padded flapper door. A surveillance camera mounted above captures the image. Meanwhile, a magnetic switch on the flapper door sends a signal to a laptop computer inside a dry box on the fishwheel. The computer is programmed to save nine frames of video image before the signal and one frame after. A waterwheel generator lowered into the current keeps the batteries charged. For as long as the fishwheel turns, the computer stores on its one-gigabyte microdrive a film fest's worth of short, silent movies of slip-and-sliding fish. Caught on the surveillance camera, the salmon look like wide-eyed shoplifters busting out of a 7-Eleven and streaking for freedom. At the end of the day, Stan simply motors over to the wheel, pops out the microdrive, which is like a standard floppy disk but smaller, and takes it back to his camp. In a small white canvas wall tent, he counts the day's catch—caught on video.

When Stan's mother-in-law, Helen Peters, an Athabascan elder from Tanana, came to camp for one of her regular visits, Stan's boy Joey said, "Grandma, go down and look at your tent." When she poked her head through the flap, she gasped, "That's my bed!" A piece of plywood on the bunk converted it to a table holding a full-sized desktop computer with nineteen-inch color monitor, a laptop computer, a flatbed scanner, a color printer, a videocassette recorder, batteries, a charger, and an iridium satellite telephone. On the monitor's screen, king salmon zoom from screen right to screen left. Stanley keys the species, and a synthesized female voice counts, "Chinook, up. Chinook, up," as a spreadsheet tabulates the census automatically. Fishwheels and wall tents may look the same from the outside, but they have changed in Helen Peters's time. And, thanks to the wise decision to bring a bushman like Stan Zuray into the biological sampling process, more of the fish intercepted by the Fish and Wildlife Service are reaching the spawning grounds.

Bill Fliris/*Ichthyophonus Hoferi*

In the summer of 1987, another couple of Tanana people, Bill and Kathy Fliris, were up at their camp cutting strips when they noticed something wrong with the fish. Highly prized all over Alaska, king salmon strips are something like jerky. To make them, the fishermen fillet the kings, then cut the fillets into long strips about half an inch wide. Before brining and going into the smokehouse for a week or more, the strips are first draped over poles and set in the open air to drip some oil and to dry out a bit. It was during this first step in the curing that Bill and Kathy noticed that one pole smelled a little funny. It wasn't an objectionable smell, exactly, says Bill. Not rotten or anything. But peculiar. That pole of strips—that fish—went into the dog pot. Maybe the strips were all right to eat, but the Flirises weren't sure.

The next year there were a few more kings like that. If one of them made it into the smokehouse, it didn't dry correctly. Fliris started asking at other camps around the Rapids, but nobody had noticed anything like he described. The year after that, quite a few of the odd-smelling kings showed up in Bill and Kathy's wheel. And they noticed something else. They cut their fish in a tent, and in that diffuse, yellow light they were able to see small whitish specks on the hearts of the affected fish. It was like they had been sprinkled with salt. Sometimes the specks showed up on the liver or spleen as well. Fliris tried to interest the biologists at the Alaska Department of Fish and Game in the mystery, but without much luck. When he sent them some tainted strips, they ended up in a freezer at the Fairbanks office. Before anyone got around to scientifically sampling them, they were sampled gastronomically. Some frozen fillets Fliris sent in did make it to a lab in Juneau, but the fact that the meat was frozen limited the tests that could be run, and nothing was learned.

Each year at meetings of the Yukon River Drainage Fishermen's Association, Fliris tried to drum up interest. But none of the downriver fishermen had seen any of the little white spots, and no one thought the fish seemed sick. At one of these meetings in 1990 or 1991, Fliris succeeded in interesting a federal biologist with the U.S. Fish and Wildlife Service named Monty Millard. The feds weren't managing the fishery—the state of Alaska was—but Millard sent Fliris some jars of preserving solution and offered to try to find some funding to get the samples tested. The next season Fliris sent properly preserved samples to Millard, and Millard sent them out to a lab in the Lower 48. The results showed the presence of a parasite called *Ichthyophonus hoferi*. Along with the lab report, Millard enclosed some biographical literature about the little bug with the long name.

"At that point," says Fliris, "I started bringing it up at the Yukon River Drainage Fishermen's Association meetings every year. After a while, people were probably saying, 'Here goes Fliris again with his sick fish talk. Let's just let him do it and we'll get on with business.'" But as time went by, the number of infected fish increased. "Basically I was trying to get through to the Alaska Department of Fish and Game that this was something that was increasing every year. By then I was seeing it in close to twenty-five percent of the fish I was catching. And some of the other people were noticing it, too, that some of the fish smelled funny. And nobody knew what it was. Everybody was thinking, 'What is it, chemical? Or is it radioactive?' I kept bringing this up at meeting after meeting for quite a few years and getting no response whatsoever. I talked to several higher-ups in the Fish and Game department and tried to coax them into doing something about it. They'd say, 'What can we do? It's natural, you know. We can't do anything about that. We know what it is, and it will either go away or not.'"

Fliris didn't know if the agency could cure the infection, but he felt there were a number of important, and frankly rather obvious, things it could do. For one thing, couldn't the department make a public announcement to the fishermen up and down the river explaining that the odd kings they were catching were infected with a disease? For another, couldn't they advise the fishermen as to whether the fish were safe for human consumption? Couldn't they recommend how the fishermen ought to dispose of infected fish? If, as Fliris had read, king salmon had contracted the *Ichthyophonus* in the first place by eating infected herring at sea, mightn't the scavenger fish in the Yukon (the whitefish and the lush, for example) become infected if fishermen threw infected king carcasses back into the river? And finally, didn't the presence of this disease have implications for fisheries management? Fish and Game's management plan was built around an "escapement" figure, the minimum number of fish that must escape the nets and fishwheels and reach the spawning grounds. If *Ichthyophonus* killed kings, then wasn't it possible that up to twenty-five percent of the escapement might not be spawning at all but rather dying en route? And if Fish and Game didn't know the answer to that question, hadn't they better find out and if necessary revise their escapement number upward before serious damage was done to the king salmon stock?

As it turned out, every one of these questions could have been, should have been, and eventually would be addressed by the biologists. There was one person at the Alaska Department of Fish and Game, says Fliris, who always gave him a sympathetic ear. "His name was Russ Holder. He was kind of a junior level management biologist at ADF&G at that time, and he kept telling me, 'You know, I think you're right. They don't want to spend any money on this, because they've got other pet projects, and they just don't want to be sidetracked. But I think there's something that needs to be paid attention to here.'" In 1999, Holder sent Fliris an article about *Ichthyophonus* occurring in Prince William Sound herring. It was authored by a Dr. Richard Kocan of the School of Aquatic & Fisheries Sciences at the University of Washington in Seattle, whom Holder described as "Mr. *Ichthyophonus*." Fliris found more about Kocan's work on the Internet. "I fired off an E-mail to him right away," says Fliris. "And I said, 'I think we've got this on the Yukon River in the king salmon because we've already had it sampled once. I'm having a real hard time convincing anybody that it's a problem, but it seems to me that it is a problem.'"

Kocan says he was astonished to hear from a fisherman on the Yukon River asking about his esoteric research into an obscure parasite. After reading the E-mail, Kocan thought to himself that Fliris was wrong about the parasite being in the Yukon River. *Ichthyophonus* had never been documented in wild salmon. "But I didn't want to turn the guy down cold," he said. So he replied that he would be willing to take a working vacation to Alaska and collect the necessary one hundred twenty or so samples if Fliris could find the money for Kocan and an assistant to fly from Seattle to two locations on the Yukon. With that, Kocan assumed he would not hear from the fisherman again. But within a couple days, Fliris had the money. The Bering Sea Fishermen's Association agreed to fund the sampling, and Kocan started packing. It was already May, and the kings would start entering the mouth of the river during the first or second week of June.

In some ways, the professor's education was only beginning. When Fliris picked him up at the Tanana airstrip and brought him home, Kocan was stunned: "The guy has more electronics in his cabin than I have at the university." Fliris happened to have five computers at the time, and miscellaneous peripherals. But the real shock came when Fliris motored him up to his fish camp and pulled a few kings out of the wheel. "He started slicing fish," says Kocan, "Holy Christ! I couldn't believe it." The salmon were teeming with the parasite. Back at his laboratory, the first thing Kocan did was write a proposal to fund a full-blown scientific study of *Ichthyophonus hoferi* in Yukon River salmon.

Kocan sampled fish at five locations on the Yukon River (Emmonak/Marshall, Tanana, the Rapids, Dawson, and Whitehorse). As a check, he sampled a site on the Tanana at the confluence of the Chena River and collected spawned-out fish on the upper Chena. Preliminary results show that clinical signs of the parasite fluctuate depending on the location of the sampling. At the mouth of the Yukon, the disease is evident in less than ten percent of the fish examined. But the percentage jumps between twenty and thirty by Tanana and the Rapids. By Dawson and Whitehorse, the incidence drops back down to 9.7 percent. So the disease increases as the fish move upriver, then dramatically declines. Kocan's findings on the

Chena River confirmed the pattern. He hypothesizes that Middle and Upper Yukon *Ichthyophonus*-infected king salmon are dying before they spawn. The disease discovered on the Yukon by Bill Fliris must be having an impact on the king salmon run. How big an effect and what to do about it is still being studied.

Dozen Islands

There is no boat at Chris and Sylvain's fish camp below Mel's, but I stop and climb the bank anyway for a self-guided tour. It's a nice, high spot that catches the sun and the breeze. And it's more than a fish camp. It is a fish processing plant. I had met Chris Ball in Dawson, and she told me a bit about their operation. She and her husband, Sylvain Fleurant, started fishing here at Dozen Islands in the 1970s. At first, they sold fish to the Dawson market, to various hotels and restaurants, but being genetically entrepreneurial, they gradually expanded the business. Today they fish three king nets, each one sized for its particular eddy. They usually have a crew of five, and any of them might go out to pick the nets. It takes an hour and forty minutes to pick the three nets, and the fish are processed as soon as they arrive back at the plant. Some of the kings are steaked, the rest filleted. They even sell smoked roe. Of the filleted fish, some are smoked, some not, some made into lox, some cut into strips. The thinly cut strips go through a secret four-stage process and come out as thin, smoky, oily pieces of jerky. Northerners go crazy over them—they are the best-selling product, at twenty-five dollars per pound. Everything is commercially vacuum packed and frozen in a gleaming, eighteen-by-thirty-six-foot walk-in freezer.

THERE IS NO BOAT either at John Lodder's camp on the left bank. I hear he has moved into town. Across the river I see that the Department of Fisheries and Oceans' fishwheel is turning at Ship Rock, which Mike Rourke's book also lists as Sheep Rock, Cave Rock, St. Paul's Dome, and Castle Rock. In the channel between Fanning's wood yard and Hall Island there is a head in the water. Moose? Bear? I cut the motor and drift quietly down toward it. The bear grows as he emerges, dripping, on the beach, though he still looks skinny until he stops at the top of the bank to shake and fling the water from his black coat.

He has himself a good look at me before bounding into the woods. I listen to his progress for half a minute before the crashing segues to absolute silence.

Fanning Creek

Fanning Creek comes out to the Yukon right where the bear came out, in a bend behind Hall Island. Rourke tells us that Old Man Fanning bought a roadhouse here from Charles Major in 1912. Twenty-two miles out of Eagle, Percy DeWolfe stopped over here on his mail run. Later, Fanning applied for a one-hundred-sixty-acre homestead. Besides running the roadhouse, he trapped and cut steamboat wood. In 1937 an ice jam and flood wiped out Fanning's roadhouse and nearly did him in as well. Percy and a Mountie reached him just in time.

Today there is a beautiful green and orange wooden boat tied up at Fanning Creek, and it belongs to Ludger "Louie" Borste, a forty-seven-year-old German immigrant who's been around Dawson for almost twenty years. Louie comes down to the beach when I pull in, and it doesn't take much to get him to show off the boat he built himself. It's a shallow V, stitch-and-glue plywood hull, thirty-three feet long, eight-foot beam, powered by a one-hundred-ninety-horsepower Volvo Penta inboard. Ten feet of its length is occupied by a cabin with windows all around, trimmed out in fir, mahogany, and oak. I'd seen the boat across the river from Dawson a few years ago and motored over just to have a good look at it and take some pictures. It looked to me like the ideal Yukon River cruiser. If it were fitted out with a galley and table and bunks, I could not imagine a more perfect floating cabin. You could tie up wherever it looked pretty and watch the river go by. But that's *my* dream. In Louie's vision, the boat transports passengers. Dawson is developing into an arts center, he says. A brand new art school is being built there at the Klondike Institute of Art and Culture. Artists and those who appreciate the arts might like to come down to spend a night or a couple of days in a quiet retreat at Fanning Creek. Back in the spruce trees, on a rise of land, Louie is building a good-sized, two-story house (twenty-four by thirty-two feet). He has title to about five acres here, thanks to a government program that proclaims that "the desire to reside in a rural environment is recognized as a legitimate land use activity." He had to have the sale approved by the

Tr'ondek Gwech'in band, and by Mel Besharah, who hunts and traps in the area. There's a review board, and he had to pay market value, less the cost of a survey. There are various requirements, says Louie, all reasonable.

Louie loves the Yukon Territory. "It's a great place to be. Few places are more real," he says. He loves Dawson too: "When I first came, I saw all these bearded guys, and dogs lying in the street. I thought it looked good." And now he has settled further into his niche. "Once I started getting out on the river," he says, "I realized this is the place to be. I like just being out here. I like the challenge. I like to build." He hauled seven hundred ten pieces of lumber down here in his boat, then carried each one up the trail to the building site. Louie is not a trapper, not interested in fishing. He likes the idea of Fanning Creek being his sole residence, of living here in the summer, with the bed-and-breakfast idea bringing in some income. But he thinks he'll continue to travel in the winters. So far, Louie has been to sixty-four countries. "Some people are homebodies. Some of us like adventure."

I mention to Louie that the very accommodating Canadian land sales programs do not seem to have drawn many takers here along the Yukon. "Along the river, no," he says, "Along the road system, yes. Up in Dawson I don't know anybody who wants to live out. They respect it, but nobody does it anymore." Well, not "nobody." Louie does. Along the Yukon on the American side of the border, where there are no such programs, one frequently hears expressed two contending explanations: "If the government opened up land to settlement, the country would be overrun with neo-pioneers," and, "Nobody wants to live out there any more, that was a phenomenon of the 1970s." I think it more likely, as Louie's occupancy testifies, that both statements are untrue.

Poppy Creek

At Poppy Creek, eighty-five miles below Dawson, there are a couple of boats, and I climb the bank to meet Gaetan Beaudet, the only full-time, year-round resident along the Yukon River in the ninety-odd miles between Dawson and the Alaska border. He has blue eyes and graying hair that looks professionally cut. Gaetan is the resident artist and philosopher along the river. His cabin walls are lined with books: psychology, philosophy, religion, classical literature, and hundreds of volumes on birds. The latter are mainly for reference. Gaetan is a master carver of birds. In a small addition off the main room of the cabin is his shop, and in it right now is a near-life-sized bald eagle. It is emerging from a block of tupelo, a soft, light wood he imports from the southern United States. Another of Gaetan's projects, also sculptural in a way, is the structure he is building nearby. It is the biggest log cabin I have ever seen. Nineteen rounds high, not counting the gable ends, dormers projecting this way and that, rooms off of rooms. He's been working on it for years and is just now getting the roof on. He sees it as a lodge that artists, or writers, or people who like to watch or photograph wildlife and scenery might like to visit.

Gaetan was drawn to this place as a nineteen-year-old. He is now fifty-one. Originally, he was a squatter, though at one point he staked a placer claim. In this, he was not unlike Robert Cameron, a Seattle Native who moved down from Forty Mile to very near this spot three-quarters of a century ago. Cameron filed for a homestead, but over the years grew weary of the paperwork and never received title. With regard to its treatment of people living on the land, the Canadian land managers have taken a more tolerant view than their American counterparts. To quote from *Squatter Policy in the Yukon*, the Yukon Territorial Government noted that "throughout the history of the Yukon Territory people have occupied land without legal tenure," that "this form of land occupancy, commonly known as squatting, has traditionally characterized frontier areas." The government thought that it was time to find "reasonable and practical solutions."

In consequence, the Yukon government established a number of eligibility criteria, application procedures, and a review panel representing various interested groups. The process took years. "I could relate to Robert Cameron getting fed up with the whole thing," says Gaetan. But eventually the government granted title to small plots around the homes of a few river people like himself. He had originally applied for the maximum two hectares, about 4.9 acres, but the review panel cut his allotment in half, expressing concern that if he were given the full parcel, he might subdivide. Gaetan still shakes his head at that one. "I'm moving eighty-five miles from town, and I want a neighbor fifty feet away? But that's OK. That's fine. They don't know me."

Cameron left trails too, as did Old Man Fanning. Gaetan and others continue to maintain the trails as if they were historic artifacts—which, of course, is precisely what they are. But, since coming into this area twenty-seven years ago, Gaetan has not trapped. It struck him as "a strange way of living." Nor has he run dogs. He didn't want the full-time commitment dogs require, and he saw little justification in killing thousands of fish to feed them. Nor has he fished commercially, though once in a while he will set a net for a few fish as a change in diet. He shoots a moose every year or two. For the last twenty-two summers, he has earned income by tagging salmon for the Department of Fisheries, which has a fishwheel right across the river from his cabin. In the winters, Gaetan carves birds and earns top prices for them. He takes photographs, he reads, and usually he travels for a month or two. He thinks living away from town permits him to do his best work, that there is less pressure to conform, leaving him freer to find his own creative expression. He believes living out in the woods is a good thing for people. He wishes the American and Canadian governments would allow a limited number of others to do the same. "To allow people to move in just for even a short period of time, just maybe to find themselves, and then go back. Maybe have certain spots, maybe even, I don't know, have a lottery—you're allowed to stay there for so many years, like an artist in residence. It's a unique thing, and we're losing it. People are becoming alienated from nature."

Robert Cameron's Cabin

In 1980, Gaetan was walking a game trail a mile below his place and a couple of hundred yards off the Yukon when abruptly an old log cabin half obscured by vegetation loomed before him. It had been invisible from just fifty feet away. It turned out to be Robert Cameron's cabin, built a half-century before. And it was in excellent shape, though it had spruce trees ten inches in diameter growing out of its sod roof. It is easy for me to find, because with fires in the area, Canadian government firefighters have set up a generator and pump on the beach and run a hose back through the brushy trail to the cabin, where a sprinkler is mounted on the roof.

The roof design is what saved this cabin. It is much more stoutly built than most. There are two ridgepoles, for example, and three purlins on each side of the ridge. A ridgepole is a large log that spans the interior space between the peaks of each gabled wall. Purlins are parallel to the ridge and help support the poles that run from the side walls to the ridge. Six purlins and two ridgepoles allowed the roof to sustain an increasing load as the trees grew on top. Gaetan cut them down, worrying that they might topple in a windstorm, maybe taking a chunk of the roof along with them. Inside, the logs are in excellent shape. The place is spare and clean, kept up by a Dawson man who comes down for brief stays every so often.

Gaetan thinks Cameron intended to farm, and that fits with the evidence out front. The ground is flat all the way to the river. And it obviously had once been cleared because the trees are not large, and there is hardly a spruce among them. The deciduous trees indicate an earlier stage—and spruce a later one—in the typical boreal forest succession pattern.

Bio Camp

Just below Cameron's cabin, I stop for a cup of tea with Crane Vangel and Sean Milligan, who are staying all summer at a camp here maintained by the Department of Fisheries and Oceans. With Gaetan, they tag the fish caught by the government's two fishwheels. As it happens, it is time to tag right now, so I join the crew to motor across the river to check the wheel. The captured fish are kept in a live box. One by one, they are scooped out with a square net that matches the shape of the box. Small fish thrash for only a few seconds, but a big one might pound itself against the sides of the box for half a minute, cutting his fins and tail on the net mesh. Crane sets the fish, nose first, into a tarp-lined trough half-filled with water and tipped forward so that its head is submerged. The fish relaxes here, as Gaetan pokes a large needle through the cartilage at the base of the dorsal fin. He threads through an eight-inch length of orange-pink plastic cord, removes the needle, and ties a quick overhand knot. Crane notes the length of the fish against a yard stick on the side of the box and calls out the number as he drops the fish back into the river. The whole operation takes a few seconds.

The tagging allows the fisheries scientists to get an idea of the size of the king run. In general, the number of tagged fish should bear the same relation to the total run as the number of tagged fish caught later by fishermen bears to the number of all fish caught by the fishermen. For example, say ten percent of the fishermen's catch shows tags. If the Bio Camp crew had tagged one thousand fish, then one thousand might represent ten percent of the total run. The run might then be estimated to be ten thousand. Various adjustments may be made to account for the location of the wheels and other variables. Tagging the fish also permits the biologists to assess the timing of the run, the speed at which the salmon progress upstream, and the harvest rates by fishermen.

Estimating the strength of a salmon run is an even more iffy proposition when it is done in advance. These estimates are based in part on the strength of the previous year's run as well as on the "escapement" of the parent run. The parent run is the cohort of fish that spawned the present group, typically three and four years earlier. And the escapement refers to the number that escaped fishermen's nets and wheels and reached the spawning grounds. In 2001, the run was predicted to be very low, and severe fishing restrictions were imposed all along the middle and upper river. Based on the biologist's predictions, eighty-five-year-old Native leader Sidney Huntington from Galena in the Middle Yukon decided not to go up to his fish camp for the first time in his memory. That disrupted the whole cycle of summer life. The teenaged kids he normally brought with him to camp stayed home. It was the first time Sidney had not planted potatoes—which he does at camp—since he was three years old. Berry picking activities were thrown off too. Later, the biologists said they may have been wrong. Where people did fish, the run was strong. On the day I visited the Bio Camp up near the Canadian border, the crew told me it had caught five hundred fifty-six chinook, the highest one-day total ever recorded in the eighteen years since the program began. Gaetan thought the run appeared to be triple its normal strength, though much of that abundance must have been due to the restrictions placed on the Alaskan fishermen.

The Border

Crossing the border into Alaska, I am entering "the country," the stretch of river and side creeks that John McPhee wrote about in his masterpiece *Coming into the Country*. "I may have liked places that are wild," he wrote, "and been quickened all my days just by the sound of the word, but I see now that I never knew what it could mean. I can see why people who come to Alaska are unprepared. In four decades being beyond some sort of road, I never set foot in a place like this." It was a great steaming pile of bear dung, in the wild country along the Yukon, not far from the village of Eagle, that so spooked and inspired John McPhee. If he were left on his own here, he wrote, "I would have to change in a hurry, and learn in a hurry, or I'd never last a year."

In his 1977 book and in an earlier series of articles for *The New Yorker* magazine, McPhee had written a sympathetic portrait of a new breed of young voyageurs who, when they decided to leave their counterculture enclaves in urban America and head back to nature, made it farther than the Berkshires or the Sonoma coast. They drove their pickups beyond the interstates, up the thousand miles of gravel road that led north to Alaska, and stopped only when they reached the literal end of the road: the Alaska villages of Eagle and Circle, two of the most remote points on the American road system. From there they headed off into the immense wilderness of the Yukon basin, recapitulating, to the consternation of federal land managers, the historic migrations of trappers, prospectors, and homesteaders.

A lot of water has flowed down the Yukon in the thirty years since McPhee visited here. And it is interesting to see what has become of the young river people. Whither this tribe of woods-wise and well-spoken renegades, now well into middle age?

Steve Ulvi and Lynette Roberts

The first camp to check is here, just below the Canadian border, at a spot Steve Ulvi and his girlfriend Lynette Roberts called Windy Corner. It's a quiet place today. Neither wind nor people. I know that Steve and Lynette moved off the river years ago, and that Steve has gone to work for the National Park Service in Fairbanks. In 1976, McPhee had found Ulvi to be an articulate embodiment of the neo-pioneer. Though he gets only a mention in McPhee's book, Ulvi's story is representative of many of the young people who moved on to the river in the 1970s. He had grown up in the San Francisco Bay Area and attended college in Oregon. There he'd read and pondered several classics of wilderness lore, hiked, backpacked, and camped. He established himself in a tepee in the coast range and commuted to school. But, inevitably, he craved escape from what he regarded as a consumptive and wasteful culture. He wanted a larger and more elemental and primitive space into which his emerging philosophy (which was tending toward Buddhism) and aesthetic (which was distinctly agrarian) might expand. And he was ready to embrace the hard work, isolation, and even danger that might come with it. So, in the summer of 1974, before he quite had completed college, Steve Ulvi headed north to see about living in the deep Alaskan woods. His girlfriend Lynette Roberts joined him, as did his brother Dana and a couple of his like-minded California buddies. They all piled into a rebuilt 1951 Dodge pickup with two canoes strapped on top and the back crammed with tools, gear, and eight or nine hundred pounds of food.

Eagle was an unusual Alaskan village in those days. Almost no one was out on the land. There were those who had come to Eagle because it was a jump-off point for heading into the wilderness. But, for one reason or another, these folks hadn't jumped. Instead, they picked up seasonal work or, in a few cases, started small businesses. Eagle also attracted a number of comfortably well-off retirees drawing government pensions. Like the first group, they sometimes kept a canoe tied up at the riverbank, occasionally checked their gill net for a salmon for dinner, but they rarely ventured farther into the country. They were the frontier equivalent of gentlemen farmers, and the value of their harvest was best measured in psychological rather than economic terms. The occasional fish had less to do with sustaining the body than sustaining an identity. It was the slender thread that connected the townsfolk to the wilderness and permitted their deeply valued self-image as frontiersmen and -women. And, finally, there was the village of Han Indians just outside Eagle. But these folks, too, had largely given up trapping and fishing and dog teams in favor of paying jobs, government assistance, and store food. Not a single one of the Han were living out in the country in 1974. In 1976, only one moose was taken by an Eagle Village resident, and that was on the Taylor Highway. A few still did some backyard trapping on lines less than a mile long, cut firewood for sale, or fished in the eddies in front of the village. But gone were the days of training good teams of working dogs, of spending a part of the winter out at a trap camp, of spending the summer at a fish camp.

In short, the traditional skills of the old-timers of this region were about to be lost, when a kind of salvation came rolling down the hill into Eagle. They emerged long-haired and smelling of unfamiliar herbs from pickups and vans with license plates from California, Oregon, and New Hampshire. In the main, they were white, urban, hippie kids like Steve Ulvi and his friends.

ULVI AND HIS PALS set up their tents at the Eagle campground and strolled downtown to look things over. Perhaps predictably, the inhabitants of Eagle tended to discourage—if not disparage—newcomers. Did they have any idea what seventy degrees below zero felt like? Had they ever lived in a small cabin with no electricity? No running water? Hell, the darkness alone drove people crazy, with the sun not up for much more than the lunch hour. But, as Ulvi would learn later, the most naysaying of the townsfolk tended to be those who had not, themselves, lived out in the country.

The group found a more sympathetic reception at the Native village. At least, they met a man there who would let them move onto land that he claimed just this side of the Canadian border, on the opposite bank of the Yukon. It was five miles off the end of the road, eight miles above the Han village, eleven miles above Eagle proper. There was an old cabin on the site (the one that stands today nearest the river) that two of the party could fix up and live in. The others—Ulvi, Lynette, and Dana—could build a new cabin. The man probably doubted they would last the winter, Ulvi thought, and was figuring that he'd shortly acquire, without cost, one new and one rehabilitated cabin. With a handshake, they concluded the deal, never putting a time limit on the occupancy.

Like old-time sourdoughs, the partners "lined" their outfit upriver. That is, they loaded their gear into the two canoes and, walking on shore, hauled each canoe upstream with a loop of rope, the ends of which were tied to the bow and stern. If the rope was held at just the right point on the loop, the bow would point slightly into the current. That meant it would stand off from shore a bit, instead of tracking right behind the hauler, where it would run aground in the shallows. If they came to a steep, eroded bank or a rock outcrop, they would have to paddle across the river, which might be two-thirds of a mile wide in places. In doing so, they could lose a half mile or more to the current before they climbed out on the other side and resumed lining.

If the group's approach to transportation seemed labor-intensive, it fit their collective notion of right living. They did not care to use outboard motors. And in constructing their cabins, they had decided they would employ only hand tools: axes, augers, and an old-fashioned crosscut saw. Ulvi had owned a chain saw in Oregon but sold it before heading north. The racket and fumes seemed almost an impiety in the deep silences of the Alaskan wilderness. And he didn't want to be dependent on gas, oil, and parts. They would cut their house logs, roof poles, and floor poles by hand. And by hand they would ripsaw what lumber they required. No plywood would taint their camp. Once, when a sheet of the stuff drifted down the river and fetched up nearby, they poked it back into the current. (Early-day sourdoughs would have fought each other over it—a great flat board made without whipsaw or adze, perfect as a fish-cutting table or for stretching beaver hides.)

Nor would Ulvi, in selecting a site for the cabin, allow himself the pleasure of a view of the passing river. Instead, he built it a hundred yards back in the trees so as not to violate the river or impose his settlement on travelers. When the fifteen-by-fifteen-foot structure was finished, the occupants settled into a style of housekeeping that suggested the relative opulence of a monastery. As near-vegetarians, and frugal ones, they parceled out their lentils, rice, beans, and pancake mix from fifty-pound sacks. Of course, they baked their own bread, grinding wheat by hand. As a special indulgence, they permitted themselves one can of fruit per week, split three ways. Candles provided the only light during the months of dark winter. And they would forego that inessential artifact of a profligate era: toilet paper. Moss would suffice.

But ascetic purity, even on this impressive scale, had limits. For one thing, there was a six-mil sheet of polyethylene under the roof sod, which was practically the only way to prevent such a roof from leaking. Squares of clear plastic film served as windows, nylon sleeping bags lay on the bunks, and a high-powered rifle hung by the door. Even the mail-order importation of bulk dried fruit or powdered milk implied the sort of industrial infrastructure that the group seemed to spurn. And the philosophy of self-denial, while sincere, seemed tinged with sanctimony:

the plaid-shirted pioneers were cultivating their image every bit as assiduously as the blow-dried kids contemporaneously making the scene at America's shopping malls. Last, Ulvi and his friends modified their canon as the country demanded (or as advancing maturity permitted). It wasn't long before they hunted for meat, took up trapping, bought kerosene lanterns and eventually an outboard motor, even a chain saw. To a remarkable degree, however, Ulvi and his friends, as well as the other young people living out along the Yukon River in the mid-1970s, approximated the frontier life of the previous century. Like their sourdough antecedents, they lived a life closely connected to the land and one in which simplicity and hard work were both the prerequisites of survival and values in themselves.

As it turned out, the Native man in Eagle Village did not fall heir to two abandoned cabins in the spring of 1975. The other three young men moved off the site, but Steve Ulvi, then twenty-three years old, stayed on until he was a middle-aged man. He and Lynette married and started a family here. During the warm summer months, while Steve and Lynette cut and hung fish to dry or hauled buckets of river water to the garden, the two kids played on the beach with the sled dog pups. When the leaves yellowed and the rank smell of cranberries filled the woods, the kids dug potatoes in the wet earth or headed out with their pails to help harvest tongue-staining blueberries, rose hips packed with seeds and vitamins, and the highbush cranberries that burst in your mouth with a small explosion of sour juice. In winter they sometimes rode in the sled over the trapline trails, spending the night in a wall tent miles from the sight or sound of another human being outside of the family. When the kids became school-aged, Lynette sent away for correspondence school materials and taught them at home.

If Steve Ulvi had jumped headlong into a wilderness life, he returned from it in stages. As the kids grew, Steve and Lynette wanted them to be able to play more with other children. Lynette, too, was beginning to crave more of a social life, and she wanted a job. Steve had begun to reach a point where a declining enthusiasm for trapping was being overtaken by an ascending interest in a regular paycheck. In 1981, he started working for the Park Service as a seasonal hire doing construction work. Two years later, he was offered a permanent position with the Park Service in Eagle, and he took it. The family moved from their snug cabin upriver to an ancient, sagging, and drafty one in town. The kids enrolled in the Eagle school. Lynette served on the school board. Steve worked a steady job.

Steve and Lynette built a nice place of their own near Eagle Village, but soon, as the kids reached junior-high-school age, Fairbanks beckoned. As Interior Alaska's hub and home of the state university's main campus, Fairbanks (area population 80,000) could offer libraries and swimming pools; ballet and drama classes; and gymnastics, soccer, and track. Eagle (population 168) could not. And both Steve and Lynette wanted to "exercise the mind," as Steve said, to finish college, for a start. Now, for the first time, they were ready—eager—to turn their energies and intellects toward some traditional career progress. So, for all the reasons that generally make more sense to people approaching forty than they do to people barely out of their teens, the family moved out of the upper Yukon country in 1990.

The front cabin still stands on a little bluff above the river, and it looks like it is used occasionally. A trail up through the woods behind it leads to Steve and Lynette's old cabin, now a beautiful, ghostly shell. The roof poles are strangely bare against the sky and painted with a green mold. Someone probably stripped off the roof moss and used it to add insulation to the other cabin. Where some of the original roof remains, a forest of little spruce trees now grows. It is a ruin like other ruins along the Yukon. The mausoleum of a dream. Steve and Lynette's reasons for coming into the country had been like those of the other river people of their era, and not especially different from those who had come before for generations. Their reasons for coming out of the country were alike as well.

Eagle

Just below the border, my engine sputters, and I point for shore in a rocky spot to land and fill my gas tank. But I don't lift the motor in time, and a blade breaks off my ancient prop. It's a sunny day as I wobble into Eagle, and I'm not fretting too much about the prop. I figure there is bound to be a match for this one lying around Eagle somewhere. It's a matter of being directed to whoever might have an old ten- or fifteen-horse Evinrude or Johnson clamped to a sawhorse among the weeds in the yard, its owner willing to convert it into cash. At the boat landing I meet a fellow named Greg Birchard, who kindly heads home to make some calls on my behalf but returns to report no luck. He points me to Chris Christensen's cabin near the well house. Chris gives me a soda and takes me on a tour of his backyard. Unfortunately, his relics don't match mine. A white-bearded fellow named Austin Nelson hops on his four-wheeler and drives eighteen miles round trip to see what he's got in his junk pile. When he comes back, he tells me he's got props from the years before mine and from the years after mine. He's got smaller props and larger props. But he does not have a nine-and-a-half-inch prop for a thirteen-tooth spline. I hike out the road toward the Native village to look for a repair shop that someone thought was still in existence but turns out not to be. On the way, I get a lift from a bearded fellow in camo pants who lives with a very large family in a very large tent compound. It's fabricated from many, many blue tarps propped up by poles and guyed down with ropes. Some clear plastic patches sewn in serve as sky-lights. It looks very much like a Bedouin encampment, set down in the sub-Arctic and colored by a child in all the wrong colors. He is a collec-tor of things, this man, notably bicycles, a hundred or two of which await his attention in rusting piles. He lives some kind of Arabian vision, I think, here on his oasis among the scrubby black spruce. His caravan of iron camels rests outside his tent. His begotten play in the shade.

If a house is an expression of self, as I think Jung said, then the range of selves to be found in Eagle, Alaska, is illustrated in a short block along this road. Not far from the tent encampment is a virtual dollhouse, painted an optimistic blue and white, with scalloped fancy work hanging along the eaves like wooden lace. Spick-and-span to the verge of antisepsis, the little house is set, like a precious stone, in a sparkling green lawn ringed by a white picket fence. American flag aflutter, the wide muddy river beyond, it is a vision of Hannibal, Mis-souri, on the Fourth of July.

From the pay phone in front of the store, I track down a prop at the Boat Shop in Fairbanks. My wife will put it on the mail plane tomor-row. Meanwhile, for the price of a hamburger at the café on the river-front, I take in a million-dollar view. The picture windows look east out over the river to the Ogilvies. For nearly one hundred eighty de-grees, one sees nothing but sky and river and mountains and trees, a view that hasn't changed significantly since the end of the last Ice Age.

Of course, from the other side of the river, looking toward where I am sitting, the view would have changed a lot in the last century and a quarter, as a Han Indian village morphed into a regional hub for prospectors, traders, missionaries, the military, and the government, then shrank to near-extinction, then revived again. All the comings and goings apparently taxed the historians and record keepers, because the names and dates of the various settlements built on or near Eagle vary almost with every published account. Probably in 1880,[*] near the mouth of Mission Creek, the trader Francois Mercier[†] found on the left bank a Han settlement of one hundred six residents called David's Village[‡] after its chief. That year, on the same bank, says Mercier, three-quarters of a mile below the village[§] and toward Mission Creek, perhaps within the present town of Eagle,[**] he built a trading post for the Western Fur and Trading Company. Mercier is quite specific about this location.[††] He does not give this first fort a name in his memoirs.[‡‡] In any event, the 1880 trading post was abandoned the following year when the trader he left in charge pulled out, taking the windows and stove. Mercier returned in 1882 under the auspices of the Alaska Commercial Company to build a new post "nearby," according to the reliable historian Melody Webb.[§§] He named it Fort Bell at first, and later Belle Isle. Mercier's chronicler places this trading post both above and below the village.[***] Somewhere in the area, during the 1880s, the Han had a semipermanent winter camp called *Nibaw Zhoh*, meaning "skin house."

------

[*]Cornelius Osgood, the first professional ethnographer to write about the Han, says 1873, an error that almost everyone repeats, although Mike Rourke and others say 1874.

[†]Osgood and others incorrectly say it was his brother Moise Mercier.

[‡]Or Johnny's Village, as Frederick Schwatka and others have it.

[§]Or a mile and a quarter below, according to Schwatka.

[**]Osgood and the local people believe the location was on the island across from the present town site.

[††]But Mercier was also quite specific when he wrote that he built Fort Reliance six miles *above* the Klondike River, when in fact the site is six miles *below* the Klondike. And he places Charley Village on the Yukon's left bank opposite the mouth of the Kandik River, when it was on the right bank beside the Kandik's mouth.

[‡‡]Several writers call it Belle Isle, which is the name of the *next* fort Mercier built.

[§§]Or he simply "reestablished" the original post, as the unreliable Mercier writes.

[***]Linda Finn Yarborough, *Recollections of the Youkon*, pp. 83 and 89, respectively.

In May 1898, twenty-eight miners who hadn't managed to find wealth in the Klondike staked a townsite near Eagle Bluff. Prospectors staked more than two hundred claims on Mission Creek and its tributary American Creek. Eagle City boomed, with more than five hundred cabins built and seventeen hundred residents on site almost overnight. But the next night, figuratively, the town all but emptied with reports of the gold strike at Nome in 1899. The same year, at the downriver edge of the town, the U.S. Army began constructing Eagle City Camp, later called Fort Egbert, to support the construction of a telegraph line intended to cross to Asia at Bering Strait. The fort grew into a complex of thirty-seven buildings housing more than one hundred fifty men. An enormous mule barn had stalls for fifty-eight mules. When the army closed Fort Egbert in 1911, Hudson Stuck, Alaska's dog-mushing missionary, recalled the scene: "Fort Egbert is abandoned now, another addition to the melancholy of the Yukon; its extensive buildings, barracks, and officers' quarters, post-exchange and commissariat, hospital, sawmill, and artisans' shops, a spacious, complete gymnasium only recently built, are all vacant and deserted. In the yards lie three thousand cords of dry wood, a year's supply; cut on the hills, awaiting the expected annual contracts, lie as many more—six thousand cords left to rot! Some of us perverse 'conservationists,' upon whom the unanimous Alaska press delights to pour scorn, lament the trees more than the troops."

Upon the fort's construction, either the Han were compelled by the military to move upriver, where they established what is known today as Eagle Village (as local Native people adamantly assert in oral history accounts), or the Native village was upriver from the fort and the townsite at the time the town and fort were built, as other accounts have it. What is known is that the area around the Fort Egbert site, and the area now occupied by Park Service buildings, is littered with chipped stone tool remains, indicating long-term occupancy by Han people before contact.

People came to this place, and they left it. The settlements themselves came and went. Assigned to these encampments at Eagle, at one time or another, by one writer or another, I find twenty-two names: Fetoutlin, Klatolklin, Johnny's Village, Johnny Village, Johnny's Indians, John's Village, David's People, David's Village, David's Camp, Eagle Village, *Tthe T'awdlin, Nibaw Zhoh, Niibeeo Zhoo,* the Western

Fur and Trading Company trading post, Fort Bell, Belleisle, Belle Isle, Belle Isle Station, Eagle City, Eagle, Eagle City Camp, and Fort Egbert. But there's a good chance that occupancy—and names—trace back all the way to the Pleistocene.

THE NEXT DAY, I am eager to jump off from this jumping-off place, so when my prop comes in on the mail plane, I hop into the back of a pickup truck at the store and ride out to the airstrip. I have to say that Percy DeWolfe could not have topped this one-day delivery service, thanks to the telephone and the daily flights of the little bush planes carrying mail, cargo, and passengers. Back at my campsite at Mission Creek, I slap the new prop on the outboard, load my gear, and push off into the river. Once clear of the rocks, I lower the kicker, pull on the starter rope, and set the throttle to a quiet putt. A minute later, I can hardly make out the shapes of human figures standing on shore. Shrinking by the second is the town of Eagle, a couple dozen tin roofs glittering in an afternoon sun shower.

Seymour Able

Leif Able emerges from the woods while I am hammering my stake into the beach at Shade Creek around the first big bend below Eagle. He looks to be in his early twenties and cheerful. I am in luck, he says, when I tell him I was hoping to catch his father in. I've wanted to meet Seymour for years and to get his story, which I have only heard secondhand. Pretty soon Seymour comes down to check out the visitor. This is the first stage of bush protocol, akin to a city person opening the door a crack, with the chain in place, to look the caller over before committing to anything more. I pass the preliminaries and am invited up to the cabin.

Seymour is tall and lanky and dressed in a clean T-shirt, shorts, and sandals. A graying mustache sprouts from graying stubble like a swatch of grass the mower keeps missing. His thinning hair funnels back from a tanned forehead into a ponytail so small it would be a proportional fit on a pony the size of a lemming. Seymour's Tennessee accent is made the more engaging by a couple-tooth gap in the front row that creates a spoiler effect on his fricatives.

He had a rough childhood, emotionally and physically. He didn't get along with his stepfather and was determined to get away from him.

Immediately after high school classes, Seymour and a buddy left Memphis for Alaska. They didn't even wait for the graduation ceremony. When classes were done, so were they. "One day we walked out of the high school doors, the next day we loaded the truck, and the day after that we left." He worked for a while in Anchorage, mostly as a carpenter, but soon moved to the town of Delta on the Alaska Highway. Delta began to boom in 1975 with work on the Trans-Alaska Pipeline, and Seymour found he wanted to move again. "I felt like Delta was not really what I'd come for after the pipeline started, and it just got really crazy. It wasn't my thing, and I didn't quite cotton to the whole concept of that pipeline and all the oil and all the waste and everything, and I just wanted to get further away from it."

With some friends he launched at Eagle and headed downriver. "I was totally green. I didn't know what I was getting myself into." The motor broke down and the group ended up at the mouth of Nation River. There wasn't much river traffic in those days, and three weeks passed before they were able to flag down a boat and hitch a ride to town for parts. His friends were going to help him build a cabin, but now, having frittered away three weeks, they had to get home. Seymour, his girlfriend Janice Waldron, and nine dogs motored downriver to a spot just about midway between the Nation and Kandik Rivers. They set up camp on a slough behind Catham Island below Glenn Creek. "The reason that I ended up where I was is because if I'd have went any further I wouldn't have had enough gas to get back to town. It was a gas thing, but it turned out to be a really nice place." They had no idea how long they would stay, and they had only a modest outfit.

Having bailed from contemporary society, Seymour and Jan jumped into the woods and survived under a sheltering canopy. That statement is only partly metaphoric. "I just had an army parachute and some Visqueen and just put up a little frame and made a tent out of all that and added some moss and stuff. And I tentatively kind of started a cabin, but after I seen that I wouldn't get it done in time for winter— and I was just so excited about everything else—we figured we'd just live in the tent. And one year led to the next." Jan and Seymour lived under the parachute for two years.

They were light on food. And they were so green, says Seymour, they didn't even know that the Yukon was full of salmon that could be easily caught with nets and put up for use throughout the long winter. "I didn't know nothing about fishing. Well, I didn't know nothing about trapping. I'd done a little bit of it but I didn't have a clue. So the first winter was really just, well, actually it was a lot of hardship, too. We didn't have a lot of food, and didn't even get an early moose. A couple of people just lost, not really knowing what to do, but we had a good time figuring it out." Eventually they got things figured out: hunting, fishing, trapping, and ordering bulk organic food through a co-op—like two hundred pounds of wheat, fifty pounds of rye, and fifty pounds of buckwheat. All this they freighted downriver from Eagle in their canoe.

They managed. Thrived, even, if propagation is a measure: by the spring of 1977, Jan was expecting a baby. The couple decided they did not want to go to a hospital. "But I did go to a doctor and get a little instruction," says Seymour, "about pressure and torque and that kind of stuff, and read a bunch of books and decided we'd have it here at Shade Creek." Charlie Edwards and his wife Cheryl had a cabin at Shade Creek then (today, it molders as a ruin below Seymour's spot), and Cheryl had acted as a midwife once before. But the river's breakup was a drawn-out affair that spring, and it took a long time for the ice to begin clearing out. Finally, when Seymour was ready to load his pregnant wife into the Grumman canoe and point it into the Yukon's current for an iceberg-dodging upriver run to Shade Creek, Jan said she thought she might be going into labor.

All things considered, it still seemed best to go anyway, so they did. Seymour cut the nine dogs loose to run along the beach, and as much as he could, he hugged the bank where he didn't have to buck too much current. The little ten-horse kicker didn't fail him, and the whole menagerie arrived safely at Shade Creek. Charlie and Cheryl arrived in camp a little later with a Dall sheep they had lucked into right on the beach below Limestone Hogback Ridge near Pickerel Slough. Jan's labor was evident now, and Seymour was trying to get things set for the birthing. "There was only one piece of plywood, and Charlie didn't want to give it up for us to make a makeshift bed for Leif to be born on. He wanted to tack the sheep [hide] on it. So he tacked the sheep on it, and we still needed it, so we just used it anyway with the sheep on the other side—we just turned it over and Leif was born, and it was something."

Before Leif entered the world, hale and whole and ultimately handsome, there had been some "what if" discussion. "You know, being out in the bush, you're alone a lot, we even talked about, you know, like we do puppies, you know, we cull puppies if they're not right when they're born. And we even talked about what if he's born weird or, are we going to cull him or—you know we could a *never* done nothing like that, couldn't of even *considered* it, but we talked about it, you know. And it's a good thing because far as I'm concerned he looked awful when he was born."

Leif's arrival in 1977 prompted the abandonment of the tent and the construction of a cabin. "We figured we needed a cabin for a kid," says Seymour. Leif may have been the more powerful force, but the decision to leave the tent was also nudged along by agents of the federal government. The tent sat on federal land, administered by the Bureau of Land Management (BLM), and in the summer of 1977 the BLM paid Seymour and Jan a visit. They served the couple with a trespass notice laced with *to wits* and *hereby notifieds* and impenetrable citations to the statutes. Seymour pointed out that they were living in a tent. Technically, they were camping, which was legal. It was a cute argument, but the agents were not amused. "They threatened me with jail, so I went to town and signed a piece of paper saying I would move, and I moved off that section that they wrote in their paperwork."

THIS LEVEL OF INTEREST on the part of the federal government in trespass cabins out in the wilderness of Alaska was a new development. From prehistory forward, anyone who took a notion to move here just did it. And the government seemed to give tacit approval to the occupation. Basically, it ignored the land during the first century of American ownership. And that seemed reasonable. The few people who were tough enough and savvy enough to handle the cold, the darkness, and the mosquitoes, and to wrestle a slim living from such a place had certainly lived up to the spirit of the government's homesteading programs. But in the early 1970s, things began to change. A new logic took hold that said no old-fashioned, dues-paying residency amounted to a "right" to live on public land.

And BLM officials started patrolling the country in search of cabins to post with trespass notices or, they threatened, to burn. Because the cabins were usually tiny and made from the natural materials at hand—unpeeled logs with sod roofs—they weren't easy to spot. And though they blended into their surroundings, though they were sometimes fifty miles from the nearest town and often more canoe-dragging miles up a side creek, the BLM had its orders. And it had helicopters. When the river people cut a tree for firewood or for some construction purpose, they took to placing a chunk of moss on the fresh-cut stump to make it less visible from the air. With townspeople, they were cagey about where, exactly, they lived.

A big part of the reason for this turn of events had to do with the discovery of the nation's largest oil field at Prudhoe Bay on Alaska's Arctic Ocean coast in the late 1960s. Alaska Natives and environmentalists halted the rush to oil development until aboriginal land claims were resolved and provisions made for establishing parks. In short order, land issues dominated Alaska politics. Out of this controversy emerged the Alaska Native Claims Settlement Act (ANCSA) in 1971, an unprecedented legislative victory for Alaska's Native people. Along with a tidy cash settlement (about a billion dollars), the Native people were permitted to select forty million acres of federal land in Alaska (roughly a Wisconsin plus a New Jersey). Also tucked away in the legislation was something for the advocates of the environment: a promise that Alaska lands for refuges, preserves, and parks would be identified and set aside by 1978.

Federal land managers from the National Park Service, the Fish and Wildlife Service, the Bureau of Outdoor Recreation, the BLM, and the Forest Service sat down together with their maps to see "which lands should go into what System," as the new law stipulated. Literally in smoke-filled rooms, with big maps on the wall, the agency people strategized like players in a board game, trading for what they wanted. At the same time, the Alaska state government also staked its claim to vacant lands. According to the statehood act passed by Congress in 1958, Alaska had the right to select one hundred four million acres of public land as its statehood entitlement, though much of this land had neither been selected nor transferred by the 1970s. So, all at the same time, the various federal agencies, the state government, the oil companies, and the Native groups all moved to acquire title to Alaska lands. It amounted to an institutional land rush. And that is how, by the mid-1970s, briefcase-toting BLM bureaucrats came to be jumping out of helicopters in the middle of the wilderness to assert the government's ownership of lands and cabins it had long ignored.

SEYMOUR ABLE COMPLIED with the BLM's order. The agency had said they wanted him off Section 14, Township 6 North, Range 27 East, Fairbanks Meridian. So he moved off Section 14. But he built a cabin on another section about a mile away, near a lake that people now call Seymour Lake. For his fish camp, he used another site on the Yukon directly across from Glenn Creek, and it too was outside the section he'd agreed to vacate. But BLM was still on his case; they visited him via snow machine in March 1978 with two of their agents and four state troopers, and again via riverboat in July. Jan decided to write Alaska's congressman, Don Young, and Senator Ted Stevens. She explained that she and Seymour trapped and fished seventy miles from the nearest village, that their life was simple, canning fish for their food, drying fish for the dogs, trapping for the cash that bought the other basics. "This land," she wrote, "has historically been available for public use and subsistence living, without patented land or any deed of ownership. It is not our desire to own the land, but to be able to continue using it as it has been used traditionally. We believe there's enough area out here that BLM should have some kind of program so that we can continue our present land use."

After Senator Stevens asked the BLM for an explanation, the BLM offered several of the river people, including Jan and Seymour, the opportunity to apply for permits to occupy existing cabins during the trapping season. But the locals were leery. It seemed best to see how the land management shuffle played out. If it turned out the Park Service was to take over the upper Yukon, maybe that agency would take the mandate to protect subsistence living more to heart and set up reasonable regulations governing the resident people. For the time being, the river people bided their time.

Eventually Seymour and Jan's fish camp across from Glenn Creek took on a form more emblematic of the 1970s than of the classic sourdough period, and it harked back to older old-timers than the prospectors. The camp's main dwelling consisted of a tepee not so different from the sort of skin tents once used by the Athabascan Indians native to this region. The occupants, too, took on an aboriginal aspect. "We used to go around every summer whenever it was possible naked all the time. I mean we'd do canoes naked, we'd line naked, we was always around fish camp naked." Later in the summer, when evening brought gradually darker nights, the muslin of the tepee glowed a cheery yellow from electric lights within. Seymour had rigged up a twelve-volt system charged by a wind generator mounted atop a fifty-foot log tower.

Meanwhile, back in the halls of government, a new law emerged from the horse-trading. The Alaska National Interest Lands Conservation Act (ANILCA) of 1980 was said by its framers to be the most significant land conservation act in the history of the United States. In one stroke ANILCA added Alaska land sufficient to more than double the size of the nation's national parks, more than double the national wildlife refuge lands, and triple the size of the country's wilderness preserves. It designated twenty-four new wild and scenic rivers, named ten more rivers for possible inclusion in the system, established four new national conservation areas and two national recreation areas, and created one new national forest and added to several existing ones. If the ANILCA real estate in Alaska were declared the fifty-first state, it would rank third in land area. Only the remainder of Alaska and Texas would be larger.

Obviously, this had big consequences for the river people. With the passage of ANILCA, most of the land adjacent to the Yukon River between Eagle and Circle was given to the National Park Service. And many of the cabin dwellers, including Seymour, found themselves not just squatting on some long-ignored BLM acreage but smack in the middle of a new unit of the National Park System: Yukon-Charley Rivers National Preserve.

There seemed to be a ray of hope, however. Wisely, Congress recognized the difference between backcountry in the lower states and wilderness in Alaska. For one thing, there were people—both Native and white—who lived in or near these wild places. Their livelihood depended on their freedom to hunt, fish, gather berries, cut trees, and so on. And this way of life in rural Alaska, the Congress noted, "may be the last major remnant of the subsistence culture alive today in North America." Accordingly, the "subsistence lifestyle" was declared a "cultural value," and its practice was to be allowed in the newly established parklands.

Furthermore, in the specific case of Yukon-Charley Rivers National Preserve, it was precisely the human use of the country that made the area especially deserving of protection. "The history of the upper Yukon River area is rich and still visible," said Congress. "Along the banks of the Yukon, the remains of many old buildings attest to the river's historic use as an artery of trade, travel, and communication." And these old cabins, roadhouses, mining works, trails, and equipment—these "historic resources," in Park Service parlance—were said to be among the primary "values" present in the preserve.

In consideration of all of this, Congress mandated that the Park Service establish regulations that would protect the subsistence lifestyle within parklands. The regulations adopted by the Park Service, however, were designed to eliminate the resident people altogether. It went like this: the most recent residents, those who built cabins on federal land after 1978, were to lose their cabins to the Park Service straight away. Those who built before 1978, but after 1973, could apply for a permit to stay in their cabin for one year. And those who built cabins prior to 1973 could apply for a five-year permit. This latter permit could be renewed every five years for the life of the occupant, but it could not be transferred except to an immediate family member residing in the cabin "at the time of the issuance of the original permit." Applicants were required to sign away any interest in the land on which the cabin stood and to agree to turn the structure over to the Park Service upon the expiration of the permit. The regulations, therefore, phased out—over the course of one lifetime—the residency of all people living on preserve land. And with them would go the culturally and historically significant activities, which, in large part, justified the preserve to begin with.

SO IT WAS that one day in the early 1980s, Seymour received another visit, this time from the National Park Service. "[It] was early summer and I think about six or seven of them showed up at my camp." Seymour met them at his boat landing and sat down for a chat. "They were all really nice and told me that this was a park now but that it was made to accommodate subsistence people and that I could stay there the rest of my life, my family could stay there the rest of their lives, my kids and so forth and so on." All this was sounding pretty good, says Seymour. "I really liked being there and I had no plans of leaving. I thought that it was my spot forever, at that point."

The bureaucratic details of occupancy were still to be written, the park rangers said. "They seemed disoriented theirselves, it was a new thing, they flat admitted it, and said things needed to be worked out, but that Congress said not only that it was all right for us to be there but that they were supposed to accommodate us, that they were supposed to help us stay there, that the preserve was to preserve the subsistence people, as well as the park. And at that point I thought that I had it made."

Like the other people living in the new park, Seymour was asked to sign a document that allowed him to stay at his homesite but which turned over any interest he may have in the property and his buildings to the Park Service. That was all right by Seymour because he wasn't living in the country to acquire property. "I didn't own the land. I didn't *care* to own it. I didn't want no ownership and I didn't move there hoping to claim anything. So I got a permit. I agreed to get a permit. I was the first one to sign it, if I remember right."

He didn't go to town much in those days, but when he did, he'd stop in at the Park Service headquarters and ask questions to double-check on his status. "And at least for that first year, and maybe the next one after that, I was led to believe nothing but great stuff."

Then things changed. "Within a few years I asked them for a permit to build a new cabin, and I got a permit written that I could build a cabin. I cut the logs and everything." Seymour let the logs dry a year, as cabin builders often do, but before he could start building the next summer, he was told he had to leave. "Somewhere along the line I made them mad at me. I just didn't fit into their idea of what they wanted. I came back from being gone all winter and was told that I was no longer considered subsistence, and they were going to pull my permit."

The Park Service had begun, as bureaucracies are prone to do, to attempt to codify things. Defining exactly what is and what isn't a subsistence life can be an oxymoronic exercise because living a subsistence life always involved a shifting, resilient, opportunistic approach to making ends meet. What subsistence was one year, it might not be the next. If game animals were in a certain area for a few years, that is where people exploited them. If the animals moved to another place later, the people moved their operations there. If fur prices were up, they trapped more. If they were down, they might cut steamboat wood instead. If a little wage work offered itself at a roadhouse, or a mine, or some geologists needed supplies freighted, people seized those opportunities as they came along. A fellow might even forego fishing altogether in favor of a summer's wages in town. One common tactic beginning in the 1950s was for bush residents to fight fires for the BLM in the summer, to return to hunt for meat in the fall, and to go out on the trapline for the winter. With their wages, they could pay cash to feed their dog teams dried fish that they hadn't caught themselves. There were innumerable combinations. They varied with the practitioner, and they were always in flux. What the federal agency was missing was that attempting to define narrowly what was and what wasn't a true and sanctioned subsistence lifestyle simply missed the point: it degraded in a Heisenbergian way the very thing they sought to measure. As Seymour sees it, park employees (with titles like Cultural Resource Specialist) were trying to objectify the subsistence life with so much quasi-legalistic verbiage that pretty soon the bush people no longer fit the definition of themselves.

"They started making all these laws, like you could only make so much money. You could only make a certain percentage of that money outside of your subsistence life. And it was a small percentage, like twenty-five percent. Seventy-five percent of it had to be made in the bush or something like that. You know, they come up with all these things. They was trying to make all these laws from that intent and they kept changing them. And one year I'd be told one thing, and the next year I'd be told another, and it started to get to where it was hard to keep up with." The Park Service says no such income limits were ever established. But these ideas were talked about, and the regulations were written and rewritten for many years. At the same time, the agency was getting an earful from the other side. Environmental groups pressured—even sued—to get the squatters out and the cabins torn down. They saw only the countryside as worth protecting, not the inhabitants, not the lifestyle.

Like most other frontiersmen before him, Seymour hadn't given a whole lot of thought to quantifying his life in the woods. "I didn't even claim to be a subsistence person. I didn't even know what a subsistence person was. And I still don't claim to be subsistence. I don't claim to be anything. But them guys came down and wanted to put labels on everything. And they were pulling my permit, and I was going to have to move out."

It was a little like a situation that developed in the village of Barrow on Alaska's North Slope in the 1950s when an overeager fish and game warden flew up and busted a few of the local hunters for shooting ducks out of season. He told the Eskimos that they had to wait until September because that's when hunting season for ducks opened. The locals thought he was crazy. Their people had hunted ducks for ten thousand years. Now comes a white guy telling them they can only hunt ducks after the ducks had flown south and the ponds had frozen over. The game warden did not consider it within his purview to factor in latitude, or history, or common sense, or even a general notion of fair play. He pointed to the regulations and wrote out the citations.

Unlike the Eskimos, who fought the government and won the right to continue taking ducks, Seymour folded his tepee. He bundled up his tribe, pulled the snow hook, whistled up the dogs, and moved out of the preserve. Now, sitting in the yard beside his spacious cabin on a birch- and spruce-covered slope above Shade Creek just outside the park boundary, he is for the most part sanguine. "I can honestly say that I am glad that it happened because my life is so good now that I can thank them for putting me in such a position."

But sometimes Seymour remembers a lot of wasted energy. "We're talking about quite a few years of dealing with these guys. And I mean if they'd have come down from the very beginning and said, 'Look, we're turning this into a park, we don't want you here,' I'd have left. There'd have been no problem at all. I would not have stayed because I would have seen the writing on the wall. I wouldn't want to be hassled all my life by them guys if they didn't want me to be there."

The park has definitely changed things, and not all for the better, says Seymour. Having the Park Service come in is about the worst thing that can happen to a pretty piece of country, he thinks. Well, not the *worst* thing. The worst thing would be having it be industrialized or commercialized. But being loved to death by the Park Service is the next worst thing.

"You know, if the congressional intent was really to have subsistence people here and accommodated, they flubbed. They didn't do it. Not only did it not work, they went out of their way to orchestrate getting rid of the subsistence people so they wouldn't have to mess with them." From where Seymour Able sits, the result is clear enough. As far as Congress's intention to recognize and protect subsistence activities in Yukon-Charley Rivers National Preserve, "it's not happening. Everybody's gone."

Calico Bluff

I get myself gone, too, as it's close to dark and time to make some ripples on the surface of this wide, placid river. In a minute, I am pointing toward Calico Bluff, where the river takes a bend to the north and crosses the boundary into Yukon-Charley Rivers National Preserve. The exposure reveals a multicolored, multilayered face that suggests a bite taken out of a giant torte. The Yukon River took that bite and digested the light and dark layers of limestone and shale. I visited Bob Satler here once. He was leading a crew of historical archaeologists excavating the site of a one hundred-year-old cabin just upstream from the bluff. They had found two butter cans from Coldbrook Creamery in San Francisco dating 1898 and 1899 as well as various cans, bottles, bits of fabric, hundreds of rifle and shotgun casings of various calibers, and assorted buttons—some military.

The 1900 census lists Homer Ford, a woodcutter, as the resident here. But Bob thinks market meat hunters may have used the cabin at some point and that, after market hunting was outlawed in 1907, a military contingent might have been posted here to enforce the law. The area is rich, situated on a strip of land between the Yukon and a large lake that attracts many hundreds of ducks. There are flats—moose habitat—east and west and north of Calico Bluff, and the easily climbed bluff provides a great lookout. Bob thinks the site has been occupied for thousands of years. He almost always finds flakes of worked stone on the beach, and he has excavated and dated shards to more than five thousand years before present. Once, he unearthed a football-shaped wad of chipped black argillite. Black argillite is a soft, crypto-crystalline rock that fractures predictably and so can be fashioned into tools. It shows up as a dark streak on Calico Bluff. He speculates that the heap of chipped stone he found resulted from a man sitting cross-legged, chipping stone as the flakes piled up between his legs.

Seventymile River

Around a big horseshoe bend, past Limestone Hogback Ridge, is an island that hides the mouth of Seventymile River. It looks like camp to me. And soon it is.

It is an absolutely silent evening. The setting sun lights up little puffs of clouds until they glow a shade of purple that, I want to say, does not occur in nature. From my pipe, I send up little puffs of rejoinder. Smoke signals. I don't smoke as a rule. I suppose I do it to break a rule. Out here, a bowl of Stoney's Blend is as companionable as the fire. It is a communion, too, with my Uncle Jim, whose teeth have left indentations on the stem.

Now it is dark, and the calls of the great horned owls are floating across the still air. A plea for company broadcast hopefully into the night. Over and over. Four notes, one a double. Short, long, short-short. The dit-dah of loneliness.

In the middle of the night, the sound of pounding feet very near my tent startles me awake. A big animal in full charge. I grab my pistol and sit bolt upright until I can tell from the clattering cobbles that it is running inland, away from me. Almost certainly it is a moose, walking the shore and surprised by the tent. Tomorrow we'll see.

IN THE MORNING, a black cloud moves through, washing down the bar like a Mexican shopkeeper up early to clean the sidewalk. The squall prompts me to lie in my bag and jot some notes. The air is lovely when I emerge to make a fire for coffee and to paw through the grub box. A raven flying over the island alters his course to check me out, his wing strokes making a whoo, whoo, whoo, directly overhead. We exchange casual squawks.

I'm packing up the tent when a green johnboat with a Go-Devil passes, heading upriver. A Go-Devil is a kind of outboard motor where the propeller is located at the end of a long driveline that projects well astern of the transom and allows operation in shallow water. I wave. No response. Wave again. No response. The raven was friendlier. Twenty-two minutes later, the throb of the motor still comes to me in faint waves from around the bend, five miles up river. He is probably up near the mouth of Pickerel Slough. He is probably looking at the morning sun lighting up the variegated strata of Calico Bluff ahead of him. I am in his past. But he remains in my present because I can hear him still. Perhaps, we are both in the raven's present, as he may perceive us both from his vantage. In another moment I cannot distinguish the pulse of the Go-Devil from the general thrum of the living world. The whine disintegrates into the air, though for a while I can reassemble it more or less accurately in my memory. It is a shadow of perception, and it begins at once to fade like a photograph left in the sun.

Unless one makes a record.

Stories are the original record of human memory in this place. My friend Bill Schneider is the curator of oral history at the University of Alaska in Fairbanks. He makes the point that human experience on the landscape invests the country not just with derelict steamboats and old cabins and tin can middens but also with stories.

That bend is where Biederman's dog team went through the ice. The current swirls there and eats away the ice from below. You have to watch out here.

There used to be a cabin at this bend. John the Baptist starved to death in it. Have I ever told you about him?

Schneider says that as people are eliminated from Alaska's parks, new stories cease to be created, and the tradition dies. "There's still some retelling of the old stories from before the park took over," he said. "And there are the adventure stories of visitors—people from elsewhere who come to the park to recreate." Of course, these folks rarely get off the main stem of the Yukon, and their knowledge and store of experience connected to this place is limited. Meanwhile, the lore of trappers and dog mushers and miners, who knew intimately the Yukon, Kandik, and Nation, is not being replenished. "What's being promulgated now in Yukon-Charley," he said, "is an oral tradition of the park employees' activities." That strikes me as an astonishing fact.

I don't know if Schneider would go this far, but it does seem that the changes along the Yukon in the last twenty years can be seen as a process of cultural succession. Like what happened when the white people supplanted the Athabascan here. Or when the Athabascan supplanted the Amerind, who came before them. With its roots in the nether regions of law and management policy, this new culture of administration, and the bureaucratic language that accompanies it, flourishes like fungi on a dung heap. The talk used to be about whose dogs could break trail when other teams bogged down; or where you can still see some old deadfall traps, and who likely built them; or the best sled runner width, and whether to use a skeg. Now the stories are, sadly, the shoptalk of a bureaucracy. More than once, around a woodstove, in a cabin along the Yukon, I have heard the talk slide into the brain-numbing argot of the civil service. It would have been incomprehensible to Jack London. It was largely incomprehensible to me, as the Park Service people spoke of E-perbs, FLET-C, SHPO, APLIC, ANHA, RAPS, O-A-S, D-I-1, I-B-P, and S-C-A (emergency personnel beacons, Federal Law Enforcement Training Center, State Historic Preservation Office, Alaska Public Lands Information Center, Alaska Natural History Association, Resource Apprenticeship Program for Students, Office of Aircraft Services, Department of Interior form number one, Incidental Business Permit, and Student Conservation Association).

Whenever I hear talk like this, I always think of a line from my friend, the Alaska poet John Haines, in his testy review of *Coming into the Country.* Where John McPhee sends up some speaker's bureaucratic gibberish, Haines swings his shotgun to it and blasts: "Anyone who can pretend to think in this jargon must be beyond ordinary human communication and should not be trusted with public policies." "Pretend to think." There's truth in that. So much of the chatter we listen to amounts to the coupling of preformulated phrases, labels for predigested ideas. There's no more actual thinking involved than there is in linking the cars of a toy train.

McPhee was only repeating the jargon, of course, but Haines's ear was cocked toward McPhee's language, too. "I found myself annoyed with his continual dropping of the brand names of our culture, as if we would not know where we are without these abundant references. . . ." And, even more trenchantly, "His grip on the words for things is not hand-worn and familiar. He never loses himself sufficiently in what he sees, but remains in a semidetached way something of the sightseer in a strange land." But I think we need, from time to time, people from New Jersey to come up to Alaska and report on this very different place, to compare us against the standards they bring with them. These things rub both ways, though, and I wouldn't be too sure as to who was taking whose measure.

A GLANCE AT the ground breaks my hermeneutic reverie. Besides the Go-Devil and the raven, the other diffident visitor, last night's charging beast, was indeed a moose. I see from the tracks that it ran into the trees on the island. Now, just as I get the canoe packed, I see a riverboat come downriver and take the left channel above my island, disappearing behind it. In a minute the motor shuts off. It must have stopped at the Seventymile, and it is probably Terry McMullin. Ten minutes later, I pull in below his boat and see last night's moose standing out in the channel five hundred yards below.

McMullin meets me at the beach and invites me up to the cabin for tea. He is square-jawed, tan and silver-haired, and might be in his early sixties. His new log cabin is a beautiful piece of work, far and away the most upscale habitation I've seen on the Yukon. The log work, done by three fellows from Eagle, is as good as it gets. The sun streams in through picture windows. The kitchen area is modern. There is even a well and a septic system.

McMullin tells me that he moved to Eagle in 1967 to teach school. There were only eighteen to twenty white residents in Eagle at that time, and none of them had kids. The school was in the Native village, and he was the sole teacher of all eight grades. Originally from Minnesota, he had taught in Kodiak and Copper Center before coming to Eagle. At Copper Center he started running dogs, and when he moved to Eagle, he brought his team of big malamutes. He was keen to get out hunting and fishing and trapping with his dog team, but the old ways of living on the land had been dying out in Eagle for some time. Only two men, Willie Juneby and Tony Paul, ran fishwheels in the Native village, says McMullin, "and absolutely nobody was trapping in Eagle at that time." Eventually he partnered up with Tony Paul, and they trapped marten out along the cat trail from Eagle that hits the Seventymile River sixteen miles up from the Yukon.

McMullin loved his time traveling and trapping in the country, and the nights spent in a little trapline cabin he built himself on the Seventymile, a mile above the mouth. A few years later he dropped out of teaching with the idea of packing up his family and going out and living in the woods for a year. He expanded the trapline cabin, and in

1970 he and his wife Mary Ann and their four kids left Eagle and moved to the Seventymile River. Instead of one year, the family lived there for five. The kids—three girls and a boy—became more and more competent in hunting, fishing, running dogs, cutting firewood, gathering berries, and looking out for themselves in the woods, summer and winter. In 1975, high wages on the Trans-Alaska Pipeline lured McMullin away to construction camps. For two years he worked as a teamster, piling up his savings. It wasn't until 1979 that the family completely settled back into Eagle, and McMullin went back to the school district, this time as principal of the high school.

The family still used the cabin, but the land around it became entangled in Native claims with the passage of the Alaska Native Claims Settlement Act. First Paul filed a claim to the land, though he said he did it to protect McMullin's right to the place. But then Tony died and his wife Hanna inherited the property. She wanted to transfer it to McMullin, but the Bureau of Land Management wouldn't go along. Finally, in an instance of fair-mindedness rare in Alaska land squabbles, the Han-Gwech'in regional Native corporation stepped in to make things right where the U.S. government would not. They deeded McMullin twenty acres of their land at the mouth of the Seventymile, and there he had this new cabin built. "It was amazing," says McMullin. "But, you know, I taught school out there. I had a lot of friends. I knew everybody on the board. And they are still my friends."

Clear title is a comfort to McMullin. Like Seymour Able's site a few miles upriver, his is just outside the Yukon-Charley Preserve boundary. For just a few miles around the mouth of the Seventymile River, the right bank of the Yukon is within the preserve, while its left bank is outside of it. McMullin's tenure seems safe, but as he reaches an age where his activities on the land are reduced from what they once were, he regrets the gradual elimination of subsistence people living on the river. "I think it's a loss to see that happen. But it's going to happen. Why would the Park Service want to keep allowing subsistence? It really goes against the grain of everything that they want to see happen. I don't think there's any compatibility with what they think a park ought to be."

These days, Terry McMullin visits his cabin whenever he gets the urge. His kids, who all grew up to become self-reliant and competent people, are gone now. But he says they remember and appreciate and draw strength from their upbringing out here. And they retain their connection to the place. His son comes every fall to hunt moose with his father. And every July, one or two of his daughters comes down to join Terry and Mary Ann in fishing and putting up smoked, kippered, or canned king salmon for their extended family, just as they have done for nearly forty years. For the McMullins, the salmon they catch and put up can't be matched by anything found in a supermarket, shrink-wrapped on a Styrofoam tray.

Seventymile City and Star City

Where McMullin's cabin stands, or near it, there was once a sizable town. In 1887, prospectors found gold up the Seventymile River, so named because of its distance below the town of Forty Mile. A man with a rocker could take out fifty dollars a day on the Seventymile. In 1897–1898, overflow stampeders from Dawson and Eagle, both of which were booming, laid out a townsite called Seventymile City on the Yukon in a spot likely slightly above the mouth of the Seventymile River. Over the years, the river took a new channel, and McMullin thinks this town was probably right where the present-day mouth is. But it was flooded its first spring, and the miners moved two miles up-river, on the same side of the Yukon, and rebuilt. They called the new town Star City. By June 1898, two hundred fifty people lived here in forty or fifty cabins. The town boasted a post office and a small store. But within a year Star City drained away, too, when almost everyone stampeded on the big rush to Nome in 1899. McMullin says the only remains are a few roughly rectangular depressions in the ground, back in the brush and hard to find.

Tatonduk River, Heinie Miller

When I come out of the big bend below the Seventymile River, I come upon one of the grandest vistas in a place prodigal with vistas. It is the view to the east looking up the valley of the Tatonduk River. If I were the expedition artist on some nineteenth-century exploration, I'd stop here and set up my easel. The way the near hills part to reveal the distant Ogilvies creates a space that would pull you into the canvas, the way the actual scene beckons you into this valley, a back room in the house of wilderness. Bands of Han people were drawn into it, less for aesthetic than for economic reasons. They traveled here to the mouth of the Tatonduk after they quit fishing in the fall and waited for freeze-up. With the rivers and creeks frozen, they would trek up the Tatonduk River valley into the Ogilvies hunting sheep and caribou, spending the winter in the higher country. Throughout the winter, they would trend southeasterly. Then in the spring, with the rivers flowing again, they would build moose-skin boats to float back down to the Yukon to fish again. Perhaps many circuits of migration like this spun like waterwheels, driven by the great river's current, one revolution per year.

In the 1920s and 1930s, Frank Charles "Heinie" Miller had a woodcutting camp here just below the mouth of the Tatonduk. He'd bought out an old-timer called Lucky Laughton. I don't know if it was to celebrate the sale, or some other occasion, but Adolph Biederman once saw Lucky and Heinie shortly after they'd left Eagle in a rowboat with a gallon of whiskey. They were caught in the eddy below Eagle Bluff, contentedly drifting in big circles, pleasurably prolonging their journey, at once in motion and not really going anywhere. When Biederman asked an Eagle man if he thought they should get a boat and go help the men out, he was told that God looks out for fools and drunks, meaning, I suppose, that Heinie and Lucky were doubly protected.

Even though Heinie has been dead for better than half a century, some maps still mark the spot as Miller's Camp. He hired six or seven woodcutters, including a number of Han men, to cut wood at various places, buck it up into four-foot lengths, haul it to the river bank with horses, and stack it there for the steamboats. Maud, a trained horse, hauled timber from the hills to the wood yard unattended. In 1930, Miller shipped in a Caterpillar tractor. The woodcutters came down in the springtime, driving their dog teams on the Yukon River ice to the Tatonduk, or to Wood Islands a few miles below. They would have gotten a grubstake on credit from the Northern Commercial Company in Eagle and piled those staples into the sled, along with a tent and camping gear. They would shoot their meat downriver. "They all take their dog team, tents, and they set up tent camp," said a Han man from Eagle named Silas Stevens in an oral history interview. "A regular tent city. Down there on Wood Island. For $4.00 a cord. Good money them days too."

When Heinie Miller needed woodcutters in the middle of the winter, the men may have been able to drive a harder bargain. A 1936 letter in the Eagle Historical Society archives, from the Northern Commercial Company agent in Eagle to Miller, lays down one Native man's terms: "Charlie Yukon has agreed to go down and chop wood for you soon after the first of the Year, but he says he would want a Cabin with a stove in it, and a good place to chop that is good timber, he will furnish his own Cooking utensils and grub, and he will chop more wood than any three men you have."

Ernie Pyle, the famous journalist, met Heinie in 1937. He took a sternwheeler down the Yukon that summer, and the boat stopped to "wood-up" at Miller's Camp. According to Pyle, Heinie was a Chicago native who had come into the country around 1900 and hadn't been Outside since. "Hell, no, and I ain't going out," said Heinie. "I didn't lose nothin' down in the States I have to go back after." Heinie was getting old. "His clothes were old and not too clean," Pyle writes. He was whiskery, with tobacco juice stains on either side of his chin, and his sky-blue eyes were weakened by cataracts. But Heinie still sounded fierce in that summer of 1937, pealing off strings of profanity as he talked about tough times. He and his men had worked all last winter and stacked up about 700 cords of wood by spring. But at breakup (when the river ice finally breaks into pieces and begins to move) the ice jammed and the river rose. It flooded so quickly Heinie had to wade to a tree and climb it. When the tree started to keel over, he made his way to the big woodpile through ice water up to his shoulders. "By the jumping _____ _____ it was cold," he told Pyle. After sixteen hours on top of the woodpile—during which time it poured rain—the ice dam broke, and the water fell. Heinie hoofed it, soaked and shivering, to a trapper's cabin. "Damned if I even got a cough out of it," he said. The Yukon had left Heinie with his life, but it made off with a hundred cords of his wood, representing 800 hard-earned but not yet realized dollars. The river also knocked Heinie's new cabin off its foundation and generally trashed his entire operation. The breakup of 1937 didn't give him a cold, but it did give him enough of the country. Not long after Pyle met him, Heinie Miller packed up and left.

Dick Cook

I cut the motor to add silence to the scene and drift languidly by the mouth of the Tatonduk. Funny how the gentle sun sinks me into a kind of torpor, until it seems I cannot move, can barely daydream. It should be ice, not paper, I'm thinking, that covers the rock that breaks the scissors. Except that the scissors could never win. But then it wouldn't lose either, not when the ice gets through with the rock. In the mountains far upstream from where I am, millions of tons of moving glacier ice reduce bedrock to specks of grit as fine as flour. The gray, powdery stuff roils the glacial outwash, clouding to a pearly translucence every creek and river downstream all the way to the sea. The suspended silt hisses now against my canoe, the aluminum hull magnifying the sound tympanically, like brush strokes on a snare drum, a quiet drum roll. Enter Dick Cook, McPhee's most notable river character.

I am seeing a July day ten years ago, when my wife and then six-year-old son and I sat right over there on that stony beach, eating lunch. We hadn't realized we were quite so close to Cook's place when we saw a canoe pull out from shore a quarter mile below and glide across the wide, sparkling river. There were two people aboard, and we watched them check a salmon net on the opposite bank, gathering lunch, perhaps. In a few minutes they began to motor back, but the outboard quit. With half a mile or more of silence between us, we could clearly hear their voices over the water, as the river swept them away and the man pulled repeatedly on the starter cord. Finally, the motor fired, and they swung around and pointed into the current. But a minute later, the air was silent again. As they drifted downstream, the man pulled and fiddled, pulled until the motor caught and ran long enough for them to make it back to camp.

After a bit, we packed up and drifted down to where Cook's canoe was tied. I gave my son a bag of grapefruit to carry up the trail. If we were to disturb this famously crusty denizen of the wilds at meal time, I figured to do so a couple of paces behind a cute kid bearing gifts. But Cook was already at the head of the trail before we started up. In seconds his flashing eyes had taken in the three of us, scanned the canoe, registered that I was running an older fifteen-horsepower Evinrude on a nineteen-foot, square-stern Grumman with a lift, sized us up by our gear, calculated its volume and weight, and followed the bag of grapefruit until it was in his hands. He received it with thanks and invited us up to his camp, where he introduced us to his friend, a woman named Pat from Texas.

Cook was as McPhee had found him in the 1970s: thin and balding, with longish, gray-streaked black hair and beard, alert as a mink. He wore a T-shirt emblazoned with some irrelevance and old pants with a busted zipper. But he was shod in new sandals. He looked like a marooned pirate in Birkenstocks: a castaway scavenger of random goods swept overboard from freighters somewhere out in the distant lanes of commerce.

It was the time of gardens, and once up the bank we inspected Cook's well-managed plot, discussed fish guts as fertilizer, cauliflower that would not head, and subsistence living generally. I mentioned seeing some fish heads on the beach where we had stopped for lunch and asked if he fished with rod and reel. No, it was the work of some floaters. For him to fish with a rod would make about as much sense, he said, as for him to take his rifle and shoot into the woods, then to take off walking after the bullet to see if it hit anything. I laughed, but remarked that old-timers in this country sometimes fed their dog teams by jigging for pike. I'd read accounts of holes so productive that a person with a spoon and a length of twine could stack up fifteen-pounders like cord wood. Cook wasn't buying it. He delivered a short lecture on the need in a subsistence economy for maximum return on invested effort. It put me in mind of a bit of McPhee's scathing tact. He described Cook's voice as soft and gentle, except "when he is being pedagogical. . . . He is not infrequently pedagogical."

But neither is he ungenerous with the fruits of his wisdom. As we moved to leave, Cook plucked from the garden a perfect, deep green cucumber and handed it to my boy.

THAT WAS THEN. Now his fish camp could hardly feel lonelier. Dick Cook was one of the very few bush people left in all of Northern Alaska who still lived year-round out beyond a village. It seemed like he was here forever, part of the place, a central figure in anybody's book. And now he's gone. Just a few weeks before I pulled up to his fish camp, Cook drowned somewhat mysteriously in the Tatonduk, the river he navigated for thirty-six years.

At times, Cook used this place, half a mile below Miller's Camp at the mouth of the Tatonduk, as his main residence. More often, it served as his fish camp and trap cabin, especially when the lynx population was high, and he ran his lines through the flats and islands along the Yukon (lynx numbers oscillate harmonically with the hares, which overpopulate, then crash). The old cabin that Cook had taken over once belonged to Max Drews, a native of Berlin, Germany, who in the teens and twenties bounced around all over the country—Dawson, Fortymile, Woodchopper, finally settling in Eagle. He had a cabin at Trout Creek too but lived here near Heinie Miller. In 1933 or 1934, Drews had a contract to carry mail as far as Nation River, until he stepped in overflow and froze his foot, losing three toes. "He had extra foot gear and socks in his sled," according to one old-timer, "but he did not know his foot was frozen."

Drews's cabin, built in the 1920s and haphazardly maintained by Cook, looks to be about fourteen by sixteen feet. Its roof is not quite one thing or another. It's like a composite illustration depicting the full range of bush construction techniques. The front is lopsidedly covered with a thick layer of sod sprouting tall green grass. The section behind that is mostly clad in rusted white gas cans, cut and flattened and lapped to shed the rain. The hind quarters feature a few sheets of corrugated tin, brown with rust, and some plywood, weathered and gray. Withal, these are all honest materials, earth-toned and dignified. But wrapped across the whole rear end of the cabin, like a bright blue diaper, is a large plastic tarp. That this jury-rigged arrangement leaks is suggested by the rotting logs, which are falling apart, and the fact that Cook tacked up plastic sheeting inside over the ceiling and walls.

It takes a minute for my eyes to adjust to the low light level inside, especially because the plastic sheeting is black, and it soaks up most of what light comes in through the small windows. The interior has the look and feel of an animal den, a sensation intensified by the mixed aromas of rancid salmon grease, damp hides and the stink of recently resident chickens. Cook had cut a low opening through the south wall and rigged up a room there under the tarp for his chickens, which he regarded as very companionable animals. Letters to his friend and lawyer, Bill Caldwell, often concluded with the sort of news that a more conventional seventy-year-old might pass along about the grandchildren. "The chickens, as usual, say hello," he wrote in the spring of 2001. "They really love being in the house. Chickens seem to be God's definition of 'spectator.' No matter what I'm doing, they line up to watch." The year before, he had grieved over the loss of a hen. "A marten caught her on the nest while she was laying. I knew the marten was stealing eggs—saw him a few days earlier coming out of the henhouse with an egg in his mouth—so I'd been closing the coop at night after the birds went in and not letting them out until late morning. He got her about noon. I took the rest of them in the house; they've not been out since." Cook set traps, and got nine marten in about a month: "five shot, four trapped." The marten were worth hundreds of dollars, but Cook lamented that the hen was "the highest flyer and most skilled at getting away from the dogs. Wish she could have raised chicks and taught them her method." In his next letter, he was still pining, "No amount of marten will replace the little red hen." Eventually, he got over the loss and started planning. He decided he wanted to get a hold of a fighting cock and breed a tougher strain of chicken.

Dick experimented in the vegetative realm as well. Friends say he had some theory about the value of importing weeds. Once, while visiting his second ex-wife, Ann, and her family in Washington state, he collected the seeds of stinging nettles. He planted them, and they grew near his cabin. Perhaps he intended them for some medicinal purpose. Or, being transplanted himself, and prickly, maybe he just liked the idea of a few obnoxious exotics on his spread.

Most years, Cook's home cabin wasn't this dank little log cabin beside the Yukon but a place about six miles up the Tatonduk near the mouth of Pass Creek. He had gone to that spot first in the winter of 1964–1965, while he was living in Eagle. Maybe he built some kind of shelter there at that time. Maybe not. In a sworn deposition he says, "I built a little cabin up there [Pass Creek] at that time, '64, '65." Ann Cook, his wife in those days, now a lawyer in the Seattle area, says he didn't have any kind of shelter at Pass Creek then. But then, Ann didn't travel with him. He probably had something up there, though probably it was more lean-to than "cabin," a few logs piled up in a ramp against the wind. Around 1971, he built a ten-by-ten-foot cabin at Pass Creek but decided to move it a year later. He took the cabin apart, floated the logs about half a mile downstream, and put it back together at a new site with a better garden spot, more firewood, and no permafrost. He added a small room on to that cabin, and when McPhee saw it, he wrote that it was trim and tidy and lined with books and tools. But that was probably because Donna Kneeland was living with Cook then. Some years later, when Donna was long gone, a friend of mine saw Cook's cabin at Pass Creek. When I related McPhee's description, my friend, who is possibly as far from fastidious as anyone I know, wrinkled his nose and shook his head. "No. It was *very* funky." Another former river resident who knew Cook for better than twenty-five years said he seemed to practice a kind of studied degeneracy. "You know, if his porch overhang was sagging, he wouldn't even prop a pole under it, he'd just let it fall down. It was almost like he was trying to out-sloven everybody. Like, he'd leave a piece of moose liver on the floor and then get pissed at you when you stepped on it."

Cook said he moved on to the Tatonduk at a time when the Native people had given up trapping, and there were almost no whites out in the country. His area hadn't been trapped for six or eight years, he said, and the country downstream toward the Nation River hadn't had a trapper on it for eighteen or twenty years. Willie Juneby had been the last to trap the Tatonduk. And Art and Charlie Stevens had trapped portions of what became Cook's trapline downstream from the Tatonduk and over into Hard Luck Creek in the Nation River drainage. Cook talked at length with these Native men, gathering information and stories. Juneby told him where he could find a trapline trail that had been brushed out not too many years earlier, and Cook incorporated it into his line. He gave Juneby the first marten he caught on that trail.

Eventually, Cook claimed a trapping area of perhaps two hundred fifty to three hundred square miles. His habit was to rotate each year into one of three sectors, leaving the other two to rest. One sector included the Tatonduk, the flats around its mouth and its tributary, Thicket Creek. Another sector was the area downstream from the Drews cabin on both sides of the Yukon. And the third sector was over the hills on into Hard Luck Creek, a tributary of the Nation River. He trapped a couple of the smaller creeks off Hard Luck, including Cathedral Creek and Harrington Creek. The Hard Luck trapline was perhaps forty miles long but might have required a hundred miles of travel, out and back. He would run the line every week to ten days. Earlier on, Cook maintained a team of strong dogs.

When he was trapping seriously, he had as many as nine dogs and as few as three. The Hard Luck line required a tough dog team. "You're dealing with long, long, long days and long trails," he said in a court deposition.

COOK WAS GIVING a deposition in 1987 because he was suing the National Park Service, which came along a few years after McPhee left. He said an airplane trapper who had recently moved to Eagle was slipping into his area and poaching his fur. He pointedly complained to the Park Service superintendent in person, and he fired off letters. He must have been pounding the hell out of his old manual typewriter because the centers of all of the o's are punched clean out of the paper. Held up to the light, Cook's letters look like they were punctuated by a blast from a shotgun. "I want that pirate off my trapline and I believe it is your legal obligation to put him off." Presenting his line of legal reasoning, he declared that in the Alaska lands act, "Congress dictated that NPS would protect the subsistence lifestyle in Alaska. It is impossible to protect my lifestyle without also protecting the furbearer population in the area I trap. . . . If the courts decide I have no subsistence priority, then subsistence priority doesn't exist. Congress says I have rights; you say I don't; it is time to find out."

Cook was fond of the declarative statement, the punchy absolute. In his deposition, he lamented the introduction of not just the airplane into rural Alaska but also the internal combustion engine, calling it the worst thing that ever happened to the country. It would strike most people as unusual, then, to find that despite his ardor, Cook owned a chain saw ("vintage 1967") and an outboard motor ("given me 6 years ago because 'it's not worth fixing'"). When pressed by the pirate's attorney about snowmobiles, Cook acknowledged, "I'm going to buy one. I mean, I don't like them for personal reasons. I'd much rather have dogs. Circumstances are changing."

Most people would acknowledge that Cook certainly knew a lot about the country he lived in. But most people who knew him probably would also say he was, in common parlance, a bit of a bullshitter. Listening to his assertions about managing the marten population on his trapline, you start to think that maybe you should set a few traps of your own in the hope of catching an actual fact. In a sworn statement he gave in the spring of 1988, Cook said, "The minute I start catching females, I pull traps." A little later, he talks of a recent catch as consisting of "one-third females, which was somewhat high for the females." Well, it *would* be "somewhat high" if a fellow pulled his traps "the minute" he caught the first one. It was Cook's view that "catching females is a good sign that the trapline's in bad shape."

THE AMERICAN MARTEN is a member of the Mustelidae, or weasel family, and includes sea otter, river otter, wolverine, badger, fisher, mink, ermine, and the tiny least weasel, the world's smallest mammalian carnivore. After salmon, the marten is probably the most important wild animal in the economy of subsistence people along the Yukon, as it is widely distributed and easy to trap and sell. The marten is closely related to Siberia's sable, having crossed the Bering Land Bridge into North America during the last Ice Age. It is secretive and rarely seen, aside from when one shows up in a trap. Its presence in an area is mainly revealed by tracks in the snow. Even allowing for an expert trapper's talent for reading tracks, it would be hard to distinguish, for example, the tracks of one juvenile female from those of another juvenile female. Nevertheless, Cook claimed to have "delineated the families" in many cases and to have "made sets in such a way so that there were two sets in each family." He would "only take two out of a family which is a family of, say, six. . . . " In a letter to the park superintendent, he said, "For 13 years I managed that fur at near maximum population density with a 13 year sustained yield of 17 to 20%."

Either Cook was in possession of data-gathering techniques that would be the envy of fish and game agencies the world over, or he was in possession of rhetorical gifts that fit pretty well into a long tradition of frontier gasbaggery. In a 1987 affidavit, Cook called himself "a trained scientist" because he had taken courses, but not graduated, from the Colorado School of Mines. In another place he referred to himself as an "engineer," even though he had never completed any degree or passed any licensing examination. Cook certainly was a close observer of the nature that surrounded him. And he did make notes in his journal and on big rolls of butcher paper about his catch and the tracks he'd seen in fur prospecting trips. He was the sort to sit and cipher, to work up numbers from this angle and that. But he was an amateur. And when he latched on to an opinion, he hung on to it like a barnacle. He was prone to overstatement, and that's an understatement.

An actual trained scientist, Dave Payer of the U.S. Fish and Wildlife Service in Fairbanks, who earned his PhD studying marten, thought Cook's notions of marten families "interesting." "A male and a female do not cooperatively raise a family," he said. The adults are solitary. They are territorial within their sex, meaning they generally cannot abide another of the same sex on their range, but they will tolerate the presence of another of the opposite sex. A male's territory may be twice that of a female's, and these territories will overlap. You can think of it like a senate district represented by a male, which consists of two house districts represented by females. The male may breed with both females, and the females are not necessarily monogamous either. Breeding occurs between late June and early August, but implantation of the egg is delayed for more than half a year until spring, a more advantageous time to birth and rear young.

Triggered by the increase in daylight, around late February or March, the fertilized but barely developed egg will finally implant in the uterine wall, and a brief, twenty-seven-day active pregnancy commences. As few as one, as many as five, but on average three kits are born in mid-March to late-April. If born on April 15, the kits will not open their eyes until May 20. Then they grow up fast. They might first sample solid food on May 25 and be weaned two days later. On June 2, they will emerge from the den into a warm, green, sunny world. They will remain in the company of their mother until July or August, when they will be nearly full grown. Beginning in September, they will disperse or be driven away. "The young won't be tolerated within the parents' range," says Payer. So, a marten "family" is a single-parent one, with the father uninvolved, and the children booted out as early as five months of age. They should be dispersed before the snow sticks—that is, before tracks in the snow might allow a trapper to "delineate the families."

On the move, and seeking territory in which to establish themselves, the juvenile marten frequently end up in traps. "There is little chance that these young will be the offspring of the adults in the area," Payer said. The idea that Cook could determine that he'd taken between seventeen and twenty percent of the marten population in his area suggested that he knew to a high degree of precision the total marten population within a three-hundred-square-mile area, much of it deeply incised with narrow valleys. Says Payer, "I don't think an experienced researcher conducting a thorough study with live trapping could say that."

Marten favor a mature conifer forest where trees fall in a complicated network on the ground. They may den in trees, logs, or rocks. They can move adroitly through the branches of trees and can swim, but they hunt mostly on the ground. Marten also explore the territory under the snow, invading burrows made by smaller mammals, resting in squirrel middens. Marten will eat more than a hundred different things. As a rule, in summer they prowl for bird eggs and nestlings, insects, fish, young mammals, and carrion. In the fall they eat berries. During the winter, they hunt for meat: voles and squirrels, sometimes hares.

When a fire burns through the country, especially when it leaves behind a pick-up-sticks configuration of downed trees, the burn area may become a "sink" for transient and young marten. Even with few living trees there, the dispossessed marten from adjacent mature woodland disperse into it. The fire clears out the trees that have presided like grand lords over their dominion, and that gives the upstart grasses and forbs a chance to take hold in the rich, fertilized soil. These plants offer food for voles and shrews and mice, and the downed trees offer them cover. Where rodents abound, the marten follow. Where the marten abound, the trapper follows.

Cook regarded recently burned rolling hills as the very best trapping in his area. Consequently, when he saw that an airplane had been landing on the fringe of one such area near Montauk Mountain, he went looking for traps. He found them, sprung them, jerked them up, and heaved them into a patch of overflow. When he spotted the parked airplane once, he let fly a few rifle shots close enough that the other trapper could hear the whistle of the bullets. But mostly—getting back to the court case—Cook wanted formal, rather than vigilante, justice. He wrote to Alaska Legal Services, which provides free legal assistance to low-income Alaskans. Just days after an attorney named Bill Caldwell wrote him back saying that the case looked interesting, Cook showed up at the lawyer's office.

CALDWELL HAS A LONG GRAY BEARD and a ponytail. He is immediately recognizable for his trademark hat, which is a jet-black, straight-brimmed, multiple-gallon, Amish-style beauty not much smaller in diameter than a sombrero. Caldwell wrote the preserve superintendent that he thought Cook had a pretty good argument. The Park Service had the obligation to protect both Cook's subsistence trapping rights and the health of the animal populations. He said, "These are two of the principal purposes for which the Yukon-Charley preserve was established. . . . " Caldwell quoted the law: "The preserve shall be managed . . . to protect habitat for, and populations of, fish and wildlife. . . . Subsistence uses by local residents shall be allowed in national preserves. . . . The utilization of the public lands in Alaska is to cause the least adverse impact possible on rural residents who depend upon subsistence uses of the resources of such lands." Another section stipulated that subsistence uses shall have priority over all other uses.

Cook liked the legal brief. He liked his chances, and he was bristling for a court fight. But there was one deposed fact that Cook discounted as meaningless but that the judge did not. To wit: the pirate trapper had signed a sworn statement a year earlier promising to stay out of the area Cook claimed. After nearly three years of writing letters, filing legal briefs, giving affidavits and depositions, and after much delay on the part of the court, the judge threw out the case as moot. The trapper had promised under oath to stay clear of Cook's territory. And even though that hadn't been good enough for Cook, it was good enough for the court. Bang. Case dismissed.

IF ONE WERE TO UMPIRE Cook's trip into the legal batter's box against federal pitching, the last mentioned episode was strike two, and a third pitch was on the way. Strike one involved the Bureau of Land Management a decade earlier. In the summer of 1977, the BLM began flying over the cabins of the river people. In August the agency started serving formal trespass notices, and Cook was one of the recipients. The BLM's file on Cook contains a number of colorful entries:

June 1977: "Has made several threats about shooting down aircraft."

December 1977: ". . . threats made to our field representatives by Mr. Cook on several occasions. These threats of shooting and shooting down BLM aircraft have been made openly. . . . On one occasion, Mr. Richard Cook stated he almost shot at one of our BLM helicopters which was, in reality, a mining helicopter doing exploration work out of Eagle."

The wrangling went back and forth into 1978, with Cook trying any angle to get the agency to leave him alone. In one letter, replying to a BLM manager in Anchorage, he starts out characteristically truculent: "The first four points you make seem to try to degrade rather than to deny my claim, don't really seem relevant to the case, and are wrong." But perhaps writing out his history in the place sobered or centered him because toward the end of the letter, the prose no longer shoots out like flaming salvos from a dreadnought but rather sounds more like a string of sighs. "I came to Eagle in the spring of 1964 on a raft before the road opened. I stayed. The spring of '65 I built a makeshift cabin at the mouth of Pass Creek near my present cabin. I knew I wanted to live there. . . . When I acquired the tools and materials needed, I built the cabin at Pass Creek and started living for a garden, a shop to putter in, and solitude."

Cook certainly got the solitude. He would live at his isolated cabin for more than thirty years. Some say it touched him in the usual ways, that he would gab a torrent to anyone who happened by. One friend, Mark Richards, said he often had to pull the hook while Cook was mid-sentence because there was just no other way to get loose. Sometimes, says Richards, when he would get his dog team over the bank and lined out on the river and turn back to wave, he'd swear Cook's lips were still moving. Even by his own account, Cook talked a lot, and whether or not people were present. It's OK to talk to yourself, he once told visiting biologists. He did it all the time. And it's no big deal either if you reply to yourself. You might have a problem, though, he said, if after you reply to yourself, you ask, "What?"

His ex-wife, Ann, who has dealt in her work with post-traumatic stress disorder, says that she is certain Dick suffered from it. He had enlisted in the Marine Corps at the age of seventeen and saw frontline combat in Korea. Once, says Ann, his squad was playing cards when Cook stepped outside. A moment later, a shell hit the structure, and every one of his buddies was blown to pieces. His mother told Ann, who was fifteen years younger than Dick, that he was a different person after Korea. He started sleeping in the daytime and pacing at night. Still a boy, really, he was permanently scarred by the war, Ann believes. He would remain habitually sleepless, often pacing the cabin floor much of the night. For a time, when they lived in a twelve-by-fourteen-foot cabin, she couldn't get out of bed in the morning and occupy any of the limited floor space until he had done an hour's pacing and had things worked out. If she tried to talk to him, he would say, "Angel, I need my space. I'm *thinking*." In their small trailer in Eagle, they slept on the floor. "Dick would be up at six pacing over me, drinking tea and talking to himself out loud." Once—and only once—Ann surprised him from behind. He spun and smashed her full in the face. Living in the proximity of grizzly bears for thirty-odd years cannot have done much to dull that edge.

But Cook had an extremely congenial side as well. He regularly visited Ann and her family in Washington and got along great with everyone—Ann's husband Greg, the kids, the neighbors. Once Ann had an invitation to attend a very tony party hosted by a relative who is a successful attorney. "It was a hot-shot lawyer party: a big house, catered food, musicians. Sailboats outside strung with lights. Dick didn't hesitate to go. He talked to one and all."

He loved children too. Ann and Greg's son John visited Dick three times in Alaska. He stayed the whole summer when he was fifteen. It was a lot of work, he says, just taking care of themselves. John's duties were to pick the fish net, to gut the fish intended for human food, and to cook whole the fish intended for dog food. Dick taught the boy to cook their meals too, just as he had taught his mother thirty years earlier. The food was not particularly varied, but it could be unusual. "Salmon was pretty much all there was," says John. "And oat flour biscuits." When they picked some greens for a salad, Cook liked to use milt, the sperm-containing secretions from the testes of male salmon, as salad dressing. He found it odd that John didn't care for it. But when the boy was seventeen, he came again to visit Cook for another summer. "I enjoyed talking to Dick," says John, who is now a philosophy student at the University of Alaska, Fairbanks. "He was a fascinating and often hilarious person."

BUT DICK COOK is better known as a battler. His unsuccessful skirmish with the BLM over his trespass status gave way to the dustup with the Park Service over the pirate's poaching on his trapline. Eventually, and luckily, a Native corporation claimed his part of the country, and Cook reached an agreement with them that gave him title to his bit of ground at Pass Creek. He had also managed to buy the ground where the Drews cabin stood from a Fairbanks man who acquired Heinie Miller's homestead through adverse possession. That the Tatonduk was truly Cook's home, as he told the BLM in 1977, can be understood by looking at how he persevered there, despite the most amazing string of bad luck. One spring in the early 1990s, the Yukon flooded while Cook was at the Drews cabin. He had a cache up on stilts. A cache is a storage structure, typically a tiny cabin atop tall poles, out of reach of animals. Cook and his dogs spent a few days up there until the water went down, just as Heinie Miller had done in the 1930s. The cabin was never quite the same after that, though, having sunk into the liquefied silt.

Then in November 1995, Cook was up at his home cabin at Pass Creek taking a bath when he noticed embers falling down into the tub. He wasn't alarmed because he'd had the stove going pretty hot to get the bath water warm. It was just bits of glowing creosote that had worked through some holes in the pipe. He had a good soak and went to sleep, waking only when the burning roof began falling in on him. The cabin was already beyond saving. Cook barely had time to pull on his snow machine suit and boots and get out. He had been saving money to pay for a trip Outside to visit his two daughters from his first marriage (Ann was his second wife). They were now middle-aged, and Cook hadn't seen them since he left for Alaska when they were tiny. He managed to rescue the money, but that was about all, according to Terry McMullin, who got the story from Dick.

Toughest to take was the loss of his journals. Mark Richards remembers hearing about it from Cook. "I'd never seen Dick cry, but when he told me about the journals, he really nearly lost it. He felt that when he died they would be published by someone, and there was a lot in there he wanted told." Richards says Cook stayed by the burning cabin all night. It must have been a complex set of emotions running through his mind that winter night, decades below zero, the burning cabin simultaneously threatening his survival and temporarily sustaining it. When there was light enough, he started off on the six-mile walk down the Tatonduk to the Drews cabin on the Yukon. He had to stop and build a fire just two miles down because his feet were freezing.

"He told me he was awful cold going down to that other cabin," said Terry McMullin. "And then nobody came for so long. Hell, nobody even knew about it." In November the river ice is usually not yet safe for traveling.

Cook hung a sign out on the river calling for help, and a passing snowmachiner stopped and took him up to Eagle. He took his trip back East and visited his daughters. He saw one daughter, Holly, for only about four hours. Ann Cook says Dick had tried to stay in touch with the girls but that his first wife had withheld his letters from them. He stayed with Ann and her family in Seattle on his way to and from seeing his daughters. She said he was worried about them. He had a plan, she said, whereby his brothers might invest in a lodge that Dick would build on the Tatonduk, and that some of his family might move there to operate it. He was always trying to get family to visit, she said. They never did, until the memorial service.

Dick returned to Eagle in March 1996 and started putting together another outfit to haul down to the Tatonduk. "He was staying in this little gray cabin with Leif Able," says McMullin. "Dick was jungling-up with him before he went down river. And he had all this stuff in his cabin that he had just shipped in to take down to replace what burned up. So he's staying in that cabin. I don't know where Dick is, but Leif is over at the pool hall shooting pool and someone comes in and says, 'Leif, your cabin's on fire.' They got over there and that whole damned cabin burned down, and all of Dick's stuff was in it that he was going to take downriver with him. So he got hit pretty heavy by fire that year. Pretty tough. Pretty tough."

If this were a fictional account, that double whammy would be about all the trial-by-fire a reader would stand for. But facts sometimes arrange themselves into unseemly melodrama, and this is such an instance. With what little gear he had left after two burnouts, Cook headed back to the Tatonduk and moved into the Drews cabin, or what he called, accurately, "a flooded-out cabin that's about to fall down." In a letter to Bill Caldwell that year, he listed a bit of his material culture. He said he had a busted Elan snowmachine, an old fifteen-horse outboard, "two pair of trousers, two flannel shirts and [I] have no socks without holes." His diet was becoming limited to fish and rice. His friend Terry McMullin said, "Boy, the last couple of years, he was living pretty tough. Pretty basic. He really didn't have much." Still, he decided to rebuild at Pass Creek, and bit by bit he readied things. In 1997, in three trips, he brought down to the Tatonduk four thousand five hundred pounds of lumber, hauling the boards up the bank in fifty-pound loads—nine hundred of them. By the summer of 1999, he had some of the construction materials and supplies up at the Pass Creek site, according to the Park Service fire officer. But in June of that year, a lightning-caused forest fire flared up on Hard Luck Creek in the Nation drainage, and it headed over the pass as if it was chasing Cook back down his trapline trail and into his camp. Like some kind of demon demanding propitiation, it torched Cook's meager pile of stuff at Pass Creek, then it turned down the Tatonduk, making for Cook's last redoubt, the wretched little Drews cabin. Dick waited there as the fire bore down on him, eating up his country as it advanced. In July, a crew of smoke jumpers arrived by boat. They cut a saw line, lit a back burn, and set up pumps. The flames were very close to Cook's place. But with the lengthening nights and more moisture, the fire burned itself out and finally let him be.

McMullin took his boat down to see how Cook was doing, now that his neighborhood had turned into a landscape of charred sticks. "He was really down," said McMullin, who was worried about his friend. "First time he ever talked about going somewhere else." But a little while later he saw Dick in Eagle. "Hell, he's back making his lists and planning, you know, he was back feeling pretty positive. Plus the fact that, you know, hell, he wouldn't have any place else to go, come right down to it." Cook was then sixty-eight years old.

He settled in to another winter at the Drews cabin on the Yukon, but he didn't like it. He wrote Caldwell, "I have no wood ahead. This cold fall has got me going overtime just to keep the fire going. Wood here is scarce and hard to come by." Without a nice wood pile stacked up outside the cabin, Cook was living close to the edge. "If I broke a bone now, or got food poisoning, etc., so I couldn't get wood every other day, I'd freeze." Cook was never one to lay in a big wood pile. One cold winter day his friend Mark Richards came through with his dog team and stopped in to visit. Richards says that he didn't intend to stay long and sat for a while on the bunk, still wearing his parka. It's hard to tell the temperature of a cabin when you come in like that from the cold and you're still bundled up. But he got a rough idea when Cook, delighted for a chance to gab, sat right down on top of the woodstove.

One good thing about the forest fire having run through Pass Creek was that it left behind a lot of dry, fire-killed spruce. It was perfect for the stove, as he wrote Caldwell: "All fall I've been thinking about moving back up to Pass Crk., burn or no burn, at least for the winter," Cook wrote. "Before the burn, wood was easy and close—now it's practically feeding itself into the stove. I'm tired of devoting my entire winter getting wood, brushing trails to wood, and repairing wood sleds." He was working himself up to moving off the Yukon and actually building something again at Pass Creek. "I think a big factor is that Pass Creek is where I chose as home; I don't really want to live [on the Yukon] with the activity in summer and the wood problem in winter, I want off the river. And the wood problem is a good excuse—hopefully a good prod to get me off my butt and get up there and do something . . . anything!"

The next summer, McMullin hauled some lumber in his riverboat down to the Drews cabin, and Cook hauled some of it up to Pass Creek. With all the labor of hauling thousands of pounds of material six miles up the Tatonduk, Dick decided he needed a tractor. Or at least a truck that might be converted into a tractor. Up in Eagle, he had a truck, an old rusty International 4x4 pickup with a winch. In the fall he built a raft. It was about the most lightly built and implausible craft imaginable. It gave the impression of a classroom design project gone mad—as if the assignment had been: "Using soda straws and Scotch tape, construct a bridge over the Grand Canyon capable of supporting automobile traffic." Floating off the landing at Eagle was a platform lashed to eight bundles of two-inch-thick pink foam insulation boards. The foam was sandwiched between a few two-by-fours connected by lengths of three-eighths-inch Allthread. A prudent person would not *walk* on the vessel, not over moving Yukon River water. Half of Eagle turned out for the launching, most of them anticipating a capsizing. When Dick drove the truck aboard, the raft sank until its deck was awash. But the thing floated.

With Cook in his loaded canoe on one side, and his friend Wayne Hall and another pal in boats beside it, they guided the raft along. Why the top-heavy contraption didn't turn turtle and send the truck to the bottom of the river, taking one or both of the boats with it, is, I guess, a tribute to the design of "a trained scientist and engineer." Wayne says Dick did perform the calculations to determine the bulk of flotation required. (It's the bulk that matters because it is the weight of the water that the flotation would displace if submerged that determines the weight that the flotation will support.) In any event, he and Wayne successfully delivered tons of freight across twenty-seven miles of roadless wilderness without significant expenditure of either money or effort.

The rest of the journey didn't go as easily, as Cook wrote Caldwell. "I spent 12 days unsticking the truck and three days freighting. The truck never got above two mile. Most of my gear is still in the slough where we unloaded, over half of it now in the ice from the highest after freeze-up rise I've seen." On top of that his outboard quit. Up at Pass Creek, Cook had been at work building a tent platform, a frame over which he stretched two wall tents set end to end. This yielded a floor area of about eleven feet by twenty-four feet, plenty of room for himself and the chickens. The door was in the middle, the chickens' quarters on the left, along with Dick's bunk, and the living area on the right. He didn't get it fully insulated before winter was in full swing, but the winter had been kind "to an old man living in a tent," as he wrote Caldwell, and, as he said, wood was handy.

McPhee had described the Drews cabin in the mid-1970s as "a dirty, fetid, lightless cabin, astink in aging salmon." Its rating had probably dropped a few stars since then, what with the flood, the roof going, the black plastic wallpaper, and the chickens. But Cook's new tent-cabin at Pass Creek must have seemed fresh and new and suffused with creamy, muslin-filtered light. To Dick, it must have felt—for better *and* for worse—like he was starting over.

I SAID THERE WAS an oh-two pitch on the way: Cook's third legal tangle with yet another federal agency. In 2000, the summer Cook built the tent frames, the king salmon run looked like it was going to be very poor. Nevertheless, as the fish moved up the river, the Alaska Department of Fish and Game allowed a commercial harvest, as well as fishing by subsistence users, as people like Cook were called. But just as the kings started to arrive in Cook's neighborhood in the upper Yukon, the state decided it was time to restrict the take to protect the escapement. The downriver subsistence fishermen had been able to fish twenty-four hours a day, seven days a week, and there had been commercial openings as well. But on July 19, as the fish reached the upper river, the state moved to restrict the take to ensure the escapement of sufficient breeding stock. The few fishermen affected, like Dick Cook, were deeply dependent on kings and fall-run chums for human food and dog team fuel. Nonetheless, they were ordered to cut back their fishing to just two days per week (one whole day, plus two half days).

This was not only burdensome for Cook—to have to fish by the clock rather than according to the myriad natural variables that normally would govern his schedule—but it simply didn't allow sufficient fishing time for him to catch enough fish to feed himself and his small dog team for the year. And the implications of that would cascade along, toppling the central pillars of his livelihood: insufficient human food meant more cash required for store-bought grub. Insufficient dog food could easily mean Cook would have to shoot some dogs. No dog team, or a smaller dog team, would mean he couldn't range as far on his trapline, and that would mean less cash income. Without salmon or wage work nearby (and the steamboats and roadhouses are long gone), it is pretty hard for anyone to survive out in the country, away from a village. If fishing was closed to him, Dick Cook, the longest-term river resident along the upper Yukon, would have to move to town.

Not without a fight, Cook figured. He defied the July 19 order and continued to fish. On August 11, 2000, Fish and Game choked down the harvest in Cook's area even further, limiting fishing to one twenty-four-hour opening per week. A few weeks later, on August 23, they closed subsistence salmon fishing in his area altogether.

Of course, drastic measures are sometimes necessary to protect the viability of the fish stock and ensure future runs. But compared to the commercial take, Cook's catch was tiny beyond the point of irrelevance. It seemed to Cook like the state wanted the entire escapement of breeding stock to come out of the small percentage of fish obtained by the subsistence people. Besides, there was a process—written into federal law—for implementing restrictions. That process gave priority to rural subsistence people like Cook, and it was not being followed, Cook said. The government agreed that section 804 of ANILCA required that before any subsistence user could be restricted from fishing, he had to be accorded a priority over other users. But the government said that the state's actions in cutting back the rural sub-sistence people's opportunity to fish was not really a "restriction," rather it was a "closure." And closures were covered under another section of ANILCA. For Cook and his attorney, it was a maddening bit of bureaucratic double-talk. Clearly, if English words meant anything, the government had not *closed* the fishery on July 19 and August 11, they had *reduced* the fishing time, first to forty-eight hours per week, then to twenty-four hours per week. If that wasn't a restriction, then, as Bill Caldwell wrote in his motion, "any type of limitation could sim-ply be denominated a closure and hence exempted from the priority scheme Congress so carefully crafted."

ANILCA requires that when restrictions on the take become neces-sary, managers must invoke a preference system such that subsistence users are the last to be curtailed. Sport fishing, for example, does not have as high a priority as subsistence use. Priority must be given to those subsistence users who are most dependent on the fish. To rank them, the act set out three criteria. First, the user's dependence upon the stock as the mainstay of livelihood. Second, local residency. And third, the availability of alternate resources. It's hard to imagine any-one in the upper Yukon River area ranking higher than Cook, who de-pended heavily on the salmon for food and dog feed, had lived for decades in the area he fished, and had few if any substitute resources.

It seems straightforward, but at the mouth of the Yukon River, the salmon fishery is big business. As the salmon swim upriver, some trav-eling two thousand miles, they degrade. Their jaws hook, their skin discolors, the flesh becomes less firm. They begin the process of dying, which they complete soon after they spawn. But at the mouth of the Yukon, the fish are bright and fresh from the sea. Naturally, the fish have their greatest commercial value there, and the fishing industry is important to the economy of that region. So, the upriver subsistence fishermen not only get the poorer-quality fish, courtesy of nature, but they have no clout either, courtesy of politics. As a result, curtailment of fishing opportunities tends to fall disproportionately on the people who take the least fish, who have access to the lowest-quality fish, and who are some of the poorest and hardest-working people on the river: the middle and upper Yukon subsistence fishermen (and that is to say nothing of the Canadians, who fare even worse). If, underneath that statement, there seems to be the suggestion that the biologists who manage the fisheries are somehow influenced by political pressure, well, stranger things have happened.

Consequently, the little guy at the end of the river takes the biggest hit, even when the law is on his side. Well, to hell with that, thought Dick Cook. He fished right through the first restriction, essentially daring the U.S. Fish and Wildlife Service, which enforced the state-initiated closures in federal areas, to pull up his net. A Park Service enforcement officer stopped in at Cook's to warn him that U.S. Fish and Wildlife Service officers would be on the river the next day, so he might want to haul in his net. Not a chance. Cook said the only way to get this issue resolved was with a court case. He would keep his net in the water through the closure. The next day, July 28, 2000, Fish and Wildlife agents pulled Cook's net and left him a note saying he should call a Fish and Wildlife agent. Cook did motor up to Eagle and got on the phone. But instead of calling the Fish and Wildlife office, he called his lawyer. He told Bill Caldwell he wanted to sue the United States. He thought the mealymouthed fishery biologists were ignoring the law out of fear of the goddamn weasel politicians, who were in turn afraid of the fat cat commercial fishing interests. Caldwell, who by now knew Cook pretty well, read the law and agreed with his client's conclusion, at least when stripped of the rhetoric. Cook's opportunity to subsistence fish could not be restricted or closed off completely without the government first taking into account his priority as a rural subsistence user. Meanwhile, Cook put his net back in the water, and on August 6, 2000, the Fish and Wildlife Service agents pulled and confiscated it, ending his fishing for the year. Cook shot two of his eight dogs and worked out with a friend a trade for more dog feed to supplement the fish he had already caught.

It took the Fish and Wildlife Service six months to get around to issuing a citation to Cook, seeking four hundred dollars in fines for fishing violations. That was February, and by then, of course, Cook was out on the Tatonduk and unreachable by phone or mail or anything but a personal visit by dog team, snowmachine, or helicopter. Caldwell accepted the citations on behalf of his client and sent a letter to Eagle for Cook, should he happen to go to town. Meanwhile, Caldwell filed suit in federal district court asking for a ruling that the government was violating the terms of ANILCA. He asked the court to order the government to hold off on its prosecution of the fishing violations until the ANILCA suit was decided. But before the suit advanced, Caldwell had to respond to the fishing citations at a hearing in early April before a federal magistrate judge (a local lawyer who stands in for a real judge and handles small federal matters, like traffic violations on the nearby military base). On April 6, 2001, U.S. Magistrate Judge Tom Fenton was characteristically dyspeptic. He was not pleased to learn that the defendant was not present, and he wanted to know why not. Caldwell began to explain that Cook likely didn't even know about the proceedings, but Fenton cut him off. Had the U.S. attorney served Cook with a notice to appear? The attorney wasn't sure. Fenton told him that if he could verify that Cook had been served, then a warrant should be issued for Cook's arrest. And if Cook hadn't been served, then the U.S. attorney should by God get him served (presumably by helicopter, two hundred miles each way, probably a twelve hundred dollar charter, for a four hundred dollar citation). Finally, Fenton denied Caldwell's motion to defer the fishing violations case. He wanted Cook in his courtroom on June 15, 2001.

All the huffing and puffing and throwing down of the rosin bag and jerking the cap brim likely did not intimidate Dick Cook in the slightest. But the blustering little windup and pitch from Federal Magistrate Judge Fenton would sure enough prove to be Dick Cook's strike three.

SCARLETT AND WAYNE HALL were worried when Dick Cook didn't show up at their place on Thursday, June 14, 2001. They knew he intended to appear in court in Fairbanks on the 15th and that he had wanted the Halls to baby-sit his chickens and dogs while he was gone. They had been worried earlier in June, on the 6th, when he didn't show up in Eagle to pick up his new chickens. Scarlett and Wayne and their son Garf, who lived on the Yukon twenty-two miles upriver from the Tatonduk, were Cook's closest year-round neighbors. They had also become among his closest friends in recent years. Scarlett had placed Dick's chicken order for him in the summer, and now the postmistress was saying she had two dozen chickens, and Dick hadn't come for them. That's when Wayne and Scarlett took a run in their boat down to the Tatonduk and found Cook stranded at his camp at the Drews cabin. His outboard had quit again. For want of a spare spark plug, he'd been there four days hoping to flag down a boat for a ride to town.

Wayne and Scarlett hauled Dick up to Eagle, where he got some new spark plugs and picked up his chickens. In fact, he had such a load that the Halls agreed to carry some of it and follow Cook up to Pass Creek in their canoe, also a nineteen-foot Grumman. Wayne says he is "an amateur" boatman compared to Dick and that the water was really wild. But following Dick's route, Wayne made it to Pass Creek, greatly relieved. Then he had to contemplate the return trip. It would be much faster going downstream, and Dick would not be along to pick the line of attack. As Wayne steeled himself for the ordeal, he found he couldn't stand postponing it and wanted to get going. Cook, on the other hand, was delighted to have company, especially Scarlett, whom he adored. He insisted on tea, and, as it is the next thing to an insult to refuse a sourdough's hospitality, all went into the tent. Wayne paced while Dick commenced his tea ritual, which was elaborate. The water must be brought slowly, very slowly to the not-quite-boil. Wayne couldn't stand it, so when Cook stepped outside the tent, he turned up the heat to full blast until the water boiled, then turned it down before Cook returned. "Your water's ready," he said. "That's impossible!" said Cook, staring hard at Wayne until he confessed. "I figure I'm going to die," Wayne told Cook, "so let's get it over with." Cook told him to just hit the waves at full throttle and he'd surf right over them. "I was terrified," says Scarlett. But they made the sharp turns, dodged the sweepers, shot the chutes, and squirted out into the Yukon intact. A mere near-death experience.

The Halls had gotten Dick squared away that time, but now, eight days later, they were worried again. Cook had told them he intended to make his required court appearance. Aside from that, there was a meeting in Eagle that very evening, the 14th, where federal and state fisheries managers likely would announce more subsistence restrictions. Cook relished both fights. But it had rained heavily on the 13th, and the Tatonduk was probably raging on the 14th. When Dick didn't show up at Wayne and Scarlett's, they assured themselves that he was prudently waiting for the river to drop. It's a treacherous little river at very high water, with nasty hydraulics to go along with the usual sweepers, ninety degree bends, and of course, the cold. Somehow Dick had been navigating it for three decades in his leaky nineteen-foot Grumman with an old outboard that someone had given him. That's not to say that Cook didn't dump his canoe occasionally, even when he considered the water navigable. But when the Tatonduk was at flood stage, he generally didn't mess with it. He'd just stay home and wait for it to drop.

Cook didn't come that Thursday, and he didn't come on Friday. Nor did he show up on the weekend. By Tuesday, the 19th, the Halls were solidly worried. They motored up to Eagle, and at about 1:00 P.M. Scarlett called Cook's lawyer, Bill Caldwell. Caldwell said he had expected to hear from Cook by the 15th but that he hadn't heard anything. He asked to be kept posted. Wayne went over to the Park Service office on the grounds of old Fort Egbert to suggest that Kevin Fox, a pilot and chief of operations at Eagle, take a plane up and have a look at the Tatonduk. At 2:30 P.M., Fox took the Park Service's Cessna 185 up and flew over Cook's operations at the Drews cabin. Seeing no action there, he turned up the Tatonduk to Pass Creek. "Did not see any activity, dogs or people," he wrote later. He flew down the Yukon a bit and noticed a motor-powered, square-stern Grumman at Seymour Able's place at Shade Creek and thought it might be Cook's. But when he reported that information to Wayne Hall, Wayne told him that Seymour's canoe was the same type Grumman as Cook's, that Fox had surely seen Seymour's boat, not Cook's.

An hour and a half later, Wayne was back at NPS offices. He thought he and Fox should both go up and have another look. At 4:40 Hall climbed into Fox's personal airplane, a slower-flying Super Cub. As they poked along the Tatonduk, they spotted debris in the water. A couple hours later, Fox called Bill Caldwell in Fairbanks to confirm Wayne's information that Cook was expected to come to Eagle in connection with his court proceedings. At 6:36 P.M., Fox called the Alaska State Troopers to report Dick Cook missing and possibly in trouble. At about the same time, he radioed down to Coal Creek, where the Park Service had a contract helicopter doing fire-related work under their fire safety officer, Marsha Henderson. Fox told her that Dick Cook was expected in Eagle, hadn't shown up, and that people were worried. He asked her to take the chopper over and check it out.

Henderson jumped into the Hughes 500D with the pilot, Robert Holbrook, whom everyone calls Sterling, and flew fifty miles east to the Tatonduk River. At Pass Creek, they saw five of Dick's dogs running loose along the bank. Sterling found a little place to land on the river bank, but he couldn't shut down, needing to hold a little power.

As Henderson climbed out, the dogs came bounding up, big and ferocious looking. But she knelt down and petted them, then eased over to Cook's tent beside his beautiful garden. Henderson took a look inside and could see a bulging sleeping bag on the bunk. But when she checked it out, it was empty. "We flew around and looked, and circled and flew all over, up and down the river and everything," says Sterling, who has an accent like the rest of the people who live in Coffeeville, Alabama. "We saw he had building material down the river that he had brought part way up and had stashed there. As we circled there and checked all that out, we saw something in the river." Sterling landed right in the river, on the gravel in about a foot of water, about two-and-half miles from the mouth. Henderson got out onto the skid and retrieved an orange dry bag. It contained some of Dick Cook's correspondence and legal papers. They didn't know it at the time because the water was so high, but Cook's canoe was only yards off the chopper's nose, in a hole on the south side. As they took off, Sterling noticed a nasty chute that led to the eddy where an aluminum can bobbed and circled. "I pointed out to Marsha that it was a pretty good chute of water right there. The river was moving pretty good and it made a bend to the left, and then a hard bend back to the right and went through a chute. And there was a little hydraulic there and a pool below it, and this can was bobbing there." Henderson reported all this that night, and "that's when they decided things didn't look good," says Sterling.

The next day, the 20th, when the troopers hadn't responded, Wayne and his friend Tim McLaughlin searched the Tatonduk by boat. They found a bucket with a dead chicken in it near the mouth, a chicken crate a mile above the mouth, and a canoe paddle a half-mile below Dick's Pass Creek cabin. Kevin Fox flew the river again. It was almost a day—twenty hours—before a trooper from Northway touched down in a helicopter. It seemed to Wayne that the troopers might not have understood that they were looking for a person who might be alive and injured, and that time was of the essence. Clearly, the debris found in the river proved that Cook had capsized the canoe, and it strongly suggested that his disappearance was due to this accident, rather than that he had gone for a hike, or some other explanation. The troopers stayed just forty minutes on the ground at Cook's Pass Creek camp, then pulled out, searching the river from the air as they left. They saw no Dick, no canoe.

On June 21, a dozen local people from Eagle joined the search. Austin Nelson brought in some searchers in his jet boat. The trooper's helicopter and the Park Service helicopter were aloft, as was the NPS fixed wing. Another of Cook's dogs showed up about three and a half miles below Pass Creek, near where he'd had to abandon his pickup truck and building materials the previous fall. Kevin Fox and the village public safety officer found another dry bag, this one with food. They also discovered Cook's logbook at his Pass Creek tent cabin.

On the 22nd, eleven villagers took up the search. They turned up a can of mosquito repellent about three miles below Pass Creek. Scarlett Hall found the canoe's fuel tank a mile and a half below that. The Yukon-Charley superintendent brought a man down from Gates of the Arctic National Park to manage the search. The man had training in "applying statistical probabilities in search planning," according to Yukon-Charley superintendent Dave Mills. Eagle people were less than impressed. "He had a big map that was all color-coded," says Sterling, "and routes that he could have taken. And when you looked at it, you're like, 'My God, where is this man coming from? Does he have any concept of what it's like out there on the ground?'" One of the theories emanating from the command post was that Dick might have been suicidal and climbed to the top of Nimrod Peak to kill himself there. Nimrod Peak, northeast of his Pass Creek camp, is rugged, very steep, and five thousand feet high. "And we're like, Dick was in fine shape for his age, but no way could he possibly have climbed Nimrod Peak. And *why*? I mean, it made no sense to anybody. But anyway we flew Nimrod Peak."

As crews searched high and low, Sterling was lucky to be searching from the high sector. "He had a group hike the winter mail route, the old winter trail. Well," says Sterling, "the winter trail cuts off a bend of the Yukon, and it goes through a wet, boggy muskeg. Hell, even across a lake, because it's a winter trail. And I'm not an Alaskan, but I know they travel those in winter because the ground's frozen. But he had people slogging through that mess. Everybody was kind of laughing behind his back, but if you were hiking that winter trail, you weren't laughing." Without a doubt, Dick Cook would have been cackling until his bony ribs ached. The absolute last thing he would have done was to go walking through the swamps along the winter trail. As Dick's lawyer, Bill Caldwell, said about that, "Dick was eccentric, but he wasn't a fool." If he'd lost his canoe and wanted help, or wanted to get to Eagle, he would have walked down his trail along the Tatonduk and stayed at his cabin on the Yukon until he could flag down a passing boat.

Another theory said that Cook might have been despondent over his impending court hearing on the fishing citation, that he so hated the government the he fled into Canada via the upper Tatonduk. Caldwell says, "Dick hated the government, but he loved to fight it. He liked *his* version of the U.S. Constitution." Sterling was continually baffled by theories that Cook might have taken off walking into Canada or some other place, as if he was escaping. Sterling pointed out that Cook already lived in a place about as remote as any he might escape to. Besides, all the theories premised on Cook walking somewhere seemed to ignore one fact: the canoe was gone too. "Once I saw the can floating in the riffles, I told Marsha, I said, 'This guy's in the river.'" Sterling's theory is that Cook dumped the canoe, and it hung up in the hole near where they found the dry bag and the can. "Then he got out and walked up to his cabin and wrote down about losing it, and that he was going back to get it. I guess that he probably waded out in there, maybe in hip boots, because it wasn't that deep of water, but it was pretty swift, gravel bottom, and he lost his footing, and it sucked him right down and through that chute. You know, and he drowned and that was that."

Even though Cook lived on private land (though within the preserve's exterior boundaries), the Park Service came through with a thorough and sustained search, Sterling says. "They dropped everything. And they were fully committed to try to find Dick, and they couldn't have done anything more than what they did. Kevin Fox in particular worked diligently at it." On Saturday the 23rd, having found neither Dick nor the canoe after four days of searching, NPS brought in two teams of nose dogs and handlers from Wilderness Search and Rescue in Fairbanks. The same day, Kevin Fox and a couple others finally spotted the canoe, submerged, about two miles up the Tatonduk, about seventy-five yards above the place where Cook's other conveyance, his pickup, had also come to rest. The dogs worked both sides of the river all day but found nothing and were sent home. Nothing at all was found on the 24th, and the Park Service scaled back the search for Cook on the 25th.

WAYNE HALL FIGURES Dick Cook probably initially sat out the rain and the high water at his camp, waiting for river conditions to improve. Notes Cook entered into his journal on June 13 say, "Tried to go to EAA [Eagle's airport code]. *Flood*. Rain all day." On the 14th, he wrote, "Flood peak. Drizzle." On the 15th, "Water dropped 1"". Overcast. Some drizzle." The next day was sunny, and the water dropped twelve inches. Blue skies again on the 17th, the water dropping another six inches. The 18th was sunny again, and with the river falling three or four inches, Cook felt like giving it a try. He packed up his four hens and thirteen chicks. The chicks may have all gone into a crate. The hens went into white, plastic, five-gallon buckets with holes in the lids. One hen per bucket. That was his system.

The buckets and crate would have gone into the canoe along with Dick's gear and fuel. Whether any of the dogs went into the boat isn't known. Often the river people will run their dogs along the river bank, rather than carry them in a canoe. Cook had six huskies, perhaps an aggregate four hundred pounds of shifting weight, and they would no doubt be excited by the near proximity of squawking poultry. It would seem almost suicidal to load all the dogs. If he did decide to load some dogs, he would have faced the question of whether to tie them in. The boat would be more stable and the ride safer if the dogs were clipped in with short chains, but then they might not survive a capsizing. Probably, he ran the dogs down the beach.

Dick liked to stand up in his canoe when he navigated side streams like the Tatonduk. The Grumman's bow has a tendency to rise under power, especially if the boat is lightly loaded, and especially if the operator is sitting in the stern seat. Cook had an extension on his tiller, locally called a "Seymour Stick" (after its inventor, Seymour Able). It allows the operator to stand forward of the stern thwart to help bring the bow down. On the motor end of the stick, there is a flexible section, perhaps a piece of radiator hose or an eye-and-snap-hook coupling that acts like a universal joint. It can both rotate and articulate, such that the tiller can be pushed over all the way in either direction while still allowing it to be twisted (to operate the throttle). If the load was light, Cook liked to run the boat with a big heavy rock up forward. He didn't put it down low in the boat but rather up on the little triangular bow deck, which of course made the canoe tippy. With his gear and chickens loaded, and the mutts tearing around and raising a ruckus on shore, Cook would have squeezed the priming bulb in the fuel line to force some of his bum gas into the carburetor of his worn-out fifteen-horse motor and shoved his leaky Grumman into the swift, icy current. Wayne says that one hole in Cook's canoe sent up a jet of water like the stream from a squirt gun. "He wouldn't fix the hole, he just bailed all the time."

If he had any dogs in the boat, it wouldn't take much weight shifting to capsize. And the chickens on board would have provided an incentive. More likely the water-contaminated gas caused the motor to quit just when he needed the steerage way. Wayne ended up with several five-gallon cans of Cook's boat gas, and he said, "Not a single tankfull allowed me to go more than a hundred yards without the motor quitting." Maybe the water was just too high and fast, and he couldn't take the canoe through the turns. Maybe, at seventy years of age, he didn't have the strength, or the reflexes, or the quick thinking that he needed. Maybe, after three decades of close calls, he'd just used up his quota of luck. The only ones who know for sure are the six huskies now sitting in Wayne's dog yard.

Whatever the cause, Cook swamped his boat on June 18. Cheating death one last time, he made it to shore. Tracks along the banks not very far below Pass Creek showed he crossed the river and hoofed it back to camp. It is possible that Cook set out again the same day. But it seems more likely that he spent the rest of that day fishing out his gear and critters and drying everything out. "He only had one set of clothes that we know of," says Wayne. The journal entry offers scant information: "Tried to go to EAA. *Swamped*. Water dropped 3"–4". Sunny." He doesn't say he had to go recover the canoe or that it was sunk or lost. It seems unlikely that Cook was swept away on the 18th while trying to get his canoe unstuck or while wading across the river because his tracks show up only a short distance below his camp, not all the way down where his canoe was found, three and a half miles below. Wayne's best guess is that on the 18th, Cook dumped almost right away, just below Pass Creek, that he retrieved his gear and animals the same day, and that he launched again on the 19th. He probably didn't make it far on the second try, as his paddle was found just a half-mile downstream.

On June 25, at about 3:30 in the afternoon, the ranger brought down from Gates of the Arctic scaled back the search and handed over the search command to Kevin Fox. Within a few hours Fox saw something while flying a fixed-wing aircraft at a couple hundred feet above surface of the Tatonduk. There was something white in a pool about three hundred yards above its mouth. On closer inspection, it was white and red. The slow current had lifted up a man's red flannel shirt exposing his white back. Fox returned to Eagle, launched a Park Service boat, and with the village public safety officer and a state trooper quickly motored twenty-seven miles down to the Tatonduk. Things looked a lot different from the river. The water glinted and reflected such that it was hard to see anything beneath the surface. But from the air Fox had noticed a dead spruce tree leaning out from the bank pointing like a grim finger directly at the body. He was facedown in three feet of water, feet upstream, as if swimming for the Yukon. The men could see he was hovering on the edge of deeper water, and they were worried the prop wash might send him over the brink and on into the muddy water that clouded the last few hundred yards of the Tatonduk before it entered the Yukon. At about 6:00 P.M., they tied up at the bank, and the trooper waded in. He grabbed the man's belt and pulled him to shore. The seven-day search for Dick Cook was over.

COOK HAD ON HIP BOOTS and, characteristically, no life preserver. His finger tips were abraded, indicating that he clutched at rocks as he was swept downstream. His body may have worked its way downstream in stages over several days or all at once. The hip waders would have made it more difficult for Cook to swim, though it is a myth that the weight of water inside the waders pulls a person under. While submerged, Cook's hip waders weighed less than they would on land, and the water within them would not add any weight at all until he tried to lift them out of the water. (The same effect can be seen if a five-gallon bucket is filled with water and hung from a spring scale. It would weigh forty pounds. But lower it into a rain barrel, and the scale would register nothing at all; even the weight of the bucket would be canceled out by buoyant forces.)

Water of forty-some degrees, as the Tatonduk may have been in mid-June, would drop a person's body temperature into the hypothermic range quickly. The longer Cook was in the water, the more his core body temperature would drop. At ninety-six and a half degrees, he would shiver uncontrollably. At ninety-four degrees, he would lose his memory. At ninety-three, muscle rigidity would set in; manual dexterity would be lost. At eighty-six, unconsciousness. Without a life jacket, unconsciousness would certainly result in drowning.

But the shock of immersion in cold water kills many more Alaskans than does hypothermia. A person can function for fifteen or twenty minutes, even in ice water, before his core begins to cool. And he should last an hour and a quarter before unconsciousness and drowning, or heart failure, does him in. But sudden death killed forty-four of the fifty-five Alaskans who died in boating accidents between 2001 and 2003, and Cook may have been one of them. Once thrown into cold water, a person will usually respond by gasping violently—a reflex more intense but not unlike the involuntary sharp inhalation that accompanies putting your bare, warm foot into an icy stream. This gasp is followed by involuntary hyperventilation for about a minute. Obviously, if a person's head is underwater when he gasps or hyperventilates, he will aspirate water, fill his lungs, and likely drown immediately. But even hyperventilating air reduces carbon dioxide in the blood, resulting in constriction of blood vessels in the brain, which in turn can lead to diminished mental function, fainting, and drowning. The shock of dunking in cold water can also cause a person, even a young person, to suffer instant cardiac arrest.

Between instant death and hypothermia an hour later lurk other ways to die. In cold water, the body loses heat a hundred times faster than in air of the same temperature. Blood flow is shunted to the brain and vital organs in the core, which causes the oxygen-starved muscles in the arms and legs to weaken. As Cook's extremities numbed, he would lose the ability even to hold on to the boat or to a bit of flotation. He would become profoundly enfeebled and stop moving altogether. Without a life jacket, he would sink. As cold water hit his windpipe, his larynx might seize in a spasm that would keep water out of his lungs, but that would also result in suffocation. As his blood became further depleted of oxygen, he would slip into unconsciousness. If he were underwater and unconscious, but alive, the muscles around his airways might relax and admit water into his lungs. Either way, water in the lungs or water not in the lungs, the result is asphyxiation.

DICK COOK WAS CREMATED, and his two daughters, Dawn and Holly, came up to Alaska from the States for a memorial service in Eagle. There was a good crowd at the old church on the grassy bluff above the Yukon, and the people hauled the pews outside and had the service there. A couple dozen of the attendees loaded into boats and canoes afterward and motored down to Dick's fish camp at the Drews cabin. Two of Dick's brothers were there; his sister; his ex-wife Ann; and his friend and lawyer, Bill Caldwell. Dawn read a bit from Dick's journal and scattered half of his ashes in his garden. A bunch of the people spent the night, camping at Miller's Camp at the mouth of the Tatonduk.

Wayne and Scarlett took Dick's daughters in their canoe and set off up the Tatonduk to scatter the rest of Dick's ashes at his place at Pass Creek. About halfway up, Wayne encountered a ninety-degree curve with a sweeper nearly across the whole river. He powered through slowly and carefully until he reached a point where he thought maybe he should just pull into shore and hike the rest of the way. But just then the prop caught on a snag, killing the engine. The boat slipped sideways, caught the current, and flipped. Everybody was pitched into the cold river and swept downstream. For a moment, the same dark thought must have occurred to them all. But, unlike Dick, they were wearing life jackets. Scarlett made it to shore fairly quickly, but the others didn't. They hung on to the canoe, which was upside down, and were swept along for a half mile, with the motor taking a beating on the rocks below. At one point Dawn made it to shore while Holly was still in the water hanging onto the canoe but with her legs tangled in a rope underwater. Dawn grabbed a line and hauled on it, trying to pull the canoe ashore, but as soon as she did, Holly went under. Holly yelled, "Don't pull on the yellow rope." Dawn had ahold of a green rope, so she pulled once more, and Holly got another dunking. Louder this time, Holly yelled, "DON'T PULL ON THE YEL—glub." It was funny later, when they saw that the yellow rope was tied to the green one. Eventually the group collected themselves on a little gravel bar and started bailing the canoe and gathering and sorting out the gear. Finally, Wayne asked, "What did we lose?" Dawn answered, "A hat, sunglasses, Dick, a water jug, and the paddles." It took a minute for Wayne and Scarlett to register the inherited deadpan humor. Then they all burst out laughing. The four of them stood sopping wet and shivering on the edge of the river that had recently claimed the life of their father and friend, doubled over, laughing uncontrollably. You can almost hear Dick telling the story about how he drowned twice in the same place.

I SAY GOOD-BYE to the Swami River and pull out into the Yukon. With the breeze in my face again, I let the wide river bear me deeper into the country. I am thinking about Dick Cook's vaporous legacy. His journals have already blown away as smoke. His dwellings will molder into compost and nurture a copse of trees. The people who knew him will die. There is, of course, John McPhee's fulsome portrait and the words on these pages. They will keep a few stories alive, just as Ernie Pyle preserved Heinie Miller's cranky rants of seventy years ago. And, too, Cook nurtured a copse of spiritual progeny. Even thirty years ago, he was the old man of the river. And to some extent, as McPhee said, he was mentor to the young people who arrived after him, all the way forward to Wayne and Scarlett, who came into the country in the 1990s. McPhee had called Cook the "acknowledged high swami of the river people." But he was not really the nonpareil he was made out to be. He was not an exemplary woodsman, in the sense of building and maintaining quality camps or cabins or caches or boats. He seemed to favor raggedy and easily soaked store-bought cotton clothing to the fur the country provided. He rarely had two sticks of firewood to pile on top of one another. He never really got very far out into the country—in thirty-six years he never made it up into the Charley River drainage to meet the trapper next door. He simultaneously deplored and utilized gas-powered machines, though he never bothered to acquire much of the mechanical skill needed to maintain them, and his equipment quickly became junk.

Still, at the time of his death, he was one of the few people in all of northern Alaska to live a non-village-based life, year-round. He was the only resident along this stretch of Yukon in the modern period who stayed out in the woods until he died. At seventy, he was fitter and sharper and feistier than most people in their prime. He was still fearlessly living a life that probably not one American in half a million could handle. He was a champion of the subsistence way of life, taking his fight to the courts, and by God if he didn't have the federal government by the short hairs! And when he died in a wild ride of raw courage, he still had a lot of spit left in him. He was the true descendant of his predecessor, Heinie Miller, and he carried forth a tradition of loose-tongued, cross-grained, vinegary occupancy of this place into the twenty-first century. That is clear. What is not clear is whether anyone now may pick up where he left off.

Wood Islands

Windfall Mountain rises to my right. In the past, lightning ignited coal seams here that smoldered underground, even through the winter. Ahead is Wood Islands, where Cook found the pirate's traps, and where in the 1930s a man from Hawaii named Bane Beechman built a cabin. He stayed a winter cutting wood and writing. Later Willie Juneby of Eagle, the man who trapped the Tatonduk before Cook, stayed in the Beechman cabin while cutting steamboat wood on the islands for Heinie Miller. Juneby must have been one of Miller's top hands, as it was he who drove the Cat, dragging the wood up to Miller's Camp. That Willie was an accomplished Cat skinner was both a good and a bad thing, as Heinie told Ernie Pyle in 1937. "Hell, them Indians come all the way from Dawson, a hundred miles, just to watch Willie drive the Cat." According to Heinie, the Indians would always show up at mealtime. "And I can't say no. I've been trying to say no for twenty years but I can't do it," said Miller, the old softie.

There are three islands in this group, and running across all three is an old wood road, which also served as the mail trail, that being the safest route to move between the flats on river right and the flats on river left. On the left bank opposite Wood Islands, before the flats begin, there is a tall, sandy cut bank. A stand of young birch trees grows on top of the bank. At the water's edge a hundred feet below I see a detached clump of grassy sod with a half-dozen more birches growing out of it. It has surfed down the steep bank, upright, all the way to the river, like a car full of teenagers on a joy ride. I see in the cut bank another rust-colored spot, like the one I saw above Mel's camp. A bit of iron-rich rock? Or the place where a four-hundred-pound beaver died, as the Native people say? I imagine beaver teeth, being much harder than bone, might survive burial for ten thousand years. And a beaver tooth is the sort of bone that would identify the animal to a hunter in a way that a hip bone might not. Did some Native people long ago find beaver teeth within one of these brown splotches and make the association that way? Or is it just the rural equivalent of an urban myth? For anthropologists, "local knowledge," as they call it, certainly has intrinsic value as lore, but sometimes it is useful as science as well.

Fred Andersen worked for many years as a fish biologist for the Alaska Department of Fish and Game and now works for the Park Service. He says that downriver around Galena, when the Yukon rises in August, the Native people will tell you that it is because the salmon are in the river. Apparently the idea is that the bodies of the fish displace so much water that it causes the Yukon River to rise. Or perhaps the people are not positing a causal relationship, but merely noting that these things occur simultaneously. My own guess is that the river rises because it usually rains a monsoon in August. But Fred says he has observed many times the uncanny accuracy of another bit of Native wisdom: that the first king salmon shows up just as the cottonwoods shed their cotton. Maybe the air or water temperature or the changing duration of daylight independently triggers responses in salmon and in cottonwood trees that tend to coincide in one region along the river.

Sometimes the Native people, particularly the old people who lived out on the land, know more about how the country fits together than they are inclined to let on. Some years ago, Fred was doing research on northern pike in the Kaiyuh Flats east of the Yukon River village of Kaltag. He was trying to figure out where the northern pike went in the winter. When he asked the Kaltag people, they all said they didn't know. Fred had a hunch they knew more than they were saying. At any rate, Department of Fish and Game biologists went out and caught some pike that summer and surgically implanted radio transmitters. Once a month they flew over the flats dialing in on the signals until they got their answer. The pike ended up in a big lake out in the Kaiyuh Flats. It had a long Athabascan name, and Fred asked around until he found someone who could translate it. It means: "Place where pike go in the winter."

Montauk Bluff

Around the bend, on the right bank, twenty-six-hundred-foot Montauk Bluff tilts its stratified slabs into the river at nearly ninety degrees to the horizontal. People often see black bears on the south-facing slopes of Montauk Bluff, especially in spring. In fact, as my hunting pal Knut Kielland noticed, they seem to appear just as the aspen trees that cover Montauk's slopes begin to show a tinge of green. Knut wondered if there was a connection, so one spring he marked a few aspen trees in his neighborhood just outside Fairbanks. At leaf flush, he collected some leaves. He collected more leaves from the same trees in midsummer, and he collected again in the fall. At his laboratory at the University of Alaska, he tested each batch in an elemental analyzer. The leaves were combusted, rendered gaseous, and analyzed for elements. The first leaves, the small, tender ones newly popped from buds, turned out to be absolutely loaded with nitrogen. Knut measured more than six percent. A formula says that you multiply this percentage by six and one-quarter to arrive at a "crude protein" value of almost thirty-eight percent. In other words, more than one-third of the young leaves' dry weight consisted of a highly digestible protein. By midsummer, the leaves' protein concentration had dropped by two-thirds. By fall, it had dropped by five-sixths. So the bears come in the spring to gorge on the delicate and highly nutritious young aspen leaves, just as they burst forth on these sunny south-facing hillsides.

SOMEWHERE ON THE LEFT BANK—though exactly where isn't known—Montauk Roadhouse operated when the mail trail saw regular use. Frontier judge James Wickersham stopped here one February night a hundred years ago, after mushing all day over a rough trail through temperatures as low as fifty-two below zero. He doesn't comment on the meals, but he was plenty happy to rest his trail-sore feet. Wickersham had only been in the country for seven months when he mushed downriver and spent the night here. He'd come over on the White Pass Railway from Skagway the previous July, then downriver to Eagle by steamboat to fill a position as one of Alaska's first judges. At Eagle, he promptly dunned the saloons for enough money to erect a courthouse and jail. When he opened his one-man shop for business,

Wickersham commenced the administration of justice in a jurisdiction that encompassed three hundred thousand square miles, an area big enough to hold Texas, with enough left over to fit in New Jersey, Massachusetts, Vermont, and New Hampshire.

The very first case Judge Wickersham adjudicated, according to his memoir *Old Yukon,* was brought by Chief Charley of the Charley Creek (Kandik River) band. The chief had paddled a hundred miles upriver to Eagle with twelve fighting men, and he was ready either for justice or a tussle. After assuring himself that Wickersham was the biggest chief at Eagle, he stated his complaint. An Indian named Eagle Jack had stolen his dog down at Nation River and had taken it up to Eagle Village. "If you not get my dog," the chief told the judge, "I get my dog. Maybe some Indian get hurt." Wickersham was impressed. "All this time the old chief sat straight as a ramrod on the edge of the chair in front of me, with both his feet resting flat on the floor, gazing squarely into my eyes." The judge had no doubt of the honesty of Charley's claim and, dispensing with such legal formalities as might constitute due process, he dispatched a deputy to get the dog and deliver it to the chief. While they waited for the dog, the two chiefs sat in the sun and talked about fishing and about building a school house for the Indian children. When the dog was produced without incident, it was a decent day's work for the new judge: dog and chief reunited, case closed, minor Indian war averted, important diplomatic ties established, and justice—Solomonic and rough—born in Interior Alaska.

AROUND THE NEXT BEND, the light and the river go steely bluegray, and the trees darken until they lose all their color. I see a canoe like mine poking slowly upriver near the right bank, and I swing the tiller over and aim for it. It's Wayne Hall and his son Garf scouting for moose in the twilight. They are camped nearby in a stand of spruce trees a mile or so above the mouth of the Nation River, and they invite me to join them for the night. I go set up my tent while they check one more slough.

Around the campfire, our talk turns to territoriality. When Wayne established a fish camp at this spot a few years ago, he found that another fisherman about four miles downriver was unhappy about it. The other fellow used to live on the Kandik River: "He said, 'On the Kandik if someone wanted to camp within ten miles of someone else's place, they came and asked permission.'" Wayne, who lives on the Yukon just a few miles outside the village of Eagle, said he figured Kandik rules were different from Yukon rules because the Yukon was more of a highway than the side creeks. He's also at odds with another Kandik River resident, a trapper who prefers to be unnamed. The dispute centers on a cabin a few miles downriver built by Dave Evans. Evans was long gone by the time the man commenced using it as a trapline cabin. Wayne's case rests on the following argument: the cabin belonged to Evans; Evans used the cabin when trapping; since Wayne has taken over Evans' trapline, he is also entitled to take over the cabin.

Rivals on the river. Actually, as Wilfred Funk tells us, the word *rival* comes from *river*. Through the French to the Latin *rivales*. It means "near neighbors" or "those who lived on the banks of the same stream." *Rivales* were inevitably competitors for fish and the other bounties of riparian life, and that sense informs our modern usage.

Disputes like the ones Wayne Hall describes are not uncommon. When Steve Ulvi lived up near the border, there was an especially productive eddy claimed by a couple of fellows from Eagle who fished it every year. Each year, after they took all the fish they wanted, they let Ulvi use the site. "Eventually I started feeling real territorial about the place," he told me, "especially when they stopped fishing it and started handing it off to other people who didn't live around there. We kind of had a show-down and I lucked-out and ended up on the spot." But the primacy-of-proximity principle doesn't always hold, apparently. For instance, there was another right-of-succession case involving Ulvi and Charlie Edwards's trapline. Charlie had decided to quit trapping the upper part of Fourth of July Creek. That area had burned in 1969 and was now loaded with marten. And even though he lived fifty or sixty miles upriver, Ulvi and his brother took it over. Worse yet, in the minds of the river people, they *bought* the trapline. "Basically what we were doing was buying the hardware and snares and such and traps that were out and maybe a little compensation for the trail work and things. We went down and met Charlie and he showed us around the line and we bought it out and that was pretty controversial. There were a lot of people living along the river, particularly neighbors of that area, who thought it was outrageous that anybody could conceive of buying country. And there was a lot of talk and negative attitude toward Charlie for doing it, and for us for doing it. But we went in there and trapped and did very well."

Clearly, the Law of the North is not always simple. I keep thinking that, long after he was gone, the country still needed a Judge Wickersham riding the frontier circuit on his dogsled. He would have settled disputes with a tough and durable justice. And that might have prevented a few tragic confrontations, like the one that befell Pollack Joe Hajec.

Pollack Joe

Perhaps rivalries are magnified out here where they involve men who tend toward macho physicality to start with. Then, too, people who willingly suffer to live far from their fellow men sometimes show an independence of spirit not readily distinguishable from misanthropy. Territoriality becomes a cultural imperative. And disputes can escalate from chest-puffing, to fisticuffs, to gunfire. John Borg, the retired postmaster of Eagle, compiled a list that accounted for all the people from the Eagle area that McPhee had written about in the 1970s. Borg has an actuarial turn of mind, and his list records that only five of forty-seven people mentioned in the McPhee book still live in Eagle. Twenty-six are dead, four of those victims of criminal homicide. If expressed in conventional terms, the *Coming into the Country* community's murder rate (including manslaughter) would make Chicago look like Mr. Rogers' Neighborhood. Chicago's murder rate is twenty-two per one hundred thousand of the population. The rate of criminal homicide for McPhee's characters translates to eight thousand five hundred and eleven per one hundred thousand.

Of that number, one is Joseph J. Hajec, known locally as Pollack Joe. Joe trapped along this stretch of the Yukon. Based at Nation townsite before the other river people moved in during the mid-1970s, he used a snowmachine and covered a lot of ground. His lines ran all the way down the Yukon to Coal Creek. Joe also worked hard gold mining up near the tiny settlement of Chicken in the Fortymile River country, and he took out a lot of gold. Most people say he was an all right little guy, not adversarial, quiet, extremely tough, resourceful. Some liked him a lot: "He was a very nice person," said one. "He'd do anything to help you out." When the river people first began crowding in on his traplines, he didn't raise a fuss, he just sort of shifted to accommodate. It was a tragedy what happened, they say, not to mention a crazy miscarriage of justice. It's not a unanimous review, however. One fellow told me, "Pollack Joe? Yeah, I knew him. He was an asshole."

In any case, in the winter of 1977, Joe and his partner Thomas DeWayne Bowers were mining quite near two young fellows named Earl David Russell (aged seventeen) and Charlie Brunn (aged twenty). Originally, Joe had brought Russell in on his mining operation, which was on ground Joe had no legal claim to. At some point, Russell's parents and sister moved out to the mining ground as well. Russell pulled out of his partnership with Joe and teamed up with Brunn. Russell and Brunn began to sink their own holes in the crowded strip of productive ground where Napoleon Creek entered the South Fork of the Fortymile River. Joe took in Bowers as his new partner, and relations were not cordial between the two partnerships. One day Russell and Brunn drove up to Fairbanks and paid for the claim. At least, that's what they asserted, presenting Joe with paperwork that they said meant the ground he had been working was now theirs. With freeze-up, the two parties started sinking shafts just feet apart from one another through the ice at the mouth of Napoleon Creek. They argued over who could dig where. Russell and Brunn said Bowers pulled a gun on them, and they called in a trooper. After listening to all sides, the trooper drew a line dividing the ground into two parts, and he got an agreement that both parties would observe a ban on firearms at the work site. The truce didn't last long.

Pollack Joe and Bowers left the claim to go trapping on the Yukon but returned just before Christmas 1977. According to court documents, Russell and Brunn said that on December 22, Pollack and Bowers threatened to kill them if they tried to work down on the ice. They say they saw a shotgun in Bowers's vehicle, an International Scout. When Brunn returned to the river later, he had a pistol in his pocket. Brunn says Bowers and Hajec were crouched beside their steamer barrel when he arrived on the ice. He says he saw Bowers take a couple of quick steps toward the Scout. At that point, Brunn, by his own account, opened up on the unarmed men at a distance of twenty feet with a 9-mm semiautomatic handgun, emptying it. Joe ran away. From a cabin above, Russell began shooting at Hajec with a .308-caliber high-powered rifle. Another miner, Ed Schwoyer, was sinking a hole about fifty yards away and looked up when he heard popping sounds. "I saw Joe running toward me screaming like a kid in a playground." Bowers ran to the side of the Scout shouting at Schwoyer, "They are shooting at us! Do something!" Russell continued to fire toward Hajec, at one point trading the .308 for a 30.06. Joe crumpled to the ice. Hit several times, Bowers nonetheless reached the Scout, pulled out a .410 shotgun loaded with bird shot, and shot Brunn in the legs. Brunn fired four or five shots, according to Schwoyer, advancing right up to the Scout, continuing to pull the trigger, not realizing he was out of ammunition. Schwoyer jumped up out of his hole and ran over to Brunn, yelling, "Don't shoot anymore!" Bowers had been hit several times, but he started the Scout and turned it, trying to escape. Russell continued to fire at the vehicle with his rifle. Brunn tried to reload, but he jammed the gun. Bowers roared away down the river ice in a cloud of snow and gun smoke.

When the bullets stopped flying, Schwoyer went over to Joe Hajec. He was dead. Bowers made it out to the bridge; up onto the road; and into the tiny settlement of Chicken, on the Taylor Highway fifteen miles away. He lived for several hours at Chicken before bleeding to death. There were fourteen holes in him, which the forensic pathologist thought were made by eight bullets. Troopers said there were twelve bullet holes in the Scout. Earl David Russell and Charles L. Brunn each were indicted on two counts of first-degree murder. At the trial in Fairbanks, Russell admitted that he shot at Bowers and Hajec with a rifle. He told troopers he hit Hajec, but said, "I don't think that it killed him," according to press accounts. The medical examiner testified that Hajec was killed by one bullet, probably from a rifle. The defense attempted to show that the "boys were in mortal fear of their life by veteran river men." Hajec and Bowers, they claimed, were hardened and aggressive men who frightened the two youngsters so badly that shooting them was justified. Apparently, the Fairbanks jury was less convinced by the district attorney's presentation than they were receptive to the self-defense claim. Russell was acquitted and went free. Brunn was convicted on two counts of the lesser charge of manslaughter and sentenced to serve ten years on each count, twenty years total. His attorneys appealed the sentence as excessive. During the interim, Brunn was released to the custody of his parents out of state, where he worked and finished college. The appeal was successful. His sentence was made concurrent, reducing it by half to ten years total. Then, five of those years were suspended, meaning the new total sentence was five years, with five years probation to follow. In the end, Brunn served slightly less than two years. The people of Eagle named the boat landing "Hajec Landing" and put up a sign "In memory of Joe Hajec (Pollack Joe), one of the last of a tough, independent breed of men that have vanished along with the last frontier."

Nation River/Dave Evans

There is a bluff just below the mouth of Nation River, and at the base of the bluff is a cabin. I'd like to spend the night here, but it's still early morning when I say good-bye to Wayne and Garf and motor across the mouth of the Nation. I pull in for a quick look anyway. A little footpath uphill through the spruce leads to a grassy clearing where a pole cache looms. Beyond it, a tiny log cabin is set into the hillside. I always think I remember the cabin well, but it always looks a little different to me. It's about twelve feet square, with an entry area/workshop added on to the front. Inside, everything is squared away and tidy. A logbook on the table advises that the cabin is owned by the Park Service but may be used by travelers. The book has a brief historical note that says the place was built in 1934 by a Norwegian immigrant named Chris Nelson, a trapper so talkative folks called him "Phonograph." Chris Nelson had lived in the Eagle area since 1920 and trapped up the Nation into the 1940s. He used this place as one of his four camps. He was known as mostly a loner, a hard worker, and a good trapper. In March 1949, after forty-five years in the north, he died in his bunk, right here in this cabin. A traveler found him frozen solid. Looking the place over, though, it doesn't seem likely that it would be standing now had it been abandoned to the elements for all those decades between the 1940s and the 1980s, when the Park Service took it over.

Though the logbook's historical commentary does not mention him, the cabin's interim benefactor was a young fellow named Dave Evans who, along with his girlfriend, Sage Patton, and their friends, Brad Snow and Lilly Allen, moved onto the Nation River in 1974. Evans had grown up in suburban Boston. His father was a professor of naval architecture at MIT, and both parents were avid hikers. They belonged to the Appalachian Mountain Club and kept a summer home in Jackson in the White Mountains of northern New Hampshire. One of their neighbors in Jackson, the Davis family, had a farm where they raised cattle and sheep, pigs, chickens, ducks, and geese. They grew hay, logged, hunted, fished, and made maple syrup. They even used horses as draft animals. Evans was immediately and intensely drawn to the north woods country farm, so much so that he soon felt as much a part of the Davis farm and family as of his own circumstances. He begged Bob Davis for a summer job on the farm and at the age of twelve began working there each summer. He learned many things, not least, he said, how to work hard. After a stint working for the Appalachian Mountain Club, he began to consider where he might establish himself on the land.

In 1973, with a pickup truck loaded with the tools and gear he thought he'd need, Evans left New England and drove first to British Columbia, then on to Yukon Territory. The Takhini River outside Whitehorse appealed to him, and he called some friends back east, including Patton, Snow, and Allen, to come join him. The group had just started building when the Forest Service stopped by to check their permit. Permit? Soon Evans and his friends were in Anchorage and looking for work. Dave and Sage, now a couple, spent the winter caretaking a lodge on the Glenn Highway and looking at maps of areas where they might like to be. They picked the Upper Yukon because the area was accessible by road, it didn't require expensive air logistics, and it offered two things that Evans says always attracted him: "mountains and moving water." After a few months making wages (Evans set chokers in a logging operation in Southeast Alaska), Dave and Sage, along with Brad and Lilly, drove to Eagle in July 1974. "We figured we'd just go to the Yukon, get on it, and go down as far as necessary to get beyond the realm of people. And that's essentially what we did." In Eagle, they learned that Dick Cook was on the Tatonduk, Terry McMullin was at Seventymile River, and Sarge Waller had a nominal interest in the Kandik. The Nation River seemed to be more open, although Joe Hajec was trapping along the Yukon by snowmachine and sometimes stayed at the Bluff cabin, just below the mouth. But even this didn't seem to be much of a conflict. "At that time I wasn't really interested in trapping," says Evans. "I never really thought about it in a serious way, never really thought about it at all. I just wanted to go out and live. I wanted to build a cabin in the woods, and the rest of it would take care of itself."

That's what he did. And when he made mistakes, the country quickly put him straight. On the Takhini he'd encroached on the Forest Service's territory. On the Nation, he encroached on the river's. After lining about two and a half miles up river, he and Sage picked a good-looking building site along a cut bank beside the river, in a stand of spruce. They dug holes and set logs as the vertical legs of a cache, which they finished before starting a cabin. But it rained heavily that late July, and the Nation, as it sometimes does, changed course. It collapsed about twenty feet of the bank, crested it, and flooded the site. The river liquefied the ground, toppled the new cache, and took out the cabin, which was only a few rounds up. Lesson one: pick your site carefully. For their third start, Dave and Sage went up a nearby slough and selected a spot that was farther away from the river and did not show signs of flooding.

Among the things that Evans had learned on the Davis's farm was that an ax need not be merely a crude instrument. It could be, he said, "a fine-woodworking tool." Cutting logs for his cabin, Evans used only an ax. He wouldn't even use a Swede saw to cut the trees down and buck them to length (though he did use a saw to cut out the door and windows). "In some people's mind it was an unreasonable thing to do. But in my mind it was the only thing to do, and the only way to do it," he says. He wanted "to replicate for my own experience what it was like to live one hundred, two hundred or more years ago." On October 7th, with six inches of snow on the ground, Dave and Sage moved into the cabin.

A couple of miles farther up the Nation, Brad Snow and Lilly Allen built their cabin, but they ended up spending the winter in Eagle. The next summer their cabin was "trespassed" by BLM, meaning it was cited for being "in trespass," and Brad and Lilly were ordered to leave. They never lived there.

For a couple of years, Dave and Sage were snug in their well-built cabin out of the floodplain, but eventually they realized that its location was not ideal. Three miles away from the Yukon, it was too far to be handy as a base for summer salmon fishing. But it was too close to the Yukon and the Bluff cabin to be useful as a stopping place when they traveled up the Nation. Cabins, they realized, needed to be about a day's walking distance apart, ten or fifteen miles. Walking distance because even with a dog team, they still might be snowshoeing rather than riding. With a canoe, they might be lining. Over the years, to support their activities, Dave and Sage built more cabins and rehabilitated some old ones that Phonograph Nelson had built. Though the Park Service neglects to credit them, it was they who rescued Phonograph Nelson's Bluff cabin. Had they not done so, it might not be habitable today.

TRAPPING BY DOG TEAM, Dave Evans confronted the same obstacles and opportunities that his predecessor Chris Nelson had faced: the windy reaches where the trail always drifted in, or the place where the current weakened the river ice from below, or where moccasin-wetting overflow ran beneath the snow, or where a spring always flowed in the winter and permitted easy access to water. Inevitably, in addressing those perennial features of the country, Evans reestablished the very same routes and camps used by Phonograph Nelson and those before him, dating back perhaps a hundred years. He found and brushed out the same trails and added some new branches to the trails made by Nelson and even older old-timers, like Ed Olson, Jim Taylor, and the Canadians Oscar Erickson and Dan Van Bibber. Erickson ran a team of about eight exceptionally good dogs, according to Willard Grinnell, a retired trapper whom Evans tracked down and wrote to in California. About Erickson, Grinnell wrote, "Of the hundred-odd trappers I have known, he was among the toughest." Erickson would take his team up the Nation, cross over into the Kandik River, and trap both sides of the border. "I think he built no cabins, but lived in a tent and ate mostly meat."

As Evans moved through the country, establishing his own trapline, here and there he came upon blazes on trees. He'd find a trap hanging from a limb, or a pole cut by an ax. Several generations of trappers had built trails and cabins on the Nation, "and as it turned out, I ended up building cabins at the exact same spots they did," he said. When he saw the need for a cabin at Hard Luck Creek and built one there, the ruins of two other cabins stood within sight of his window. One, collapsed to about six rounds high, was Nelson's. The other, just a couple logs high and built by some earlier trapper, decomposed nearby. When he fixed up and used an old cabin that Nelson had built between Tinder and Waterfall Creeks, he found another ruin at that site, too. And when he established a tent camp at Jungle Creek near the Canadian border, the ruin of a Chris Nelson cabin moldered not far away.

One reason he moved into the woods was to get away from people, says Evans. "But," he laughed, "when I got out there one of the things I enjoyed most was encountering human sign. I liked to see man's sign." As the years passed, he almost felt he knew his immediate predecessor, Phonograph Nelson, who had died a generation before. "Everywhere I traveled I could see sign of his: old trails, traps that he'd left. He and I were using the same country." Evans says he would have liked to have met Nelson, then pauses and says, "In a way, I have met him."

About six years into Dave Evans's tenure, the National Park Service loomed as the new landlord. Evans didn't like it. "Through having to deal with the Park Service at all—the government in any way—I'm being exposed to, confronted by something different, something beyond the scope of the country." He even wrote letters to his congressman, hoping to keep the Park Service out. When they came anyway in 1981, Evans was persuaded to join them as a seasonal ranger. "I went to work for the Park Service because I thought I could have some effect on what was going to happen." He thought he might guide the policy makers: "If nothing else, I could at least show the people who were supposed to be managing the country a little bit about what it was really like and what they were supposed to be taking care of."

But it was the beginning of the end. In 1983, after nine years, Nation Dave left the Yukon. He left for a variety of reasons. He and Sage were splitting up. He felt he had reached "a point of diminishing return," where trapping and fishing offered less in the way of exhilaration and discovery than of repetition. He wanted more intellectual and social stimulation. And, finally, he just didn't care to live in the woods with a federal agency looking over his shoulder, supervising, regulating, permitting. "I truly thought I was going to spend the rest of my life there, and happily so," says Evans. "And that's O.K. I would not go back out there to live. No way. Too much is different—probably more so in me than in the country—though the country has changed—the Park Service being a primary instrument of that change." He and Sage "came out of there with virtually no money," he says, just "a bunch of trails and cabins that you can't take with you." But he did have skills, and there was an employer at hand. Evans put his ax to work for the Park Service as an expert restoration carpenter, rehabilitating old cabins in Denali National Park and elsewhere. That led to a Park Service desk job in Anchorage, and then to the American Southwest, where today he is cultural resources manager for Chiricahua National Monument and Fort Bowie National Historical Site in Arizona.

ONE SOMETIMES HEARS that the would-be pioneers like Dave Evans simply didn't have what it takes over the long pull, that, unlike the old-timers who died in their cabins, the modern-era homesteaders somehow broke faith. But talking to the river people who have come out of the country, one is struck by how their stories resonate with those of more legitimated American rustics who re-created themselves in the wilderness. Henry David Thoreau said: "I left the woods for as good a reason as I went there. Perhaps it seemed to me that I had several more lives to live, and could not spare any more time for that one . . . Perhaps if I had lived there much longer, I might have lived there forever. One would think twice before accepting heaven on such terms." Alaska's great poet, John Haines, who lived on a homestead in Alaska, trapping, hunting, and fishing for about twenty-five years, wrote in a similar vein: "Trapping for me was not the single, lifelong occupation it has been for others . . . But what I did had its own seriousness, and I learned from it what I wanted. Another lifetime, perhaps, I might have remained and let the wilderness take me."

Federal land managers may not yet recognize Evans's tenure as "history," says Melody Webb with regret, but one day they will. Webb is now retired from a career as a Park Service historian and superintendent who for her doctoral dissertation wrote both a history of the Yukon basin and an invaluable compendium of the historic buildings within the proposed park. In the course of her research she hired Evans as a guide to help her find the old sites of occupation. "The Park Service does this all the time," she says. "They move into an area and they think that its most recent history is no history." At Ozark Scenic Riverways the Park Service bulldozed all the cabins on the river, says Webb. "Very characteristic. Very short sighted." Again, at Big Bend National Park they knocked down all the ranchers' cabins. "And now we regret it," she says.

The same notion of history reveals itself when one talks to certain Park Service planners or reads the agency's policy papers on subsistence living in parklands. It is a view inclined to regard white old-timers (personified by the sourdough prospector) as true-blue subsistence users on a nearly equal standing with Alaska Natives, while managing to suggest that the young people heading out into the woods in the 1970s tended to be greenhorn malcontents from suburbia indulging in such trifling impulses as "social experimentation," "the novelty of the experience," or a "departure from the mores of modern society," as one Park Service policy draft said.

This view strikes me as both supercilious and seriously at odds with the more perceptive chronicles of the Klondike gold rush, the signature event of the sourdough experience. From Tappan Adney's to Pierre Berton's, most accounts bolster an opposite interpretation—namely that of the eighty thousand people rushing north in the late 1890s, the average argonaut looked a whole lot more like a bank teller from Cincinnati or a shoe-store clerk from Des Moines than like Daniel Boone; that every species of grifter, pimp, con man, and gambler rushed north along with the gold seekers; that greed, as contrasted with a wilderness ethic, was a dominant ideology ("everybody was money mad," as one '98er wrote); that the fortune-seekers were on a "sordid mission," as John Muir put it. And, as Bob Marshall, a seasoned Alaska outdoorsman who knew many of the stampeders, said: "Many of them knew nothing about the outdoors, most of them knew nothing about gold mining, and all of them knew nothing about the requirements for existence in the North."

Another puzzlement is the idea that "departure from the mores of modern society" is somehow an ignoble rationale for setting out for a new country. Did the writer suspect the motive was absent from those who boarded the Mayflower? or the prairie schooners? or from every other wave of colonist, settler, pioneer, and mountain man in the history of this or any other country? And what sense of the history of the American Revolution must one possess to brush off "social experimentation"? I wouldn't presume to offer the definitive summary of the spirit of North American pioneering, but I would imagine it would include a lot of those attitudes the Park Service writer seemed to belittle, such as a rebellion against wasteful modernity, against an increasingly frivolous culture with dubious ethical standards, against modern man becoming soft and inept and timid; a desire to redeem oneself on the frontier, to be largely self-reliant, to build one's own house, to fix what breaks, to approach problems with ingenuity, to wrest some measure of freedom from the cash economy, to take a large portion of one's food from the land, to be free of unwanted safety nets and supervision, to accomplish these things by trading ease and convenience for labor and hardship, and to face all manner of asperities and bum luck with a laugh.

Lost also in the Park Service writer's analysis is the historically interesting proposition that some of the 1970s-era river people may have routinely accomplished greater feats of woodcraft and survival than did many of their turn-of-the-century forebears. Park Service papers and publications steer clear of this heresy, of course. But it seems at least worth considering the idea that, compared to the sourdoughs, the hippies were a tougher breed. For one thing, at various times during the gold rush, there were many hundreds, maybe some thousands, of people living along the Yukon. In 1900, besides Dawson City, which may have swelled to 30,000, there were several towns between Eagle (pop. 1,700 in 1898) and Circle (pop. 700 in 1896), including Star City/Seventymile City (pop. 250), Charley River (also called Independence, pop. 180), Nation City (pop. ?), Ivy City (pop. ?), and Coal Creek (pop. 75). But by 1973, a graduate student at the University of Alaska named Bob Ritchie counted just sixteen people living the subsistence life in the entire one hundred and sixty miles between Eagle and Circle. In 1977, Rick Caufield, another grad student, found twenty-eight, counting kids. Obviously, it was a much more wild and lonely country in the recent period. In the early days, the federal government, in the form of the mail carrier, and the territorial road commission kept open a system of trails between camps. And strung along the trails, never more than a day's travel apart, were the roadhouses, providing food and beds, trade goods, and company gathered around the stove. By contrast, the latter-day pioneers broke their own trails. There were no roadhouses. You slept in your sled or maybe on a caribou hide rolled out on spruce boughs. In summertime, in the sternwheeler days, the boats kept the same corridor open: a lifeline of transportation and commerce that stocked the roadhouses with bacon and beans, canned goods, and hardware; brought in fresh recruits; and hauled out those the country had broken. But in the modern era, there was no stern-wheeler to flag down and step aboard. If a trapper at the mouth of the Kandik wanted supplies in 1972, he tied a rope on his canoe and dragged it upriver to Eagle. Dragged it eighty miles upriver to Eagle!

THE RIVER PEOPLE'S ingenuity and perseverance and their re-creation of the earlier era had impressed *New Yorker* writer John McPhee, says Dave Evans. Though he had declined to talk to him, preferring to keep a low profile, Evans says that McPhee's series of articles in the *New Yorker* and his 1977 book *Coming into the Country,* published three years before ANILCA was enacted, helped the cause of the subsistence people. "McPhee's book," says Evans, "had a lot to do with the enabling legislation specifically saying that the subsistence lifestyle is perceived to be a value: 'we don't want to threaten it, we want it to continue.' O.K., that was Congress's intent if you read the enabling legislation, particularly if you read the committee reports behind it. But the *wording* of the legislation is such that it makes it very difficult to do that if you move there subsequent to 1973." Beyond that, the language of regulations written to implement the law further thwarted congressional sympathies. "Everything—or many things—were going to need to be done under permit. And these permits had to follow certain regulations. And these regulations—I don't think with intent, but almost by accident—were written in such a way that a lot of people were going to be excluded from doing what they had been doing. They got caught in the maws of the machine, and there you are. It's no one's fault, if you will, it just happened. But happen it has."

Originally, says Evans, the Park Service sent in nice guys to reassure the river people. "The Park Service was saying at that time 'you can continue to do what you've been doing, this is part of the reason that Yukon-Charley is created.'" But it took a while for regulations to be promulgated, and the first group of nice guys rotated Outside, thousands of miles away, and were replaced by other nice guys breaking the bad news. "In the end, you deal with nice guys," says Evans. "But behind the nice guys is the bureaucracy, the letter of the law, or the interpretation of the regulation, and that's all coming from the Great Beyond." As a long-time Park Service manager, Evans's understanding of institutional inertia has matured somewhat, and he sympathizes with the Yukon-Charley managers who ushered in the changes he laments. "I didn't realize nearly to the extent that I do now that they didn't have the control that I thought they did. They were as much manipulated by forces as we all who lived out there were. Who's in charge here? Does anyone know? I don't."

Until Park Service ownership, human occupancy of the Upper Yukon had likely been uninterrupted for seven to ten thousand years. "For the good of the country and the society out there," says Evans, "you need to have a replenishment of people." But even where the regulations permit one or two longtime residents to stay until they die or choose to leave, the law and the Park Service forbid any replacement of these people.

A FINE SUN is flashing silver off the dewy fireweed and willow leaves when I emerge from the cabin at Nation Bluff. Peregrine falcons call in high whistles from their aeries in the cliff face above. I poke around in Dave and Sage's old garden, many years overgrown, and find where Phonograph Nelson kept his several wooden boats, now pinned implacably to the land by trees growing up through them. I was here a few years ago with two Park Service employees, Mary Ann Sweeney and Eileen Devinney. We rooted around in a few of the trash piles. Mary Ann and Eileen could read the garbage. They are historical archaeologists, meaning they study the leavings of people who lived in historical times. I remember Mary Ann squatting down at the edge of the pit and turning a Hills Brothers' coffee can over in her hands like Louis Leakey examining a skull. If it's a red can with a key-strip opening, and if you can see both slippered feet of the Arab, she said, then you figure 1936 to 1942. If you can see only the striding Arab's rearward foot, date it before 1932 and after 1927. Then there is the mocha-java can. Mary Ann calls it "the Clovis point of can archaeology," after the famous class of projectile points first found near Clovis, New Mexico. Before 1906, coffee sold as "Mocha-Java" purported to blend Arabian coffee (called Mocha after the Arabian port city of that name) with coffee from the Dutch South Pacific colony of Java, a couple of the farthest-flung commercial coffee growing outposts in the world. But the truth is coffee roasters often used Brazilian beans as stand-ins for mochas, and coffee from anywhere in Indonesia passed for Java. That was the case until the appearance of the Pure Food and Drug Act, which went into effect in 1906. No longer could the outside of the can claim mocha-java if it wasn't actually on the inside. Coffee labels had to be redesigned, and that established a can-dating benchmark.

The junk gives us dates, but it also speaks to matters of commerce and transportation and economic health and the individual tastes of the occupants. In the movie that plays in my mind, I can now do a bit of product placement. Where I see Phonograph Nelson rustling breakfast at his cookstove, I can liven up the black-and-white with full-color props on the shelves: red and yellow Hills Brothers' coffee cans, red and blue cans of Eagle evaporated milk. On my audio track, I imagine him singing a period send-up of the Carnation ad jingle:

> Carnation milk is best of all,
> comes in cans both short and tall:
> No tits to pull,
> no hay to pitch,
> just punch two holes
> in the son-of-a-bitch.

In one spot, in a heap maybe thirty feet in diameter, we found Hills Brothers' coffee cans from the 1950s, Darigold butter cans, five-gallon oil cans, galvanized metal buckets, parts of a wooden sled, old flashlights, beer cans, stovepipe, leather boot fragments, gas cans flattened for roofing, a barrel stove, broken traps, and modern machine-made bottles. These things are from about 1950 to 2000. But in another area we found more interesting things, previously unknown. The 1999 fire that started on Hard Luck Creek and burned up Dick Cook's territory also came through here. Fire crews saved the cabin with a back burn, but spot fires flared up here and there. In two places where fire burned off the brush and moss, it revealed underneath long-hidden trash middens. One pile contains a fragment of a Gilbey's gin bottle that was manufactured between 1932 and 1964. There is an MJB coffee can, along with a number of other cans that were made after the period when lids were soldered on. But the other newly found midden contains a number of hole-in-cap cans. These cans have an opening in the top of about an inch in diameter, and through it the can was filled with food. Then a cap with a small vent hole was soldered in place to close the opening. As steam poured out the vent hole during heat processing, a blob of solder was dropped on the hole, sealing the can. Canners used this technique from about 1810 to 1930, although evaporated milk cans were still sealed with these closures into the 1980s.

Bottles also tell a historical story. Glass that shows an amethyst tint is pre-1917. That's when the United States entered World War I and could no longer obtain German manganese dioxide, which was used as a decolorizing agent, reducing the greenish tint caused by iron impurities. The manganese tends to impart a purplish hue to glass after long exposure to sunlight. As a substitute, the United States bought selenium from Canada, and its use was preferred thereafter. Prohibition ended in 1933, but from then until 1964, bottles were required to be embossed with "FEDERAL LAW PROHIBITS THE REFILL OR REUSE OF THIS BOTTLE." In 1903, Michael J. Owens patented the automatic bottle machine, which quickly dominated bottle manufacturing. Bottles with seams over the lip indicate machine-made bottles and are post-1903. This midden proved easy to date. The pile contained two butter cans from the Coldbrook Creamery of San Francisco, and they were stamped 1898. A majority of the cans were hole-in-cap, which, by 1904, were mostly replaced by the familiar, modern, crimp-end "sanitary can."

These cans and bottles in the oldest middens probably were left by the workers at a coal mining operation that started up at Nation River in 1898. The Alaska Commercial Company hired the men to sled 2,000 tons of bituminous coal down to the Yukon from a mile up the Nation. The AC Company sold it to the steamboats or shipped it up to the Dawson market. But the deposit was spotty and therefore expensive to mine. It only lasted a few years, closing before 1902. There are still fragments of overgrown roadbed visible, and a pile of coal sits not far from Nelson's cabin. It is interesting that in a park where littering is anathema, the most intimate glimpse of the men who labored here a hundred years ago—our most personal connection with their history—comes from heaps of trash. Lucky for us the old-timers didn't adhere to the modern ethic and "leave no trace."

Nation City

A couple miles below the mouth of Nation River, but on the opposite bank, is the abandoned town site of Nation City. At the turn of the century, Nation City was a supply center for mining operations on Fourth of July Creek, which empties into the Yukon just below. For a mining camp, it survived a long time, with its heyday between 1908 and 1922. Pollack Joe Hajec revived a couple of the cabins and used them as his base of operations when he trapped from here. Other cabins Joe used in a way that showed less sensitivity for historical preservation: he cut them up and burned them in his woodstove. In any event, the ice knocked everything apart in the breakup of 1989. I stop briefly at what I take to be the old steamboat landing, then shove my canoe back into the river. I don't explore as much as I'd like. I think the fellow in the johnboat lives near here, up a trail off the river a ways, and I don't want to surprise his wife and daughter when he is not home. It probably would not be a breach of river manners to do so, but, as he had been unsociable earlier when he passed me, I suspect he would prefer I not visit while he is gone.

Taylor's Place

In 1905, a thirty-year-old Wisconsin native named Jim Taylor staked a claim on the Seventymile River. The next year he moved on to Washington Creek and later to Fourth of July Creek, where he bought up claims from miners leaving for Fairbanks. By 1910, he employed twelve men. He sold his Fourth of July properties in 1919 to a consortium from the States and went to work for the Washington Creek Coal Mine until it went bust, owing him twenty-four hundred dollars. In 1924 when the government closed the post office at Nation City where he was postmaster, Taylor turned to trapping. He established his base of operations on the right bank of the Yukon, just below Nation Bluff. He built a fine two-room house, another large cabin, a blacksmith shop, and a shed. Game warden Sam White remembers that the house had a dumbwaiter. Taylor would "just turn the crank and the waiter raised out of the basement and everything on it was nice and cool." And that wasn't all for modern kitchen gadgetry, said White. "In the far corner of the room sat a cookstove. Beside the cookstove was a trapdoor in the wall on hinges, and a wood box full of wood right under the trapdoor. On the outside of the wall was a chute full of wood, and when one opened the door the wood rolled into the wood box automatically." Taylor kept everything neat and clean, said White.

"When Jim put a stick of wood in the stove, he grabbed a brush and dust pan and swept up all sliver and bark and put them in the stove also." The late Al Stout of Eagle remembered that "when you visited him, you slept between sheets."

The outside of the Taylor place was full of marvels too. His winter dog barn had individual stalls partitioned with pole walls. The dog houses were built of peeled logs squared on the exposed faces, and they had fenced-in thirty-foot runs that gave each dog access to the creek in summer. Taylor's last move was to Seattle, where he sought medical treatment for cancer. He didn't make it back but died there in 1933.

The main cabin burned up in 1968, but the other buildings, one of them rescued by Dave Evans and Sage Patton, stood for years as some of the finest examples of the woodsman's art on the river. The Park Service did an extensive restoration of the dog barn in 1998. But on June 13, 1999, a thunderstorm touched off the Hard Luck Creek fire, along with a couple other blazes in the preserve. On the 16th, Park Service crews cut safety zones around the Taylor complex and started a few small backfires. A bit of rain quieted the fire down until July 2, when it flared up again. On the third, crews spotted a wall of flame moving along the river downstream from Taylor's. On July 4, it was too late to do anything. All evidence of Jim Taylor's occupancy of this place disappeared. Whatever wasn't incorporated into the soil as ash drifted away as vapor.

Ivy City

Somewhere along the left bank below Nation Reef and above Schley Creek was the town of Ivy City, now vanished. Even thirty years ago, Melody Webb and Dave Evans couldn't find it. Just about every available force of destruction contributed to its disappearance. First, its rival, Nation City, was more conveniently situated to serve the Fourth of July Creek mines, so Ivy City declined. Rain and rot and the regrowth of vegetation worked away at the remains until a man named Alvin Arp assisted the reclamation. He built a cabin nearby and cut up the old buildings of Ivy City to burn for firewood. Then in 1969, a forest fire erased the whole shebang. Now, with the trees grown up again, it would take a metal detector to prove the town was ever here—to find the spikes and hasps and tin cans hidden between the trees, beneath the forest duff.

I drift by in silence, pondering a country where towns are as ephemeral as footprints in the snow. I can see no sign of the old settlement, but I sense an absence hereabouts. It's a condition of emptiness that I feel in my gut, as if the town had vaporized in an instant, and the vacuum tugs at my viscera. It's like when matter converts to energy in a nuclear explosion, only this was cultural matter, and it converted to a psychic energy, the best name for which is loneliness.

Rock Creek

A couple miles below Ivy City, I see a microscopic black dot on an island most of a mile ahead. With the motor cut, I drift silently for ten minutes or more until I am within yards of a black bear unwarily exploring the beach. A mile or so farther on, a bald eagle, whose great wings might measure eight feet from tip to tip, jumps from a spruce tree and lumbers off to another perch. Later, I see another bird, not much smaller. A golden eagle. I keep still, and he permits me to cruise slowly beneath his lookout on a leaning snag, his coppery head swiveling, his dagger eye never leaving me. For people who come from highly populated areas, seeing these three in the space of a few miles would be, I suppose, a wildlife trifecta. For me, seeing people would be the rare and interesting event. Someone in a poling boat, someone tending a net. Mostly, I have to populate the places from memory and imagination. Like here at Rock Creek.

The mouth of Rock Creek, on the right bank of the Yukon inside a batch of islands, is an unprepossessing site for a cabin. The nondescript little stream is less than a jump wide. It doesn't seem any sort of key location. Which shows what I know. There are at least four cabins, or their remains, here. The creek offers a direct route over into the upper Kandik River country and the upper Nation River. The trail may have been used by the Han people for eons. About eight miles up, the trail climbs out of Rock Creek and crosses the hills, dropping over into a tributary of the Kandik. Fourteen miles from the mouth of Rock Creek, the trail hits the Kandik just above Johnson Gorge. But another branch of the Rock Creek trail veers east a couple miles up from the

Yukon, and this branch hits the Nation River opposite Hard Luck Creek. Trappers have occupied the site here at the mouth of Rock Creek, on and off, for at least eighty years. For details, I turn again to the Webb: Melody Webb, the historian. Her 1977 book *Yukon Frontiers** is a large, thick, library-bound photocopy of typescript pages. It adds four pounds to the weight of my pack, but I wouldn't be without it. Nor without her book *Yukon: The Last Frontier*** (one pound, three ounces). Webb says Pete Summerville trapped along Rock Creek to the Kandik in the early 1920s. An old ruin of unpeeled logs, eleven by thirteen feet and sitting now about ten feet from the creek, is thought to be his. Willard Grinnell, who trapped the Kandik in the 1930s and 1940s, said a trapper named Kid Allen trapped without dogs from Rock Creek downriver to Biederman Bluff and caught two hundred lynx in one year. Chris Peterson, a Canadian, and Larry Dennis, an American, used the Rock Creek trail to get into the Upper Kandik and on up it to the border, where each man trapped in his own nation. A younger ruin—thirteen by fifteen feet, sod-roofed, and long ago fallen in—may have been occupied by Harry Parker and his partner (maybe called Phillips). One day Parker shot a cow moose. When his partner ran over, he saw that he had not only all the butchering to do by himself but a grave to dig as well. Parker had killed the moose, and the moose had returned the favor. Likely not too many tears were shed for Parker, as he seems not to have been a favorite on the river. Willard Grinnell said, "Parker was never a hard trapper and very seldom caught enuf fur to pay for his grub; made money as a cat skinner & repair man." He was also the "son of a bitch" who Al Stout said had failed to haul in food for the Canadian trapper, Rudolf Bauer, but that story will be told later.

There's a large tent frame at the site too, likely built by some hunters in the 1970s. Then came Nation Dave Evans for his hitch. In about 1978, he built a trapline cabin here, the fourth known habitation at this spot. It's a little sod-roofed cutie, maybe seven by ten feet, about

---

*Published under the name Melody Webb Grauman by Cooperative Park Studies Unit, University of Alaska, Fairbanks.

**Lincoln: University of Nebraska Press, 1993. Earlier published as *The Last Frontier: A History of the Yukon Basin of Canada and Alaska* (Albuquerque: University of New Mexico Press, 1985).

the size of a Fairbanks sauna. Some of the river people who used to pass around the J. R. R. Tolkien books called it a "Hobbitation." The walls are made of eight-inch logs, peeled on the inside and outside, but not the tops and bottoms. The roof is low pitched, gabled, and made of peeled poles covered with a blue tarp and a neat layer of grassy sod. The side walls rise to about five-foot-six, and somebody five-nine, like Evans, can just stand under the ridge. That clearance would have been greater once because the cabin now has a floor of chainsaw-milled lumber. In Evans's day, the cabin had only a dirt floor and no door, only a blanket over the opening. The roof is new too. The trapper who uses the place (and who prefers to remain anonymous) asked the Park Service for permission to make some needed repairs so that he could continue using it in his trapping as he had done for decades. The Park Service said "no." Mysteriously, the cabin was fixed anyway. The tiny space is spare and tidy. There's a plywood bunk, shelves on pegs, and a small cast-iron woodstove. The low door is set in the gable end facing the river, and each side wall has a window. The door stands agape, so the curious bear needn't rip things up to have a look inside, and so that he has a clear way out when he finds no food. The cabin is nearly thirty years old, and Evans has been gone more than twenty of those years. The anonymous trapper has kept it alive, just as Evans kept Phonograph Nelson's cabin alive.

The Rock Creek cabin is the height of low impact. A model of re-spectful use of the land in the historical tradition. But when the big Nation River fire of 1999 licked its tongue into the corner of these woods, the Park Service declined to protect the cabin. River people heard the radio traffic. The firefighters called in for instructions, and the Park Service said: "Let it burn." The cabin was not on the agency's list as a structure to protect. It was on the anonymous trapper's list, however. He threw some tools in his boat and sped downriver into the smoke. With Pulaski and shovel, the man grubbed out smoldering roots that were then burning to within six feet of the cabin. With buck-ets, he carried water up from the Yukon to douse the hot spots until the threat passed.

Reading the Fire Management Plan written by Yukon-Charley pre-serve is a lot like walking through one of those funhouse gauntlets where you are knocked about and battered by spongy truncheons and spinning bolsters. You eventually reach the other side, but you feel queasy and are not completely sure how you got there. Mind-dulling terminology is the agent of this gentle assault ("management-implemented ignitions" and "incident-specific implementation procedures"). But I think I can put the basic idea into English. Fighting forest fires in Alaska is an interagency effort coordinated by the Alaska Fire Service. Annually, the Park Service sends the Alaska Fire Service a list of the structures within the preserve that should be accorded one level or another of fire protection. The Park Service ranks the cabins based on various criteria, such as whether the building is occupied or of historical significance, and they are assigned one of four levels of protection. The highest priority is called "critical," and these sites are defended aggressively. At present, of all the older, unoccupied structures, only three places are given critical status (the Coal Creek mining camp and two cabins that have been recently occupied). The next category is called "full," and at this level of protection, fires also would receive an aggressive initial response. But full-protection sites would have a lower priority than those designated critical, and the effort might be directed at minimizing fire damage rather than at complete protection. Slaven's Roadhouse is accorded "full" status, as are the public use cabins, like Phonograph Nelson's cabin at Nation Bluff. Interestingly, one of the criteria that might place a structure in the "full" category is whether the Park Service has expended funds for its restoration. Consequently, if the Park Service neglects a cabin's maintenance, it puts it doubly at risk, first from entropy, then from fire. Next comes the "nonsensitive" category, and the policy here is to let the fire burn the building down while protecting human life. Essentially, the plan is to preserve the fire, not the structures. Letting fires burn in wilderness areas is considered an ecologically sound practice, as fuels do not artificially accumulate, and because fires naturally restart the sequence of forest succession. Dave Evans's Rock Creek cabin is in this "let it burn" category. So are George Beck's fifty-nine-year-old cabin near Washington Creek, and a beautifully made thirty-two-year-old cabin up the Charley River at Hanna Creek. The final category is called "nonsensitive/defensible space." These structures, too, will be allowed to burn up. Most or perhaps all of the buildings in this category have lost their roofs. But they can still provide important historical information that would be lost to a fire, such as size, construction techniques, and artifacts.

Glenn Creek

For miles, I've been seeing the sun shining off the tin roof of a cabin across the river at the mouth of Glenn Creek. I know it to be a nice enough cabin, but it holds little attraction for me. Maybe because it is as prominent visually as it is insignificant historically. Apparently a Dr. LeFevre from Fairbanks built it in the 1950s and used the cabin as a hunting base. LeFevre does not seem to have had any deep connections with this area; he never lived in the cabin. But it may soon be considered "historic" by the Park Service. A historic structure, according to standard protocol, is one at least fifty years old, though in some cases, if the evidence is very persuasive, that status might be accorded to select younger properties. I can appreciate the difficulties of having to make determinations as to the historic value of hundreds of ruins and standing cabins in various states of disrepair. But I distrust the practice of drawing a line across the past, of declaring one side the sacred and the other the profane. It's a magic-number approach to history and is bound to yield some results that are obviously wrong. To wit: the Glenn Creek cabin soon may be assessed as historic, while Dave Evans's cabin at Rock Creek is not. Clearly, as local histories of this area are written, Evans will receive approximately as much attention as the other trappers of significant tenure who preceded him in earlier decades (he stayed exactly as long as Willard Grinnell, for example, nine years). After all, writers to date have not ignored Phonograph Nelson, who trapped in the 1930s and 1940s, in deference to the trappers of the gold rush period. (In fact, he gets more coverage.) Meanwhile, treatment—even mention—of Dr. LeFevre's brief appearance would be quite unlikely. So, the Rock Creek cabin's value as tangible history is greater than the Glenn Creek cabin's, but it is not recognized as such, and the less significant structure is currently repaired, maintained, and protected from fire, while the more significant one is slated to become a ruin or a pile of ashes. Put me in the camp of whichever historian it was who said, when asked how recent an event can be and still be regarded as history, "I draw the line at tomorrow."

Actually, I don't believe for a minute that the Park Service doesn't understand or appreciate the historic associations these cabins offer, or that they don't value the tangible "fabric" of these sites of occupation. But I think another management objective trumps these considerations.

And that is that cabins tend to draw people, and from the park managers' perspective, people are a problem.

I DECIDE NOT TO STOP at the Glenn Creek cabin this time, but motor on by. I am remembering being up there once in the late afternoon and hearing a strange crying sound. I wasn't really paying attention to it, filing it away preconsciously as a loon, perhaps, until I noticed it was getting closer. When I walked down to the river, I saw it was a young cow moose walking up the shoreline toward me. Normally, a moose will run away on seeing a human so close, but this one did not. Below her, the river piled into a steep bluff that would have stopped her if she had been moving that way, unless she cared to jump into the fast current and swim. This moose continued to walk toward me until, at a certain point, she walked into the river and crossed to a not quite emergent bar. She stood there looking back and bleating continuously in the most mournful and despondent way. Had she lost a calf to the river at the bluff? Was she sick? All I know is that her need to wail must have been great to cause her to broadcast both her coordinates and her predicament to every predator in the region. And I knew that whatever comforting she needed, I could not give it.

Seymour's Old Camp

About 3:00 in the afternoon, I pull up into the little slough where Seymour Able and Jan Waldron had their camp. It's a shallow back slough with the sort of oozy mud beach that you know you'd better scoot across or you'll sink to your shins. There's a barrier of ice-bent alder above the beach, and in from there is a mixed forest, now largely burned. The little stream that enters the slough above the camp is dinky, off-colored, and mud-bottomed. I find a trash pit and a trail but, aside from some stovepipe, no sign of the parachute dwelling. The biggest impression I get is of how quickly nature reclaims a place—like a conquering king smashing the stone tablets of the vanquished, erasing one history and writing the new one. A family's history in this country is not the blight it may be in other places. Evidence of that presence is easier to erase than to maintain.

I think I've found the trail to Seymour Lake, the place where Seymour built a cabin after the BLM trespassed him. But a 1999 fire killed the timber, which toppled and is now strewn crosshatched. Now it is grown up in grass five feet tall so that all this deadfall is concealed. It's a good place to break a leg. I pick my way carefully for a while, climbing over each tree and feeling blindly with my feet for safe footing. Then I give up. It looks like it will take all day to hike the mile in to the lake where Seymour and his family spent a decade. Besides, I understand there isn't much left of the place since a Park Service crew went in there in the summer of 1999. The big fire was burning at the time, and if the wind had shifted, the crew could have been in danger. I have been told they found the cabin in rough but fixable shape and that they knocked it apart until it was unusable. It is not clear to me why the Park Service would destroy the cabin, but I decide to try to find out. I'm told they burned some trash too, as well as some keepsakes Seymour had stored in a couple of cache drums. There were "schoolwork keepsakes" and "keepsakes from Jan's childhood," says Seymour, possibly referring to an earlier "cleanup." "But they poured kerosene right in the drums and burned it right in the drum," he says. One member of the Park Service crew who, I think, did not care for the assignment at all (who, I think, felt like a Visigoth in green drill, sacking and torching an outlying homestead), remembered especially a child's highchair made from peeled spruce poles. "I think we didn't have the heart to tear it apart."

I think it would not matter to the Park Service if it had been Henry David Thoreau who lived on the edge of this pond, not if he came in the 1970s.

WITH THE MOTOR OFF, I make a spot of lunch and drift in the sun along river right. I lean back against the motor and bob along beside bluffs that rise up out of the water to 3,000-foot Kathul Mountain. It is so completely peaceful. The only sound is the hiss of silt on the hull and a soft gurgle up ahead. The sound comes from a rivulet, the off-spring of a crease in the bluff. The tiny stream has backed itself up at the brush line with sticks it has gathered and lodged there. It jumps these in a little waterfall and bounces through the coarse gravel below, showing its authority by cutting a miniature canyon. It's a dauntless little toughie, charging into the wide world, but it never quite reaches the Yukon. The gravel that it shoved aside where the slope was steep holds its ground where the beach flattens. The pup's momentum, its music and flash, are all spent yards short of the river. A nice little run, but the obstacles exceeded its energy. It is essentially erased.

I'm thinking about what Seymour had said when I told him that his cabin had been wrecked. "I don't understand why they would do that," he said. After a moment, he said, "You know, there is really only one reason that they'd do that, and that is to keep anyone from staying in it." That seemed kind of obvious to me, but I think what Seymour was getting at is a policy, codified or otherwise, that regards good, usable cabins as "nuisances" insofar as they might attract "people to take up residence illegally," as one Park Service manager said to me. But maybe Seymour meant that the agency didn't want anybody spending even an occasional night there, in the way a trapper or a traveler might do. A trapper might be inclined to set out a branch line if he knew there was a cabin where he could spend the night, or that he might use for a warm-up, or in an emergency, or to cache some food and gear. A dog driver, too, might be more likely to travel in cold weather—or to bring the kids along—if he knew he could duck into a cabin along the way. In the Far North, cabins have always held a special status. They are sanctuaries. At fifty, or sixty, or seventy degrees below zero, they are nearly as essential as would be a life-support module on the moon. Even among the sort of back-of-beyonders who inhabit these north woods—from the merely hard-bitten independents to the dedicated hermits—cabin ownership verged on the communal. The etiquette seemed to have as much moral heft as a commandment: cabins were left unlocked. Kindling and wood were there, ready. Always. It is not the slightest exaggeration to say that when your plane goes down in the extreme cold, or your sno-go quits, or your dog team gets away from you, or you're burned out of your cabin, or you step in overflow and wet your feet, the distance to the nearest cabin may be the measurement of whether you live or die.

Officially, subsistence activities, such as trapping, are allowable (the law says they are *valued*). But by tearing down cabins, by not protecting the older ones from the elements or from fire, and by not allowing new ones, the Park Service forces trappers to operate from a base outside the preserve boundaries. The preserve includes about one hundred twenty-five miles of Yukon River. To trap in the heart of the preserve, say, around the mouth of the Kandik, would require an eighty-mile jaunt from either Eagle or Circle just to get to the trapline. By dog team, that's at least a two-day trip—possibly three, even four days, depending on the condition of the trail. Then the trapper would have to work his line, maybe thirty, forty miles, then make the eighty-mile return trip to Eagle or Circle. In other words, without the use of cabins, trapping deep within the preserve is a dubious proposition. It is being managed out of existence. And it's hard not to come to the conclusion that the Park Service's unspoken policy is to discourage and limit subsistence activities within the preserve, even though these uses are specifically enumerated in the law that created the preserve as being valued cultural activities.

The Steam Tractor

Kathul Mountain, a three-thousand-foot hill, rises on the right as Washington Creek valley opens on the left. Two miles below the mouth of Washington Creek and thirty feet from the river stands a mechanical monster. It is thirteen feet high, twenty-six feet long, with iron wheels eight feet in diameter. Littler front wheels have curving old-timey spokes like the arms of a galaxy. The Alaska Coal and Coke Company brought the steam tractor into the country, probably in 1897. For a while, it pulled boxy sleds, each loaded with ten tons of coal, down from the mine twelve miles up Washington Creek to the Yukon River. The sternwheeler *Sarah* gave the coal a try, and even though it was better than most Yukon River coal, it was still of poor enough quality that it did not prove out. The venture folded. But in a way the tractor continued to aid commerce. It served as a parts store for iron-poor locals. According to local accounts collected by Webb, George Beck loaded the boiler onto two dogsleds and hauled it off to serve as a rain barrel at Ed Biederman's camp. Biederman's fishwheel was pinned together by bolts made from the wheels' spokes. Beck even made off with the lumber from the cab to use in building doors and windows for his mining cabin. One of the sleds became a prospector's cabin. Another use, in my mind anyway, is sculptural. The tractor is a roadside monument, marking the spot where a dream died.

George Beck's Cabin at Washington Creek

Behind an island, a mile below where Washington Creek comes in on the left bank, stands George Beck's old cabin. It measures ten by twelve feet, with a shed roof maybe six feet high on the river side and five feet high in the rear. It has one window about three feet square. Beck built it in 1947 as a stopover cabin and a place to store goods that he would haul up to Washington Creek, where he was mining. Beck came into the area from Minnesota in 1934 at the age of eighteen. He worked a stint at the Coal Creek gold mining operations, then married Nellie Biederman and built a cabin at her father Ed Biederman's fish camp a few miles below here. He hunted and trapped and fished and mined throughout the Yukon-Charley country. To the young people on the river, "he was almost a culture hero," wrote Melody Webb in 1977. When she and Dave Evans spent almost sixty days in the summer of 1976 searching along the main river and up the side tribs for these old structures, they found this little one of Beck's to be "in excellent shape." "The roof still stands," she wrote, "The door is still hinged." Webb recommended to the Park Service that "the cabin should be protected. It has not yet suffered the fate of vandalism. Life along the river from 1920–1950 could be easily interpreted here. Adaptive use is suggested." For thirty years, this recommendation has not been heeded. The cabin has been photographed, measured, and plotted with GPS. But absent some attention, one day soon its roof, which has a hole, will fall in. And though the cabin is "historic" according to Park Service criteria, if a fire starts near here, the agency will let the cabin burn.

Washington Creek Roadhouse

Just downriver I find the site of the Washington Creek Roadhouse built in 1895 by David Koontz. The roof has fallen in now, and the walls are only eight rounds high, but it was a big structure in its day, seventeen by thirty-six feet. Written accounts say it was pinned by dowels, but when I visited here with the historical archaeologists, Mary Ann Sweeney and Eileen Devinney, I could see that as the left-hand wall leaned outward, the logs on the front and back walls slid with respect to one another until those walls took a trapezoidal shape. That couldn't happen if the logs were attached to each other. In fact, I found I could lift the topmost log right off the wall. Maybe they were once doweled, but if so, every one of the dowels broke or rotted. It would have been odd to put up the walls without pinning the logs together somehow, as they would twist and bow. But maybe there wasn't time to make dowels, and spikes were simply not to be had. The innkeeper papered the inside with newspaper, and Eileen found clinging to the wall a tiny scrap of paper dated April 14, 1904.

Out behind the roadhouse is a dog barn, mostly collapsed. But the stall partitions still hold up a section of roof just enough to see inside. There I could easily make out the numbers painted on the posts beside the first two stalls. The number "2," ornately curlicued in the old-timey way, was for me the one feature in the whole complex most powerfully evocative of the long-gone era. On the other side of the roadhouse is another ruin, likely the bunkhouse. Of course, it is not remotely practical for the Park Service to restore such structures as these, where there is no foundation or roof and where every single log in the walls is completely rotted and would have to be discarded. These buildings have already died. For a while they lie in state, collapsing by degrees, settling gradually into the ground. A blanket of moss covers everything, like a sheet pulled over the eyes. It is enough that we can visit these sites as we might a grave.

Judge Wickersham stopped here in the winter of 1901. In 1904 a man named C. A. "Bert" Bryant came down from Eagle in a drift boat to the Charley in October when the river was running ice. In the dark, in an eddy swirling with slabs of ice, Bryant barely landed his boat here with the help of Koontz, the innkeeper. Bryant's unpublished memoir, held by the Alaska Historical Library, offers a glimpse of the welcome warmth of this roadhouse. "It does not take a pioneer woman long to get a meal if she has the makings, and she had it. Koontz got the fire going in the bunkhouse. After getting some of the ice off the outside, footwear changed for dry socks and stags, inner being filled to capacity with baked beans (which are always on tap), a few slabs of moose steak and plenty of fresh coffee, the table was shoved back, pipes loaded and fired, tongues began to loosen." Warmth, food, conversation, and a bunk: roadhouse staples.

In later years, a woman who was notoriously aggressive in her solicitation of custom kept this inn. Hudson Stuck, archdeacon of the Yukon, remembered her in a memoir: "There was a roadhouse in my time, kept by a lady who is said to have had the interesting habit of taking shots with a rifle at people who would not stop at her road house, but I cannot speak of this from personal experience, though I well remember the intimidating and cajoling placards she posts on the trail, a rival roadhouse nine miles below being the exciting cause."

Stuck was a charitable man, but a tough one, and not inclined to suffer sloth. Nor did he mind letting rip with his opinions, which is one of the great features of his book, *Ten Thousand Miles with a Dog Sled*. The subject of roadhouses frequently received the deacon's attention. "The cost of transporting supplies to the road-houses on this trail justi-fied the high prices charged—one dollar and a half for a poor meal of rabbits and beans and bacon, or ptarmigan and beans and bacon, and one dollar for a lunch of coffee, bread and butter, and dried fruit. But no exigency could be pleaded to excuse the dirt and discomfort and lack of the commonest provisions of outhouse decency at most of these places—'twas mere shiftlessness. There is not often much middle ground in Alaskan roadhouses; they are either very good in their way or very bad; either kept by professional victuallers who take pride in them or by idle incompetents who make an easy living out of the ne-cessities of travelers."

And again, he says, "It has been said that road-house keeping in Alaska is like soliciting life insurance 'outside,' the last resort of incom-petence. Certain it is that a thoroughly lazy and incompetent man yet may make a living keeping a road-house, for there is no rivalry save at the more important points, and travelers are commonly so glad to reach any shelter that they are not disposed to be censorious."

Of the inns along the Yukon River, Stuck found them to be among "the most notorious, dirty road-houses in the North," which "hold its menace over one all day and amply fulfill it at night."

Charley's Village

About thirty miles below the Nation River, near the mouth of the Kandik, is the site of Charley Village, named for Chief Charley, Judge Wickersham's first litigant. He was a handsome man, as an old photo-graph attests, with graying hair and a white beard. His forehead is wrinkled chaotically, like wind ripples on a stream. He has clear eyes under heavy brows and nostrils like a pair of bullet holes. With a better haircut and a wool suit, he might be a Victorian preacher or scientist. Forty-eight Han Indians resided here at the time of the 1880 census. Fredrick Schwatka saw it in 1883 when he floated by on his raft. Hudson Stuck said it washed away in a flood in 1914. It hasn't all washed away, though. A careful look at the cut bank shows a layer of leavings a foot below the surface. It is illegal to remove artifacts from federal land, but I can look. I see bones, mostly. Osseous shards of all sizes. A moose jaw, a scapula, leg bones cracked for the marrow. The jaw bone of a porcupine, maybe. Some strips of tin verify occupancy in the modern period, and in the rubble at the toe of the slope I see a square of blue glass, a bottle bottom. When I poked around here with Mary Ann and Eileen a couple of years ago, I found an actual item of personal adornment, or applied art, or whatever archaeologists might call a pocket watch. Actually, it was only the brass perimeter of a pocket watch, the mechanism quite gone. Brass doesn't rust, so it was like new. Timeless in a way. Timeless in another way. The right sort of clock for living out here.

Sarge Waller's Cabin

Up ahead, at the edge of the Kandik's dry mouth, I see the spot where Sarge Waller built a cabin in 1970. A Park Service ranger told me that everybody who floats the river who has read McPhee's book says that they want to see Sarge's cabin. Sarge and his family were living in Eagle when he decided to build the place and bring his wife and two girls down here to live. They ended up spending only a winter, as the cabin was poorly built and none of the family was comfortable there. A fellow named Rich Corazza spent a more notable winter in the cabin as a novice trapper, alone and lovesick for the stateside girl he left behind. He also left behind an endearing journal that McPhee found and reproduced in part. It isn't the site of Sarge's sojourn that people are moved to see but rather the place where this pining, aspiring sourdough lived. It touches readers and makes them want to visit the cabin. When Brad Snow saw the structure while canoe-chauffeuring McPhee, he pronounced it "the most poorly built cabin you will ever see." I also happened to see it at about the same time—in fact just a few weeks before Corazza moved in, in the fall of 1975. My memory may have magnified the image, but I remember walls that looked something like rail fences. I have a clear recollection of seeing daylight in strips. Only the gaps survive, now joined one to the other. In 1976, the BLM served a trespass notice on Sarge, the nominal owner, though he was by then long reestablished in Eagle. When the Park Service came in, they tore the place down.

Waller's cabin isn't the sort of history the agency is inclined to conserve for posterity, and maybe it was a good candidate for removal. But if I were writing the policy, I think I might want to save such a cabin as Waller's, even such a one as Dick Cook's place near Miller's Camp. I can hear those hollow-eyed cabins crying out like Sojourner Truth: "I've had stinking trappers within my walls, and dead animals skinned on my floor, and been abused at every turn, and *still* I stood all these years. Ain't I history?" It's too late to enshrine Waller's misbegotten structure, but not Cook's. We could seal off the entrance with Plexiglas so that it could be preserved just as it was when he left it—the black plastic, the chicken feathers, the dank hides. I'd keep the narrow wooden bunk with its squirrel-eaten mattress sprinkled with vole dung, the old magazine on beekeeping. I'd leave the bottles and cans, the white plastic buckets, the wooden barrel, jars, plastic jugs, crumpled paper, cardboard boxes, plastic bags, egg cartons, pipes, and over all this the heavy layer of grime. And if it burned down, I'd have a replica built based on photographs, right down to the vole turds. Why isn't it history?

Ricketts's Cabin

It is nearly dark, with black clouds gathering, as I pull into the lower channel of the mouth of the Kandik River, into a sloughy arm of black water, a good hole for pike. There's a snug little cabin here, built in 1981 by Larry Ricketts and Jean Trainor and now taken over by the Park Service. In the past, I've pitched my tent in the yard here, using the cabin as a place to cook and eat in the pleasant glow of lantern light. Tonight, a Dutch gal has pulled in just ahead of me, a kayaker I had seen on the river. We'd been leapfrogging all day—though she was out in the middle, and I near one bank or the other. I'd go past her, stop at a cabin, then putt by her again. It was the tortoise and the hare, and sure enough, it was the tortoise who first tossed her gear ashore at Ricketts's. If it had seemed a welcome thing, I would have pitched my tent on the grass near the bank and maybe combined forces on an evening meal, or just shared an *après diner* drop of sour mash and a spot of conversation, in the way people do at trekker huts all over the world. But this country invites the solitaire. And I sense that it is not for nothing this young woman is alone in the middle of a far-flung land. We chat a bit about the awesome scale of the river, especially as viewed from a kayak, then I shove out onto the murky river.

Biederman's

I want to stop in at Biederman's camp, across the river, but I don't want to spend the night there. The cabin is dank and musty. On the other hand, it's 10:30 at night, and the temperature is dropping toward freezing. I know that the present owner is Eddie O'Leary, who lives outside Circle. Eddie's father was the well-known mail carrier Maurice O'Leary, who ran the route out of Circle over Eagle Summit toward Fairbanks. I understand that he has the old-time attitude: spend a night, just respect his property and leave it clean. I talk myself into and out of and into staying there, then beach the boat and climb the bank.

I don't know Eddie, but I know his brother George, and I knew his sister Dianne and his uncle Bill. For all its vastness, Alaska is a small town. Thirty years ago I stayed a winter in Dianne's cabin after she and her husband Seward were killed when their plane crashed. I inherited her dog team. Though they lived twenty miles away, Dianne and Seward were my second-nearest neighbors. George and his uncle Bill O'Leary came to my wedding the next year, and Bill did something there that you only see in the movies. The ceremony was very informal; we were standing beside the Chena River with a bunch of friends around us and a judge officiating. I guess we'd picked a fairly old-fashioned text because it included that line about if anyone present knew a reason why these two should not be joined in matrimony, let them speak now or forever hold their peace. Bill had made a trip or two to the keg at that point, I believe, and burst out with, "I object!" I thought it was pretty funny, but I don't think the judge did. He hurried along before Bill could lay out his evidence.

Anyway, on the strength of all that, I figure Eddie won't mind me flopping here at Biederman's. The cabin is nearly forty feet long, built in sections over the years. I remember having a look inside ten years ago. There were shelves full of books, oil cloth on the tables, kerosene lanterns—a homey feel. The place must have been even more true to its era when Melody Webb saw it in July 1976. It was, she said wistfully, like "a nostalgic return to the Yukon River of the 1930s." But most of those furnishings have been removed. It looks like porcupines have been the most recent tenants, and their rank smell remains. I don't make a fire but just rustle up a bowl of Ramen on my camp stove, tossing in chunks of this and that. Ten minutes later, I brush the ubiquitous vole turds off a cot by the window overlooking the river, roll out my bag, and drop instantly to sleep.

I don't move a muscle all night until I open my eyes to an unbelievable vision. The river is molten gold. All the sky is a dazzling, luminous yellow where fiery clouds flash gilded edges. It's as if I awoke to a dream. Or that I didn't survive to wake, and now glimpse the glory. And then I remember that the whole spinning world is a miracle, and that sometimes reality dawns more golden than dreams.

WHAT BIEDERMAN'S lacks in tidiness, it makes up for in history. Ed Biederman was a mail carrier. Among sourdoughs, that's saying a lot. Born Max Adolphus Biederman in Bohemia in 1870, it wasn't long before the boy showed signs of an uncommonly brave and independent heart. At thirteen years of age, he persuaded his father, who was in the export business, to help him with steamboat passage to America. According to family accounts, Ed first worked as an apprentice baker in Philadelphia, then tramped around the States. He walked across Florida subsisting on oranges and even made it to Cuba. In 1899 or 1900, then just twenty, Biederman left for Alaska. Joining the stampede to Nome, he was among the thousands too late to stake good ground. Biederman signed on with the Northern Commercial Company, cutting steamboat wood on the Yukon and boarding dogs in the summer. After some time feeding the mail carriers' dogs, he landed a contract with the company to carry the U.S. mail along the Yukon River, first between Tanana and Rampart. In 1912, Ed took over the route between Circle and Eagle. Seeing the advantage of basing his operations midway between those two points, he selected this hillside across from the mouth of the Kandik River. And he selected a wife, Bella Roderick, the daughter of the chief at Medicine Lake. They married in Circle in September 1916 and left for the homesite to build a cabin. Lining a boat full of provisions up to Charley Creek (which was the name the old-timers often used for the Kandik), Ed walked along the shore and hauled on the rope while Bella sat in the boat and steered. If she allowed the boat to angle too much across the current, Ed would get a laugh out of her by mentioning that he wasn't a horse. He must have been something close to it, though. The boat was fully loaded, including Bella and an old-fashioned, cast-iron treadle sewing machine, and they were going seventy-five miles upstream.

It grew to be quite an operation, with the house, bunkhouse, cache, greenhouse, steam house, meat tunnel, several large wooden boats (still moldering away here and there in the willows), and a huge pole shed covering a fish drying rack that could accommodate three thousand six hundred fish. The family grew too, with the birth of "seven or eight" kids, as two different accounts have it. The Biedermans operated two fishwheels, their twelve-foot baskets continuously plunging to a depth of eight feet. Once, on a very good day, in a good year, Ed's two wheels produced four hundred king salmon in twenty-four hours. Typically, the Biedermans caught, cut, smoked, canned or dried, and baled three tons of salmon for human food and for dog food. An eighty-pound bale of dried dog fish (chum salmon) brought twelve dollars. At the same time, the family boarded as many as sixty dogs in the summer. Twenty-four were their own; the rest belonged to local trappers who went elsewhere in summer to mine or work for wages.

In the winter, Ed carried the mail, often five hundred pounds of it at a time, on a sled pulled by between six and nine dogs. The mail above Eagle was delivered by Percy DeWolfe, and below Circle it ran in relays down the Yukon River—Fort Yukon, Rampart, Tanana, all the way to Nome, sixteen hundred miles in all. The run between Eagle and Circle took six days. Ed would lay over a day at each end, then start back. He spent the night at cabins and roadhouses spaced roughly twenty-five miles apart, a distance he could cover in as little as four hours or as many as eighteen, depending on the weather, the load, and the condition of the trail. Leaving Eagle, Biederman stopped the first night at Miller's Camp, then at Nation, then a night at home, Woodchopper Roadhouse on the fourth night, then either Twenty-Six Mile Way Station or Twenty-Two Mile Roadhouse, and finally Circle. He kept that schedule for twenty-six weeks, traveling better than four thousand miles each winter. He said he never rode the runners but rather ran or walked all the way.

I knew an old dog driver in Fairbanks, a Native elder named Moses Cruickshank, who as a boy used to travel with the missionaries, including Hudson Stuck, in winter and summer. Stuck once snatched him out of the Yukon after Moses had fallen overboard. Moses used to say, apropos of winter travel in the days before search and rescue, "You made a mistake them days, you *paid* for it! Yeah!" Ed had been carrying the mail for more than thirteen years when he made a mistake. It all started the summer before, when his dogs were being moved by steamboat between Eagle and his fish camp. The steamer was pushing a barge, and for reasons that differ with the telling, the barge went under, flipped, and floated downriver bottom up. All Ed's dogs drowned. While crossing a creek with inexperienced dogs the next winter, he ended up in overflow, a condition where water pools on the surface of the ice. Paradoxically, it is often extreme cold that accounts for the unusual presence of liquid water. As the ice in the stream freezes deeper, the pressurized water finds a way out via a crack. Insulated by the overlying snow, the overflow can remain unfrozen, invisible, and deadly to travelers.

The green lead dog didn't handle the situation as well as his trained leader would have, and Ed got his feet wet. Under his moccasins, he wore three pairs of socks. They were soaked through. It was forty-two below zero, and it was four miles down the trail to Twenty-Two-Mile Roadhouse. Ed had two choices. One: stop, build a fire, and dry his gear (probably he carried some extra socks and moccasins). Two: hustle on to the roadhouse. The rule is you stop. Even if the trail had been good, it was still probably more than forty minutes to the roadhouse. And that's too long with soaked feet at that temperature, even if you are as tough as Ed Biederman undoubtedly was. Still, I wonder if he might have saved his feet if he hadn't resorted to a folk remedy. As Ernie Pyle heard it from Ed, after he got to the roadhouse, he took off his moccasins and socks, "and then he went outside, at forty-two below, and walked around in the snow in his bare feet." The final stage of this folk cure is usually, I bet, amputation. Another one was to daub coal oil on the frozen part, which did nothing, or to just rub vigorously, which only exacerbated the vascular damage. The right thing to do is to immerse the part in warm water to rapidly warm it. Ed was sledded to Fort Yukon, where the doctor at the Episcopal hospital amputated the forepart of both feet. After that, with poor circulation and lousy balance, Ed Biederman's days as a mail carrier were over.

The next year, 1926, Ed's son Horace left school at the age of fourteen to take over the mail run, but the Biedermans lost the contract soon thereafter. Horace brought the contract back to the family in 1934, and his younger brother Charlie became the regular mail carrier the next year. Charlie Biederman held the mail contract until 1938. After that, the Biedermans, like the other dog team mail carriers all over Alaska, lost their jobs. The winter trails ceased to be maintained, and most of them grew up in brush. Innkeepers abandoned their roadhouses, which soon tumbled in. A six-mile-an-hour way of life gave way to a new, faster age, typified by a more glamorous breed of hero. The mail contracts went to the aviators.

Charlie Biederman was the last of the Upper Yukon dog team mail carriers. Just before he died in 1994, he got a call from a woman from the U.S. Postal Service. For two and a half years she had been looking for an authentic dogsled used by an Alaskan mail carrier. She wanted it to serve as the centerpiece of a museum exhibit. Charlie said he didn't own a sled anymore, but he thought his nephew Max Beck in Eagle had the last sled he used on the mail run. The woman flew to Eagle and with Max hacked through the fireweed and horsetail out to the shed. Max dug out the door of the settling shed, and when they opened it and their eyes adjusted, there was Charlie's seventeen-foot hickory sled in almost perfect condition. Max said sure, the Post Office could have it. Now it resides in the National Postal Museum at the Smithsonian Institution. Charlie was failing from cancer, but he made the trip back to Washington for the dedication, where he was commended by the postmaster general, praised by a speechifying Alaska senator, fêted and fussed over. Three weeks later, he died.

Judge James Wickersham, who traveled the trails, heard the stories, and met the men, said, "No hardier, braver, or more capable men ever drove a stage across the plains to California than these pioneer mail carriers of the Yukon."

Kandik Trappers

The Dutch girl has stolen a march on me again, so I will conduct a rear action by motoring over to her just-vacated berth at Ricketts's cabin and walk up the trail to have a look at Gordon Bertoson's old place. Kandik means "Willow Creek" in the Han language. The old-timers invariably called it Charley Creek as a consequence of the nearby Charley Village. But it was confusing to have Charley Creek coming in on the right bank and Charley River entering on the left bank, both within twelve miles of each other. The mapmakers at the United States Geological Survey used to put both names on the topographic sheet, but they have now settled on calling this river the Kandik. The river is rich in recent history. Ed Olson was one of the real early trappers, working on the Kandik and Nation around 1910. The Fish boys, brothers Frank and Al Fish, trapped the Kandik from around 1910 or 1915 to about 1930, when they left for the States. They built cabins all over the area, including one three and a half miles above the Kandik on the Yukon, one where Sarge Waller built (Ed Biederman bought that one, took it apart, rafted it across the river to his place, and put it back together), and at least five or six additional cabins up the Kandik, including ones two miles up, seven miles up, fourteen miles up, thirty-three miles up, and one up Judge Creek under Snowy Mountain. "At one time or another," says Willard Grinnell, who came in a couple of years after the Fish boys left, "they had trapped about every square foot of the Kandik drainage and had built at least 5 or 6 cabins up the Kandik."

Pete Summerville trapped the Kandik too, coming in from Rock Creek. Charlie Biederman ran a trapline here for a few years after he lost the mail contract. George Beck trapped the Kandik. So did an Athabascan man from Fort Yukon named Paul Solomon. And Chris Nelson worked his way over a pass from his cabins on the Nation.

Morris and Silas Gundrum, half-brothers from Circle, trapped marten and wolf in the lower Kandik in the early 1930s. In a letter to Dave Evans, Grinnell says, "Silas was in his early 20's walked an average of 4 miles an hour [which would be very fast on pavement], snowshoes the same [extremely fast], always had 8 or 12 good dogs, used a racing sled mostly [a very light sled], seldom loaded his dogs heavily, ran behind most of the time [rather than riding on the runners] and made 6 or 7 miles an hour [good for the conditions—modern race teams of sixteen or more dogs on hard, fast trails average twenty miles per hour]." Grinnell met Silas Gundrum when the two worked on the road crew constructing the Taylor Highway into Eagle in the summer of 1934. "He invited me to come down to the Kandik, and he would show me how to trap. Said it is big country, which it is." That September, Grinnell "bought a drift boat, and with 2 dogs and a load of grub and some traps went down to the Kandik and up it about 2 miles to a 12x18 cabin built by the 'Fish Boys.'" Late that month, Morris and Silas Gundrum mushed up from Circle "with a dozen dogs and a good outfit. We shot a moose apiece and a few caribou." For a winter's worth of dog food, they cut willow stakes and made a fish trap on a shallow bar. "We caught 4 or 5 tons of grayling, whitefish, etc. the last two weeks before the Kandik froze—the last two nites we had to go down and unload the fish box every two or three hours—it was full. We fed all our dogs till May and gave away several sled loads to other trappers." That winter, Grinnell trapped about twenty miles of the Kandik above Johnson Gorge. Morris and Silas trapped several of the side creeks. Grinnell caught thirty-five marten; Morris and Silas got about one hundred seventy-five.

Grinnell's several long letters to Dave Evans, laden with precise details and rendered in the language of the Yukon River trapper of seventy years ago, offer a marvelous peephole on the past. "Harry Parker and Rudolf Bauer came up the Kandik in March 1935—with two dog teams loaded. There was broke trail all the way to Indian Grave Creek & they got some stuff from Tiny & Slim . . . who were leaving. Parker had agreed to bring a boat load up to Indian Grave if Bauer would stay there all summer and build cabins for them. Bauer told me he built three. . . . Parker never showed up in the fall, stopped at Rock Creek instead. He may not have had enuf money to buy outfits for two, or figured he could not boat up there alone. I think he was very scared of Rudolf Bauer, and when Parker did not show up, Bauer told me he would beat Parker 'to a pulp' next time he saw him. He told me he had killed two men—one a Catholic priest in Germany—he fled across the Swiss border; the other a game warden. Silas G. visited him a few days after the Kandik froze and I spent 4 nites with him during the winter. Once he was out of meat and came down to see me—I had shot 6 cariboo the day before and gave him a load, about mid-winter I killed a moose and took half to him. I found him dead about the last of Feb. The fry pan on the stove was full of burnt caribou steaks."Grinnell figured Bauer collapsed suddenly, perhaps of a stroke, while cooking a meal. Maybe he hit his head and that killed him. Or maybe he was only knocked unconscious but lay there until the fire in the stove went out and he froze. Grinnell left the body as it lay and informed the authorities in Eagle.

Al Stout, the marshall's son-in-law, was "the dumb one elected to go get him," as Stout said in a 1991 tape-recorded interview in Eagle just before he died. It was a real slog, with the trail mostly underwater due to overflow. He found Bauer frozen beside his bunk with his face in the wood pile. There was very little food in the cabin, just a little caribou meat. "Harry Parker was supposed to haul this guy's grub in for a share of his trapping, and he never did get there," said Stout. "He never hauled him grub. So, I'd say that son-of-a-bitch killed him." Bauer was obviously not eating well, and Stout figured he fell, knocked himself out, and then froze to death. Stout made his way back, ninety miles down the slushy Kandik to the Yukon, with the body loaded into his little sled on edge, limbs jutting. He was tempted but forbore doing a little trimming with his Swede saw. At the mouth of the Kandik, Stout pulled into Biederman's place to spend the night just as Charlie Biederman pulled in with the mail on his way up from Circle. Stout was trying to unload the body and had grabbed a stick to help break it loose. "I guess it was the Old Man's [Ed's] walking stick. I had that and I was beating the ice off him. Charlie couldn't take that. He said, 'Jesus Christ, you're beating the hell out of him, and he's dead!' I said, 'I don't think he feels it.'" In the morning Stout set off for Eagle, another eighty miles up the Yukon. "I didn't say nice things to that corpse all the way to Eagle."

Willard Grinnell trapped on the Kandik for nine years, from 1934 to 1943. In 1941 he married Evelyn Berglund, a "girl trapper" from the Porcupine River area, who later wrote a wonderful autobiography called *Born on Snowshoes*. After that, he and Evelyn trapped on Beaver Creek west of Circle for another nine years. In 1952, after twenty-two years in Alaska, Grinnell moved with Evelyn to the San Francisco Bay Area, where he had connections. His father had been a professor at Berkeley, and his brother a professor at Stanford. Evelyn lasted only a year Outside, divorced him, moved back to Fairbanks, and remarried. In the end, she decided she liked the Bay Area after all and relocated there. Willard and Evelyn lived near each other, remained friends, and saw each other several times a year before he died. Of his time trapping in Alaska, Willard Grinnell wrote, "they undoubtedly were the happiest days of my life."

Randy Brown

By 1963, the Kandik country was totally empty of trappers. That's when Gordon Bertoson built a cabin at the mouth and, for a couple of winters, trapped upriver as far as Johnson Gorge. In the late 1960s, Morris Gunderson ran a trapline out of that cabin, then he too left. Apparently for old times' sake, when Willard Grinnell was about sixty years old and had by then been Outside for twenty years, he spent the fall and early winter of 1972 in the cabin with Morris Gundrum (not to be confused with Morris Gunderson), who was older yet. Grinnell cut wood and looked after camp while Gundrum walked a snowshoe trapline into the hills and caught fifty marten. It could be here that Grinnell earned his new nickname, "Sleepy," but I'm guessing. Earlier, he had been known as "The Eagle Milk Kid" in consequence of his fondness for the stuff. After that, the cabin stood empty for a few years, until 1975, when a fellow named Fred Beech—"Dirty Fred" to his friends—moved into it. But from 1977, for about ten of the next fifteen years, the Kandik was the stomping ground of Randy Brown. "Old cabins are here and there and everywhere out here," says Brown, "there are dozens of old trails." Brown hunted for and found those trails—then choked with decades of overgrowth—and cut many of them out.

As a kid, Brown did so much hiking and camping in New Mexico that by the time he was eighteen, he had formulated one definite career objective: "I wanted to be out in the country to such an extent that I would travel by canoe or by foot beyond the mountain range that you see in the distance; to travel by foot there; to go by your own power; to know the country enough to be able to take off and walk up a river valley, over a ridge of mountains, down another valley, beyond the mountain range on the horizon."

In the summer of 1976, Brown, who was then eighteen, and a partner named "Little John" Gaudio, who had come from California with

Steve Ulvi, packed up a few supplies into their two canoes and pushed off into the Yukon at Eagle. Little John had trapped for a couple of years with Mike Potts in the Fortymile country, and Randy had joined them one year too. They had both learned from Potts how to take care of themselves out in the country. Their idea was to keep things simple. They had along a twenty-five-pound sack of rice, a twenty-five-pound sack of beans, and a five-gallon bucket of tallow for the dogs. That was it for store grub. Brown and Little John planned to be gone for a year. And they were heading so far beyond the horizon that resupply would not be easy. While Little John and Ulvi had built their first cabins five miles off the end of the road past Eagle Village and a couple hundred yards off the river, Brown and Little John would travel eighty miles down the Yukon and build sixty miles off it, lining their canoes that distance up the Kandik River.

The float down the Yukon was easy enough. Lining the loaded canoe up against the current of the Kandik was slow, heavy, wet work. They spent two weeks lining up to Indian Grave Creek and began work on a ten-by-twelve-foot cabin there. They got about five rounds of logs in place when they decided to head back to Eagle for more supplies and to walk over into the Fortymile country to collect some traps that belonged to Little John. For much of the trip upriver on the Yukon, they could ride in the canoe, steering as the dogs trotted along the beach, pulling. On the return trip, they ran into Fred Beech, Jan Waldron, and Seymour Able on the Kandik. The group decided to collaborate on the construction of three cabins, which they all would use in pursuit of their separate trapping plans. They finished the ten-by-twelve-foot cabin at Indian Grave Creek, sixty miles up; then built a ten-by-ten-foot cabin above Johnson Gorge, about thirty miles up; and another, just six by nine feet, near Judge Creek, about ten miles upriver. When the construction was done, Little John set out a trapline from the Johnson Gorge cabin, while Randy put in trails out of Indian Grave Creek. Fred went back down to his place at the mouth of the Kandik, where he did a very modest bit of marten and lynx trapping. Seymour headed back to his lake cabin and worked his trapline, which now incorporated some Kandik cabins.

With all this lining of boats and building of log cabins, Randy and Little John's rice and beans went pretty fast. There were still some beans left when they shot a moose. Eventually they learned where to find, and how to hunt, the winter caribou that came through the upper Kandik in small bands. They learned to render every ounce of fat from every animal. Fat is a crucial nutrient in a lean country, says Randy. "If you just eat lean meat, you'll go downhill."

Besides food, the young men needed tough, warm clothing. Using a sewing awl and caribou skins with the hair left on, they sewed their own clothes: caribou parkas with hoods and wolf ruffs, caribou pants, caribou liners in their mukluks. Sometimes they attempted a brain-tanning method Little John had learned from the Han people (animal brains blended in water make a good tanning agent). But other times they just forced their way into the garments, which were as stiff as cardboard boxes, and allowed their sweat and movement to soften them. Like early aboriginals of the North, they were dressed completely in skin clothing, eating an all-meat diet, and living—literally—from kill to kill. They had some "hungry times," Brown says, but they didn't starve.

FOR RANDY BROWN, "starve" is not a figure of speech. "There was a fellow who did," he says, "He starved. He died. That's the way it was." That's the way it was in Alaska in the early days, and that's the way it was in the fall of 1978 when two fellows came downriver intending to head out into the woods. They launched their boat at Eagle and floated down the Yukon, stopping and staying with various people living along the river and ending up at Sarge Waller's cabin at the mouth of the Kandik. During the night, one of the partners slipped down to the boat and took off with all the gear. The stranded man was left with only the clothes he wore and a double-barrel, 20-gauge shotgun. The same day, the man hailed Dirty Fred, who lived about a mile away on the other side of the Kandik.

Fred was an easy-going sort who loved to show floaters the country around the mouth of the Kandik: the cabins and trails, the lakes where he had stashed canoes, his caches of grub and ammo. But the stranger was strange. At various times, he claimed to be one or another biblical character. Eventually, the river people referred to him as "Smeagol," after the two-faced character in J. R. R. Tolkien's *The Hobbit*. But Fred, who liked a bit of company and wasn't too fussy, let the fellow stay with him. He made it clear to Smeagol, though, that he had to hitch a ride out of the country with one of the moose hunters who soon would be motoring back to Eagle or Circle. Fred himself left in the fall on a two-month trip to the States. When he returned in November, the Yukon was running ice, and it was starting to jam up. He had to pull his canoe on shore a few miles above the Kandik and walk home. Arriving cold at his cabin, he found no lamp, no sleeping bag, and no stovepipe. There was a note explaining that the gear had been moved to a cabin three miles up the Kandik. It was signed "John the Baptist."

Fred spent the night in a spare sleeping bag, without a fire in the stove, and walked upriver the next day. He found Smeagol settled in the cabin surrounded by Fred's cache of winter food, as well as ammunition and gear belonging to Fred and Randy Brown. Smeagol had done a pretty good job of eating up Fred's moose meat and jarred salmon, particularly the precious buckets of rendered moose fat. Fred lived "pretty darn marginally," says Randy. "He didn't have a whole lot of extra."

Dirty Fred was hopping mad. But the fellow claimed to have shot a moose ten miles up the Kandik near Judge Creek. He said he'd dried the meat and cached the fat in a tree. Well, said Fred, in that case he had better get his butt on up there and bring back some of that moose. Fred meant to get his food replaced and then kick the freeloader out. Because it wasn't likely that Smeagol could walk there and back in a day, Fred told him about the small cabin he'd helped to build near Judge Creek. Next morning, Smeagol set off up the Kandik with three days' food (which may only have been a few handfuls of split peas and beans), carrying Fred's .22 pistol, and wearing a pair of Randy Brown's brand new store-bought snowshoes.

Two weeks later, Brown showed up at Fred's cabin at the mouth. He had hiked sixty miles overland from his main cabin up the Kandik to the Yukon. He was traveling on homemade snowshoes which were now broken, and he was looking forward to strapping on his new pair. When he heard Fred's story about Smeagol and the filched meat, salmon, and snowshoes, he decided that he and Fred ought to take a walk upriver to "have a talk with him and get our stuff back."

"Well, there was a lot of snow that year," says Brown, "It snowed and snowed and snowed." And Fred didn't tend to keep his trails broken out. After a whole day's work, Brown and Fred had covered just three of the ten miles. Faced with the prospect of spending three or four days breaking trail to retrieve his snowshoes, Randy decided that he had better things to do. The two turned around and went back to their respective cabins and traplines.

Smeagol never came out. Because of the deep snow, no one visited the Judge Creek cabin all winter. Whenever Randy or Fred or Dave Evans met over the next six months, they speculated about Smeagol. Maybe he walked out and slipped by Fred. Maybe he flagged down an airplane. He'd said something about walking over into the Black River and down it to the Gwech'in village of Chalkytsik. But that was a long way. Nobody believed he could do it. He's up there, Randy Brown figured, and he's dead.

As was his custom, Brown spent breakup at the mouth of the Kandik, watching ice from the two rivers go out. Then he and Fred hiked overland to Randy's cabin above Johnson Gorge to bring the canoe down the Kandik for the summer's fishing on the Yukon. When they stopped at the Judge Creek cabin, Randy saw his snowshoes leaning against a tree. He knew Smeagol was in the cabin, and that meant he was dead.

He was lying on the bunk, or what was left of it. His body was emaciated, but his feet were gigantically swollen. Apparently he had frozen his feet, then starved. No longer able to walk outside to get wood, he had been burning the bunk poles. The bunk's length was down to just four feet. "Oh, it was a pretty tough scene there," says Brown. "He didn't have any light. There were no candles, and there were no lamps. There was no reading material, no writing material." The cabin was only six by nine feet, and there wasn't even a window. The only light to enter the dark cell came in through a plastic-covered three-inch gap between two logs—and then only for the few hours that the sun was up that time of year.

Brown carried the man out and laid him on the ground. They thought about burying him, but they had no shovel. Even if they did have one, the ground was frozen. They could have taken him down the Kandik and then on down the Yukon eighty miles to Circle. But there were several problems with that idea. They had no money with which to buy food while in Circle. They had no motor to use to get back. Nor could they line back upriver—which would have been a week's work— because it was spring and the Yukon would be running high with all the gravel bars under water. And they felt that Smeagol had been warned to leave, that things shook out about as one would expect, that

"that's the way it was." When Randy returned later in the summer, Smeagol's body was gone. No bones. Nothing. Maybe a bear dragged him off, or a wolverine. More likely, it was the wolves that denned near Judge Creek.

IN 1981, RANDY BROWN married Karen Kallen. She was a schoolteacher from New Jersey, and not immediately drawn to the six-by-nine-foot cabin recently vacated by Smeagol. Nor did the comparatively commodious ten-by-twelve cabin at Indian Grave Creek seem a good fit. So they built a new home cabin above Johnson Gorge very near the cabin Willard Grinnell built in the 1930s, now a ruin. Randy and Karen left the next winter when Karen got a teaching job, and over the next six years, during which time they had two children, they were only on the Kandik one winter. But they spent every summer at their fish camp on the Yukon. In 1988 they returned to their Kandik River cabin. The cabin was located outside the preserve, but the land was transferred to Doyon, Ltd., a Native corporation established under the Alaska Native Claims Settlement Act. About 1990, Doyon got interested in developing the land's oil potential. They wanted to allow an oil company to drill prospect wells, and they asked the Browns to leave. They couldn't move to Randy's other cabins either above or below the gorge because the land above was now owned by Doyon or the State of Alaska, and the land below was now owned by the Park Service. The kids were thriving in the bush life, but town offered advantages too. The family moved off the river and into Fairbanks in 1991. Randy attended the University of Alaska and earned first a bachelor's degree in biology in 1996, and then a master of science degree in fisheries in 2000. He has worked for the U.S. Fish and Wildlife Service since 1996.

TALKING ABOUT HIS LIFE on the Kandik makes him "homesick," he says. Thinking about the influence of the Park Service and the Native corporations discourages him: "Most of the people out there didn't want to have anything to do with anybody in an official way. They didn't want to own the land. They didn't want to get kicked off. They didn't want anybody telling them how far the outhouse had to be from the—. Heck, most people didn't even *have* outhouses. Then all of a sudden here's these rules and regulations." Superimposing a gridwork of permitting procedures, he says, seems to violate in an intrinsic way the very activities for which authorization might be sought. Building an authentic birch bark canoe, for example, has got to be the apotheosis of wilderness craft. Randy Brown is one of the few people who can do it anymore. His canoes have been bought by museums. It would seem that the Park Service would nurture this sort of faithful continuance of a traditional activity within Yukon-Charley. Not so, says Randy's wife Karen: "If you read ANILCA, Randy building a birch bark canoe to sell for a quarter or a fifth of our income each year is a subsistence activity. And yet [the Park Service] looked at it as, well, if you are going to *sell* your birch bark canoe, it's a commercial activity—even though you can only make one in a year," she laughed. "If it's a commercial use, you have to get a permit to cut a tree larger than *three inches* in diameter. Well, to get your long, straight-grained gunwales, you have to cut a tree bigger than three inches in diameter. So, you get your permit to cut your one tree. Well, what happens if when you're bending your gunwales you split them, and you have to cut a second tree? Do you say, 'OK, well, let me line [the canoe] back up to Eagle [one hundred forty miles one way]—let's see, that will take me six days if we really hustle—and get a new permit'? Or do you suddenly become illegal and you cut a second tree?" It baffles Karen that the Park Service would insist on a permitting procedure so onerous for the building of a birch bark canoe. "It's absolutely absurd," she says. When she thinks about the agency setting up these kinds of obstacles for the few tenacious souls laboring so hard to barely survive in the traditional way, Karen says, "I really question whether it's unintentional."

Randy doesn't dispute his wife's recollection, and he thinks her reaction is justified. But, he says, "In the beginning the rules weren't exactly formulated yet. They were kind of making the rules up as they went along. But nobody ever cited anybody. We were never stopped from doing anything, and eventually we had wood-cutting permits for something like twenty trees."

Still, Karen laments the changes. "In our fish camp, every year we've had people stopping by, and we've shared our salmon," she said. "We've had people come and spend a month, lining up the Kandik with Randy, coming back in the winter to visit and see what it's like in the winter, people we continue to write to. We think that probably for the park, that's probably better than any interpretation center they could do. People that stop by with Randy building a bark canoe, people stopping by with Jed, helping to pole or line the canoe upriver, or talk about the dogs, and yet that's not going to be there." The presence of the Park Service, says Randy, "has definitely resulted in the depopulation of the country, as has Doyon, the state, BLM." And attrition of the woodsmen already there is only half the story. "Nobody new can get in. . . . [In the past] there was a constant circulation of people. People would come in, stay for a year, two years, five years, and then leave." Now, by law, they can only go one way.

PARK SERVICE HISTORIAN Melody Webb said almost the same thing: "A large part of the problem with the Park Service is that it still manages scenery. It manages natural resources. It cannot manage people, so they want the people off. . . . There is no provision for a continuation, a continuum [of residency within the preserve] to occur, which is the way that the Yukon-Charley area always existed. That was its historic tradition." In other parts of Alaska, says Webb, a subsistence culture was traditionally passed from father to son, mother to daughter. "You don't have that in Yukon-Charley. It is a culture that each individual acquires as they go into the area. And it is different. It is an individual culture. And, yes, the Park Service is incompatible with it."

In the 1970s, Webb worked on the early data-gathering and the planning preliminary to the establishment of new Alaskan park lands under ANILCA. Part of that was her work finding the historic structures in the proposed Yukon-Charley preserve. She had great hopes that the Park Service would "recognize the meaning of a white, subsistence lifestyle" and that regulations would demonstrate "compassion." But even though that lifestyle was declared in the law to be culturally important, it was ineluctably at odds with the agency's own institutional culture: "They are trying to make parks in Alaska like parks in the Lower 48. And they've done so. That was our greatest fear."

In a 2003 retrospective on her career, Webb explains more about how she sees Alaska parks as different. Park managers in the lower states, she said, tended to focus on "making parks accessible, enjoyable, and comfortable to visitors." There were "roads, trails, visitor centers, rest rooms, restaurants, lodgings, and viewing vistas," not to mention "swimming pools, golf courses, ski runs, even bars and liquor stores." The natural setting was at risk of being overwhelmed by traffic, congestion, and noise. "In Alaska we looked at such developments as distractions and intrusions. Alaskan parks could not be improved; they could only be perverted. Our ideal management plan was 'leave it like it is.'"

Webb and her Alaska team opposed building employee housing, fancy visitor centers, campgrounds, trails, restrooms, and roads within the parks. Finally, she and her Park Service colleagues in Alaska believed that parks here differed so much from parks in the Lower 48 that they required "separate regulations" that were "sensitive and thoughtful." Chief among the differences was the fact that people were living in or near the Alaska parks who made their living doing such things as killing animals and peeling their skins off. Not an easy sell.

Nevertheless, they did it. They established in law the concept of permitting subsistence activities within park lands in Alaska. Title VIII codified this revolutionary concept into the Alaska National Interest Lands Conservation Act: "The Congress finds and declares that . . . the continuation of the opportunity for subsistence uses by rural residents of Alaska, including both Natives and non-Natives, on the public lands . . . is essential to Native physical, economic, traditional, and cultural existence and to non-Native physical, economic, traditional, and social existence." Webb credits her old boss Zorro Bradley with getting the Park Service to see that the law ought to allow subsistence activities on park lands. But the law only established the objective. Regulations written by the agency, ostensibly to implement the new subsistence policy, effectively killed it instead. If Bradley had been able to keep such key people as John Cook, Bill Brown (Randy's father), and Bob Belous in Alaska, says Webb, "I don't think what happened would have happened. I think subsistence would have been a viable part of our national parks. Without them, you had plastic people who came from other parts of the Lower 48 who had no understanding, no perception, no compassion."

Dirty Fred's Cabin

Along the trail up the right bank of the Kandik I see a large electrical breaker box nailed to a tree. One of Dirty Fred's ammo caches, no doubt. In a few hundred yards the trail crosses a dry creek and enters a clearing in the spruce trees. Here is the cabin, looking like somebody stepped on it. The roof is pushed in; the door frame is trapezoidal; poles stick up at odd angles. Weeds thrive without and within. It is a shame because when Dave Evans and Melody Webb saw it in 1976, they found the cabin to be "in excellent shape." In her report to the Park Service, she said, "it should be preserved." A tent-frame cache has fallen down. Off in the fireweed I see an old dogsled with steel-shoed runners. It's quite narrow, maybe fourteen or sixteen inches, sized to track in the trail of a tandem-hitched (single-file) dog team. I can see parallel undulations in the ground next to the cabin—likely Fred's garden—where he had heaped up raised beds to help warm the cold ground and give the plants a chance.

The cabin was built by Gordon Bertoson from the Circle area in about 1963. He had been living and trapping downriver at Eureka Creek, but he liked to move around every couple of years to let the fur come back. Nobody was on the Kandik, he told me, so he put up this cabin at the mouth and trapped as far as Johnson Gorge. Gordon was an old man with thick glasses, living in a trailer outside of Circle when I talked to him fifteen years ago. The Kandik was good marten country, he said. He also said that "a lot of guys will crawl into a cabin, but they won't build one." Bertoson's successor, Fred Beech, had more of the crawler than the builder about him. One trapper who partnered with Fred for a season found him to be "lazy and no good." Fred ended up doing a fair bit of rabbit trapping. People say he was a home-brew alcoholic, a con man who pilfered when he visited their camps, and that he gradually wore out his welcome everywhere. "At one time or another," said Seymour Able, "everyone ostracized him, kicked him out of their camps and told him not to come back." Still, somehow, he was likable. Seymour visited him on the East Coast after Fred moved there. People say he married a Jamaican woman, moved to Jamaica, and died there of a stroke or maybe a heart attack.

I think I met Fred in the fall of 1975 when I was canoeing down the river. A fellow who fit his description was putting in upstream, as I re-call, a double-ender canoe with a tiny side-mount kicker. We inter-sected above the Kandik, floated along side-by-side for a while, chatting, then pulled to shore so he wouldn't lose ground. I thought he might be a couple of years older than I (I was not quite twenty-five). He said he had a cabin on the Kandik, that he "trapped cat," and that he was heading Outside to look for a woman. At different times, he'd found different women to move in with him, he said, but they seemed always to have a problem with the climate. I remember him saying "climate" with emphasis, like it was a great peculiarity that anyone could grouse about temperatures of sixty degrees below zero and three hours of sunlight in midwinter. This fellow I met also mentioned finding a dead king salmon along the riverbank and that he'd made a meal from this riverine roadkill. As soon as I mention the washed-up salmon to people who knew him, they all say, "That was Fred."

Mail Trail Way Station

Back on the water, I don't go far but cross the Yukon again and stop inside a little island just below Biederman's. It isn't easy to find, but there is a little ruin here in the thick spruce woods. A blazed trail runs along the high bank parallel to the river. It is the old mail trail. Biederman's was situated as a logical stopping place for the mail carriers, but when Ed froze his feet in 1925, the contract went to Johnny Palm of Circle the next year. Seeing the need for a way station near Biederman's, the Alaska Road Commission, which maintained the mail trails, put up a cabin here. Actually, they hired a good cabin builder to do it—Sandy Johnson, a Finnish immigrant who had been in the Yukon River area since maybe 1898, trapping and prospecting. The cabin is no longer a cabin. It is a mound of rusty-colored wood chips, with the odd gray board and shell of a log strewn about, and a thirty-foot spruce tree growing out of the heap. Out back I find a scrap of trail that looks to be a loop. A loop would allow a team and a sled to pull in off the trail and then be able to get out again without having to horse a heavily loaded sled around. Probably there isn't a man alive who saw the inside of this place when it was functioning. But in his 1938 book, Judge Wickersham left us a glimpse of the scene at way stations like this one, as the mail carrier—with his wolverine-trimmed denim parka and gaudily beaded gauntlet gloves—pulled his team into the yard: "When the mail-team reaches the station or the roadhouse at the end of the day's run, the driver unhitches the team and turns all the dogs, except the leader, loose to rustle for themselves. His leader, his parka, gloves and whip, he brings into the roadhouse, puts the leader under his bunk, hangs his wet garments on the best wires around the stovepipe—and woe unto him who complains about the leader under the bunk! All other vehicles are required by the United States laws to give the right of way to the mail-teams, and so the mail-driver is the most important personage on the trail, in the mail-station, or at the over-night roadhouse. He is given the best seat at the table, the first service of hotcakes at breakfast, and the best bunk at night. Today, at a few cabins along the river, you will see the same deference shown the dog drivers who race in the Yukon Quest sled dog race between Dawson and Fairbanks.

Crazy Man Island

I don't know where Crazy Man Island is. My Rourke volume doesn't have it; the inch-to-a-mile USGS map doesn't show it; Donald Orth's *Dictionary of Alaska Place Names* doesn't list it. What I need is an old-timer. Charlie Biederman is the man, but he isn't around any more. He used to tell a story (Laurel Tyrrell of Central got it down on tape) of the Fish and Game flying down to the Kandik River in the spring and counting eighty moose on what he called "Crazy Man Island." "They wouldn't listen to me or someone who had been there before. Sure, in March [the moose] always do that. They come down from the creeks on account of deep snow to these islands where there's good feed. And they'll just gang up. Well, they feed up and go on to another one. And then as soon as the snow starts getting soft, then they'll go back. The bull moose will go back further up those creeks, and the cows will stay down there and have their calves," Charlie said. "But they got the idea they're going to overgraze the country. So they opened a season up for two moose, a bull and a cow. So everybody come in, a lot of Outside hunters, non-residents come in there, and come down and just because they *could* shoot two, they shot them. Whether they need them or not. Well, that's what ruined that whole country. In about three years' time, there was no moose. They killed all the cows off. It's going to take years to build back up."

Charlie said the fish and game authorities did the same thing with the caribou. "In later years when they got more hunters and highways and more hunters come in, like they did with the Fortymile Caribou Herd, Fish and Game just opened it wide open. They could kill five caribou, and sometimes more. And they just slaughtered them." When the herd came near the new highway into Eagle, and the bag limit was five, the road hunters showed no restraint. "It was really awful to see them on the highway there. They'd get a herd of caribou down in a draw and have them surrounded. And they'd just keep shooting until they shot every one of them. The Game Commission: Oh, that's all right. We've got an oversupply of them. Couple years later they said, Oh, gee, they depleted so much."

LOCAL KNOWLEDGE is a favorite topic of a fellow who lives in this general area, though not very near, and not within the preserve. Mark Richards is too far off the Yukon for me to visit, but he can beam me E-mails via satellite. As I write this, I've never met Mark or his wife Lori, though we have sent messages back and forth for years. They met when she was sixteen—"high school sweethearts," says Lori. Mark's dream was to live in the wilderness, far from roads or towns. "His dream soon became mine," she says. When Lori graduated from high school, they moved into a tiny apartment in Los Angeles while they worked, saved money, and read books on Alaska. On a map of the state, they put an X to mark where they wanted to live. They still have the map. If the X actually existed on the ground, they could see it from their window. For twenty-five years they have lived here, from the tail end of childhood to the brink of growing old. Both of them are still as passionate about living in the bush as they were before they had any real idea what they were getting into. Even the arrival of children did not change the plan, as it did for many others. They have three kids, one grown and moved away and two teenagers at home. There is a difference, they say, between them and most of the other bush people they have known. Others came into the country to live out a dream for a time, to measure themselves against the standards of a bygone day, to acquire an experiential basis of knowledge, to conquer fears and tap buried sources of strength, and to do those things until they had taken from the experience what they had sought. By contrast, Mark and Lori always intended—and still affirm—that they came to stay until they die.

Meanwhile, they have kids to raise and educate and income to earn by selling crafts and fur. And they have time left over to follow their interests through the Internet and books. Mark, it seems, reads everything, is into everything. From geology and hydrology to taking a stab at writing a novel, from solar power and satellite communications, to Native place-names (toponyms, he calls them). One day a hydrology professor showed up on his creek to sample the water. "I asked him if when they did the water sampling if they used the stream gauge to correlate it with just how high the river was when the sampling was taken. He said No. He didn't seem aware how much and how fast rains and high water influenced the water quality (acidity, carbon content, etc.)." In other words, if the scientist doesn't know if the river is high or low at the time of the sampling, he won't know if the chemistry he records is a typical condition or associated with an unusual water level. "What I'm getting at here is that a stewardship plan of some kind should, I think, involve some kind of monitoring of the ecosystem that may be beneficial to various agencies. From snow depth, to water quality, to temp records, to the first duck arrivals, and on and on." Mark's idea, still gestating, is that a few widely separated people or families might be permitted to live out in the deep woods on public land, offering their local knowledge and their labor to assist the work of scientists, scholars, and land managers. A "stewardship allotment," he calls it. When some forestry scientists were in his area once, they were telling him about various ways that trees may have advanced into new regions following the last Ice Age. Mark asked if they had considered trees rafting down the rivers in high water. Like the little clump of birch I'd seen upriver, trees can sometimes break off from the shore with a chunk of real estate attached. Sometimes the river will carry the whole unit, relatively intact, for a long distance, then fetch it up on an island or shallow place. When the water recedes, the trees can grow again and propagate. Uh, no, actually, they hadn't thought of that. There is no doubt that curious and observant people like Mark Richards, out in the country for decades, could add much to the inquiries of city-based researchers whose field time is limited.

Ed Gelvin's A-Frame

Below the Kandik and Biederman's, one leaves Eagle's sphere of influence and enters Circle's. From here on down, the river people will use Circle (pop. 99) for access to the road system, telephone, mail, and some supplies. The river follows a camel's-hump bend now, with Biederman Bluff defining the northern limit for several miles. I've got the kicker at about one-third throttle, just enough RPM for the water pump to cool the engine. But I have my earplugs in, and that removes me from the glories that surround me. As earplugs turn down the volume on my surroundings, they turn up the volume on my thoughts. Under-my-breath colloquies, previously inaudible, now transmit themselves like unwanted radio signals. It's like I'm listening to myself think, which should only be possible for someone with multiple personalities.

"With what?"

"Multiple personalities."

"Oh."

With the motor off now and the earplugs out, the air is still, the sun gentle, and the world wonderfully quiet. Splitting the islands in the bend, a big sky opens up to the south. From my vantage on the water, no hills appear above the spruce trees on the left bank. But as I come out of the bend, I can see farther to the south and raise the six thousand-foot hills that enclose the Charley River. The vast sky is a smorgasbord of clouds. It's a textbook for cloud identification—an important skill, one mastered by any competent guide. The entry in my field book contains, I believe, the accepted nomenclature: "Every kind of cloud: high wispy things. Broken, horizontally oriented things. Puffy ones atop the hills to the south. High gray clouds to the southwest, downriver. Will probably look for Gelvin's."

Right. Well, at least I found Gelvin's place.

"Place" in the sense of "location," not in the sense of "house." Gelvin was a pilot, prospector, cat skinner, mechanic, and all-around independent operator and homesteader from Central who figured heroically in McPhee's book. In 1960, he put up a little A-frame cabin on a high bank here, just below Chester Bluff. It was a place to go to just get away and maybe to look for moose. He could have staked the ground as a recreation site, but he never did. The BLM had told him—dishonestly, he felt—that there was no point to it, nobody was going to bother him. Shortly, the Park Service came along and removed the cabin. The square spot of grass that remains has an eerie look, as if the cabin had been vaporized by a spaceship. There's nothing left but Ed's view and a couple of cut stumps to sit on while taking it in. It's a pretty scene, across the Yukon toward the mouth of the Charley River. I know that there are archaeological sites here on

Chester Bluff. Prehistoric men probably sat up here and worked on their weapons while looking out over the flats for game. Which is pretty much what Ed did, I imagine.

Ed Gelvin died a few years ago. I'd interviewed him some years before that. By all accounts, he was an archetype of independence, amazingly competent with all manner of machinery. There's probably nobody in the world you'd rather be with if you were out in the country—in Alaska, in winter—and dependent on a cat train or an airplane or a snowmachine (or all three) to get you in and get you back. He was a soft-spoken man, too, and modest. I laugh, remembering what he said about Dick Cook, who represented the opposite pole of personality in McPhee's pantheon. Ed said he met Cook once and that "he had the biggest line of BS I ever heard in my life." With Gelvin, I found a lot to admire but, interestingly, not a lot to agree with. The Park Service—and all bureaucrats everywhere—were irredeemably malevolent. There was not one aspect of the establishment of the preserve that had any beneficial aspect. An environmental extremist was someone who thought that any degree of restraint or reclamation might be asked of miners who chewed up pretty creeks on public land and left their messes behind. The river people were into dope, couldn't have made it without their food stamps, and didn't get very far out into the country anyway. When the talk turned to one particular long-haired trapper, Ed said he'd heard the fellow had gotten out of dogs and into dope. Ed wondered how he got around now. But I had just visited the man. He was at his fish camp, putting up fish. His dog team was right there, and he was getting ready to go up to his home cabin to hunt moose and get ready for winter, just as he had been doing for seventeen years. Ed was a strong man with strong opinions, but sometimes those opinions were born of rumor and intolerance, not fact.

Charley River/Charlie Kidd

As I sit here at the place where Gelvin's A-frame used to be and look across toward the valley of the Charley River, I am thinking about how huge it is. It is hard to imagine that for a couple of decades there was only one resident in the whole of it. Now he is gone. And I'm thinking about how little a difference, and how big a difference, that makes.

A few years ago, a crew from the National Geographic Society were in the Circle area working on a film about bush life in interior and northern Alaska. As people on the river tell the story, the filmmakers were especially keen to get an interview with a certain trapper who for many years had been living alone in the upper reaches of the Charley River, one of the most remote places in interior Alaska. He was Charlie Kidd or, inevitably, Charley River Charlie. The film crew chartered riverboats, and even a helicopter, to look for him. But all they accomplished, besides providing a welcome boost to the local economy, was an occasional aerial glimpse of the reclusive trapper as he slipped out of one of his cabins and ducked into the woods.

I MET CHARLIE KIDD at his fish camp in 1991. I was with my wife and six-year-old son, and we had been told to look for his fish camp about a mile and a half below Slaven's Roadhouse on the left bank. After floating by the bluff below Slaven's, I saw an old, battered, sixteen-foot, square-stern, aluminum canoe dragged up on the beach. Nearby there were a couple of spruce poles set into the ground. A few cross-member sticks were tied in place, and a sheet or two of corrugated tin leaned against this tiny structure. It looked to me to be too small an operation to fit any definition of the term "fish camp," and I started to cruise by. But then I thought I had better stop and check it out.

My boy was the first to see the man coming toward us on the beach. He was perhaps in his mid- to late-thirties, with brown hair trailing down his back and a long brown beard reaching about as far down his chest. He was shirtless and barefoot, wearing a fur headband and leather-patched jeans that had seen some mud recently. Slim but muscled, he walked purposefully with his arms hanging loosely at his sides. His eyes were light brown and clear. It was impossible not to see, for a moment, Jesus, or one of his fisherman apostles, walking the shoreline of a Northern Galilee.

Charlie knew who we were right away. At that time I was doing a research project for the Park Service, collecting on tape the stories of people along the river, and Charlie had said it would be all right for me to talk to him. He invited us up to his campfire, and we dug out of our canoe a sack of apples and grapefruit we'd brought for him. By the time we climbed up the bank to his camp, he had stirred the coals of a campfire to life and disappeared into the brush. He was staying at—or perhaps beside—a cabin where an old-timer named George McGregor used to live. It had been built more than half a century earlier, and the roof was partly fallen in. Charlie came back with a few green alder branches from which he stripped off leafy twigs. Tossed on the fire, these made a smudge that kept the mosquitoes at bay. That done, he rustled in the willows behind the cabin until he'd rounded up three five-gallon gas cans (left over from some previous occupant) and dropped them by the campfire for us to use as seats. He muttered something about tea and headed back into the woods like he was going to the cupboard. When he returned, he had a fistful of a green shrub whose common name is Labrador tea. He stuffed this into an amazingly battered and blackened kettle and turned up the fire with two split sticks of dry spruce. He filled the kettle with Yukon River water and put it on a bit of expanded steel set across a ring of stones. When it had boiled, it made a good, dark brew. Charlie rinsed out for us a discarded can that had been opened with a knife. I don't think we could have been shown more complete hospitality or observed more efficient domestic skill if our tea was being poured in Buckingham Palace. When it started to sprinkle, Charlie pulled on a very tattered homemade vest of what I took to be dog fur.

Everybody said Charlie Kidd was the guy who came into the country with practically nothing but the intention to "keep it simple"; that he didn't deviate a degree over the course of (then) eighteen years; that he still used the original pot and pan he arrived with; that he was never lured by outboard or chain saw or big dog teams; that he was incredibly tough, snowshoeing 120 miles into Circle once a year over the Woodchopper trail. "I take a tow once a year from Circle to the mouth of the Charley River," he told me. "That's all I need." I said I noticed he had a square-stern canoe and wondered if he ever thought of getting a kicker. He said no, then you're depending on it and gas and parts and the whole nine yards. Charlie had heard from the Park Service that I was coming down the river, and he'd understood I was interested in the history of the gold dredge at Coal Creek, where he used to work in the 1970s. I said I was more interested in hearing about his life in the woods, but Charlie didn't see the point in talking about himself. He seemed uncertain about his future. War-gaming Air Force jets dropping flares had just started a forest fire in the Charley

River drainage, burning about forty thousand acres, right up to the doorstep of Charlie's home cabin at Hanna Creek. He didn't care for the changes that had brought so many people onto the river. "It's a goddamned circus," he said. I assumed he meant near-daily sightings of rangers in jet boats, and the occasional scientific crew running around in boats and helicopters, sticking bright plastic tags on every critter they could net or dart. Also, like the other river people, Charlie had had to sign over any interest in his cabins to the Park Service. But he was willing to work with the agency, willing to follow their rules and hope that things would work out. Like everybody else, he never had wanted to own anything—land or cabin—just wanted to be able to live way out in the woods.

The afternoon of our visit, Charlie had been invited to dinner by his neighbors, the volunteers working at Slaven's Roadhouse, a mile and a half upriver. It was about five o'clock, and I didn't want to get between a man like him and his grub. He tossed a piece of burlap over his few things piled under a tree, fed his two dogs, and pulled on a pair of army boots. He grabbed an old T-shirt but not a life jacket. I offered to tow him up, but he said he'd line. We said good-bye at the beach, and he ran into his dented canoe all the way to the stern, stopping short so that his momentum forced the boat into the river. Kneeling in the stern and pointing toward the far shore at an upstream angle, he stroked powerfully against the current, first on one side, then the other. Slaven's was on the same side of the river as Charlie's camp, but there was a bluff in between. He had to cross the river, then line his boat far enough above Slaven's so that when he recrossed he could reach the bank above the roadhouse and not be carried into the swift current at the bluff. I watched him cross until he was a tiny figure jumping out of the canoe in shallow water just off a long gravel bar. As he strode upriver, splashes shot up from his feet and flashed in the low-angle sun. He was moving through the shallows so that the canoe would ride far enough offshore to float. But it looked like he was walking on water.

Ames Cabin

Across the Yukon from Ed Gelvin's site, the mouth of the Charley beckons, so I motor up its blue waters for a few bends just to get a feel of it. I scare up a black bear who runs along the bank beside me for a bit—his fat rippling under glossy fur—before he veers off into the spruce trees. I drop back to the first bend and beach the canoe above the upper of two islands. Moose, wolf, and bear have signed the mud registry in recent weeks, and I make my own prints, climb the bank, and look for a trail into the Ames cabin.

I find it in a yard full of weeds, squatting like a soldier in ambush, camouflaged with little trees and bunches of grass sprouting from its roof. A fellow named Al Ames built the place in the summer of 1941, according to most accounts. But I trust Willard Grinnell's memory. In April and May of 1943, Grinnell and his wife Evelyn stayed at another of Ames's cabins, the one at Bonanza Creek, nine miles up the Charley. Grinnell says Ames had been trapping alone out of the Bonanza Creek cabin for three or four years at that point. Ames had gotten married that year, 1943, and decided to trap up the Black River out of Fort Yukon with his in-laws. So Grinnell and his wife moved into the Bonanza Creek cabin and trapped beaver. After the river broke up, they whipsawed lumber to build a twenty-four-foot boat and on the first of June floated back to Fort Yukon. Ames returned, now married, and probably built this larger cabin at the mouth then. He lived here with his wife and several kids. But after a few years trapping, he owed the Northern Commercial Company so much money for supplies that they offered him a job. He and his family moved to Fairbanks, where Al fired boilers at the NC store.

It's a nice cabin, or was. With two rooms adding up to thirty by fifteen feet, it's probably one of the largest in the preserve, and one of the very few in which kids were reared. It has a real board floor, a store-bought door, and logs that are hewn flat on the inside. But the roof is partly fallen in, making the still-sound barrel stove a dubious appurtenance. But I am wrong about that, as a neat stack of birch firewood attests. Somebody comes in here to get out of the wind and rain and to warm up. When Melody Webb visited in 1976, she noted "glass windows and doors are uncracked. Stove, tables, benches, and beds complete the furnishings." The Bonanza Creek cabin was in good shape then too. "Livable," she said, "with wood floor, root cellar, stove, table, beds." She recommended maintenance, preservation. Nothing was done, however, and both are ruins now.

Charlie Kidd used the mouth cabin on his trapline for years in the early 1970s, as well as other cabins farther up the Charley River. The mouth cabin and the one at Bonanza Creek are examples of "demolition by neglect." The Park Service won't repair them, so they fall in. At least one can still look at the elegantly aging remains. But in other cases, the destruction has been abrupt. Kidd used a cabin at Everett Creek, maybe eighteen or twenty miles up the Charley River. A good carpenter, a Swede named Ole Beckloff, built it in 1974. Dave Evans, himself an expert craftsman, said it was a nice cabin, well-made. In June 1999, however, the preserve superintendent authorized its demolition. According to several accounts, a crew of mostly seasonal Park Service employees working out of Eagle was assigned to do the dirty work. Traveling with the crew was a cultural specialist, new on the job. On seeing the relatively intact cabin, she held up the operation for several hours, insisting that the Eagle office be raised on the radio to verify that the demolition was authorized. When the authorization was confirmed, she insisted that Park Service headquarters in Fairbanks be contacted to be sure that Superintendent Dave Mills approved of the tear-down. He did. The crew knocked the cabin apart and threw the logs in the river.

After hearing, through back channels, of this and similar "removals," I set up a meeting to ask Mills about it. But shortly before the appointed date, Mills said he wanted written questions in advance. I sent him questions, including, "Which cabins have been removed since the establishment of the preserve?" The evening before the morning meeting, which had been scheduled for three weeks, I found a letter on my door. It was from Mills, and it provided some general answers to my questions. On cabin removal, he said:

> After careful evaluation, a small number of unoccupied, not historically significant structures on federal public land deemed to be unauthorized and an attractive nuisance, or considered to be endangering public safety, have been removed since the establishment of the preserve. Each and every case of such structures on public land is a unique situation requiring a decision in the best interest of the public and resource values. 2 non-historic structures have been removed from public land (the "A-frame" near

Chester Bluff and "Sarge Waller's Cabin" (roof collapsed) at the mouth of the Kandik River). Procedurally, the Superintendent makes these determinations on a case-by-case basis, after consultation with appropriate park and regional staff.

Mills's letter also said he would not be meeting with me in the morning, but that his assistants, including Steve Ulvi, would be available "if any further clarification is necessary." I opted for "further clarification" and showed up the next day with a tape recorder.

Steve Ulvi had been off the river for many years at this point and had risen within the Park Service to become one of the key administrators of Yukon-Charley Rivers National Preserve. Mills had not acknowledged that other cabins, besides the two he listed in his letter, had been demolished by the Park Service, and I pressed Ulvi on the point. He said the number of demolished cabins was small, that the decisions were made at the top and only after careful evaluation and consultation with staff. How hard could it be then, I asked, to remember so few cabins so carefully evaluated? "Those are the only two," he insisted. Finally, I mentioned the cabin at Everett Creek and Seymour Able's lake cabin but got nowhere, except that Ulvi offered to double-check. The next week I got a letter from him. It was an acknowledgement wrapped up in palliatives, like a dog's pill inside a ball of hamburger. "In 1999 several non-historic cabins were removed from public lands as they were unauthorized, non-historic, causing confusion for fire suppression/monitoring personnel, an attractive nuisance and a potential threat to public safety." These threatening and confusing nuisances, the Park Service now acknowledged, included the Everett Creek cabin, Seymour's lake cabin, and one on Logan Creek (where, local people tell me, they ran a chain saw down through the walls and let the logs fall into a heap).

NOT ALL YUKON-CHARLEY employees approve of these tactics, of course, but they are afraid to speak openly, even within the office. Neither does the Alaska State Historic Preservation Office approve. In a signed agreement with the fifty state historic preservation offices, the National Park Service promised to follow certain procedures before altering potentially historic structures. This "programmatic agreement," as it is always called, isn't just a courtesy, it responds to the law, namely the National Historic Preservation Act. The Park Service is bound to work in concert with the state historic preservation offices (SHPO). "Cabin demolition," says Stefanie Ludwig of Alaska's SHPO, "is something that NPS should contact us about."

When the rules are followed, the first step is for the Park Service to fill out one of its own agency's forms, called an Assessment of Effect. In the case of nonhistoric cabins, like the ones at issue here, it might be a very simple exercise. The proposed action is described, the superintendent checks a box that says "No Effect," and that's it. What the agency would be certifying is that it had considered the matter and judged the property to be nonhistoric and not eligible for listing on the National Register of Historic Places. Hence the action would have no effect on historic assets. The next step is for the Park Service to write the SHPO a letter describing the plan. The SHPO would look over the project and decide whether or not they concurred that, for example, George Washington had not slept at Seymour Able's lake cabin, that it did not qualify for the National Register of Historic Places, and that tearing it down wouldn't have an effect on historic properties. As Stefanie Ludwig says, the letter should "request SHPO's concurrence on the findings of eligibility and effect." But these demolitions that the Park Service initially did not acknowledge to me (twice) were also not disclosed to state officials as required. Nor did the Park Service complete the Assessment of Effect forms. Other reporting requirements may also have been ignored that have to do with environmental law, including an opportunity for public comment. I don't know if the words "secret" and "illegal" strictly apply, but at best these demolitions violated the programmatic agreement and were improper.

CHARLIE KIDD IS GONE from the river now. He left for his own reasons in 1997, having stayed for about twenty-four years. I wonder if anyone has ever lived longer on Charley River. Maybe Phil Berail did. Berail was a legendary figure, at the top of everyone's list of "the toughest men I ever knew." He trapped and mined in the country between Coal Creek and Circle for thirty or forty years. Maybe there were a few others of long tenure. Since the park no longer issues resident permits, there likely never again will be a person with a longer tenancy than Kidd. In a little while, Charley River Charlie will be considered a historical figure in this drainage. But by then much, if not all, of the material record of his occupancy will have been destroyed.

I would propose a thought experiment. Imagine a couple of raft-loads of Park Service VIPs who have wrangled spots on the coveted annual fly-in float trip down the Charley River. It's a sparkling day on the river when the rafts pull into the beach where Everett Creek bounces into the Charley. The visitors pile out and hike up a trail through the dark spruce into a clearing where a tiny, nicely built log cabin sits. The old logs are a lovely raw sienna in the filtered light. The roof sprouts green grass two feet tall. The door is so small the visitors will have to stoop to look inside. Every one of the VIPs—the assistant deputy director and his policy aide from D.C., the congressman from Ohio, the historian from Santa Fe—will shoot a few pictures of the little log cabin in the clearing in the woods. Every one of them will poke his head in the door to see what it looks like inside. You know they will. But why? The answer, I think, gets at something important. It is that even the Park Service policy wonk is helpless to resist the attraction of an image so powerfully and classically evocative of this country, of this preserve. With those gestures, they are saying, "This is what it looks like. This is what living here involved. Can you imagine yourself living through an Alaskan winter in this tiny cabin!? What must the people have been like who did it?" That is how they feel. But they have a great capacity for dissonance, and the feeling will not survive a journey through the bureaucracy. The feeling will only survive a journey through photo processing and on to showing the pictures to family and friends.

Excepting the handful of public use cabins that the Park Service maintains, the life cycle of a log cabin in this preserve is a short arc into the moss: No one is allowed to live in the cabin and thus to maintain it. No one is allowed to repair the cabin when deterioration shows. The Park Service does not employ so much as a tarp to protect the structure from water damage and rot. Protection from wildfire is not recommended. Inevitably, the roof begins to go. Either the cabin burns or neglect continues until the cabin falls in by natural processes. Alternately, the cabin is declared a threat and a nuisance and demolished. Yukon-Charley administrators deny this is a tacit policy to eliminate cabins within the preserve, even as they continue to watch the cabins go, one by one, thirty years after their own specialist, Melody Webb, recommended their protection. Of course, the cabins are only the outward manifestation of the larger thing that is being demolished, which is the subsistence way of life.

The Park Service policy may be lamented by many, but it is applauded by some. Beginning twenty-five years ago with the passage of ANILCA, such groups as the Sierra Club and the Northern Alaska Environmental Center have pressed the Park Service to correct what they considered overly lenient policies on trespass cabins. Why are they tolerated in a national preserve at all? Why aren't they all taken down immediately? The spectrum of strongly held opinion in Alaska bends into a full circle, and the Park Service managers are in the middle of it, pulled and pushed in several directions at once.

I DRIFT DOWN THE CHARLEY to its mouth. After being on the milky Yukon, it is strange to see the rocks slide below the hull, to feel like I am hovering a foot over the bottom. It's as if the canoe is held up on a film of Saran Wrap that the hull deflects but does not puncture. A few paddle strokes, and the silty water fogs the bottom like clouds below an airplane, and the sense of vertical elevation vanishes.

Sam Creek/Carolyn Kelly

Below the Charley, the country opens up on the right bank where Andrew Creek Flats begins. On river left, Sam Creek rolls down from the hills. Here, off the river a few hundred yards, is another little old cabin. Little, as in eleven-by-thirteen feet. Old, as in possibly the oldest standing structure in the preserve. Sandy Johnson and his partner Albert Johnson stampeded into the country in 1898 and floated down the Yukon on a log raft. They staked claims on Sam Creek and its little tributary, Ben Creek, which showed good prospects. A prospector named Cap Reynolds had a cabin near here too. Phil Berail found him dead in the trail in the 1940s, apparently murdered by a freeloader Cap had put up. Among the other miners in the district was Max Drews, who built the cabin Dick Cook used at the mouth of the Tatonduk. Sandy Johnson was a talented carpenter, and before 1917 had built this cabin, another large one up on Ben Creek, the mail trail way station upriver, and Slaven's Roadhouse just downriver. He took the trouble to shape the bottom of each successive log to fit the top of the one below, and the fit is still tight. Charlie Kidd used this place as a stopover on his trapline. And someone, probably George Moore and Carolyn Kelly, put some corrugated tin on the roof, though it's just nailed to birch poles laid across the old moss roof. The rain isn't kept out completely, as the sheets barely overlap, and there's no cap along the ridge.

IN THE WINTER OF 1977, Carolyn Kelly, who had come to Fairbanks from Santa Rosa, California, a few years earlier, met a young man named George Moore. Moore had fourteen dogs, a tent, and a notion to get out of town. Kelly was drawn to the idea of traveling with a dog team. "I was fascinated that he would put a stove and a tent in his sled and travel," she says. "And so I sort of nagged my way into involvement in that." They became a couple and spent a winter trapping and living in the tent on the Tolovana River northwest of Fairbanks. Carolyn ran her own dog team and her own trapline. In the spring they decided to look for a place to live where they could fish for the dogs. George had spent some time in Eagle Village and knew Mike Potts, an experienced trapper. Potts suggested George and Carolyn might look at Andrew Flats, nearly a hundred miles downriver from Eagle.

Not all the river people were as welcoming as Potts. George and Carolyn had too many dogs, people said. They'd be shooting moose to feed them. And they were the wrong kind of dogs. Too small. And they had basket sleds, for Christ's sake, instead of the narrow toboggans with moose-hide sides. "Everybody had the huge malamutes," says Carolyn. "And the sleds and stuff we brought in were different. Everybody did everything the same way. And that was the only way, and that was the right way. So we were wrong and we obviously weren't going to make it." If not making it was what they did, they did it for six years.

And the dogs did fine, though Moore and Kelly did have to pare down to five or six. (Eventually, most river people saw the disadvantages of their big, hundred-pound Malamutes: you had to *shovel* the food into the big galumphing beasts, they ran at a walk, and they loved nothing so much as a murderous fight. Eventually, all but the big-dog die-hards converted to the smaller, Iditarod-type dogs—like those George and Carolyn ran—which were around sixty or seventy pounds, had better dispositions, and could trot all day.)

In August, Carolyn and George started a cabin near the mouth of Andrew Creek. They used only hand tools, having a strong aversion to gasoline engines of all sorts, their noise especially. The fall came cold. By October, the cabin was late and the winter early. They were still camped out, and Carolyn was pregnant. Seeing the circumstances, Charlie Kidd offered to let them use the Sam Creek cabin, so long as he could continue to stop over there. They moved in straightaway.

The baby was due on March 29, and as the date approached, George was sticking close to home, not running his trapline, to be sure to be on hand when Carolyn went into labor. The cabin's square footage is approximately that of a medium-sized Persian rug, and George was developing a case of "cabin fever." "George was hanging around and hanging around. By the twenty-ninth he was going nuts," remembers Carolyn. "So we went over from Sam Creek to Andrew Creek to our tent. And I snowshoed. I probably snowshoed about ten miles that day. And about ten o'clock that night I went into labor in the tent. And at dawn, George put me in the sled and ran me back over across the river to Sam Creek, because I didn't want to have the baby in this little five-by-eight tent with nothing in it."

Carolyn had seen Jan Waldron in September but had not seen another woman in the intervening six months. She and George had debated about going into Fairbanks to have the baby. Or maybe, they thought, they should go down to the Coal Creek mining camp, where Arlene Bell and her husband Ray were caretakers. If things went badly, there was both a radio and an airstrip at Coal Creek. All they had at this little log cabin on Sam Creek was a book: *Spiritual Midwifery*— "the greatest book ever written," according to Carolyn. Back at the Sam Creek cabin, George just had time to get the cabin warmed up and some water thawed and the book opened to the pertinent page. "It was pretty quick," Carolyn says. "Pretty easy."

When the baby was two weeks old, George made a dog-hide carrier, lashed it to a showshoe, and attached pack straps. Sort of a Pleistocene Snuggly. They wanted to get the baby checked out by a doctor, and Carolyn was nervous about rocketing down the steep hills to Coal Creek with a newborn in the dogsled. The sled could easily flip, become separated from the driver, and crash into a tree. So she walked while George took the dog team. Over the hills, down along Coal

Creek to the mining camp, then on down to the roadhouse at the Yukon. On the map, it looks to me like nearly fifteen miles, with about a two-thousand-foot climb. But her story gets better. She and the baby, Zach, check out fine in Fairbanks, and they get a lift home from a friend with a Taylorcraft on wheels. He buzzes George at the Sam Creek cabin and then tries to land on a slough at the mouth. It is now mid-April. What looks from the air to be ice turns out to be slush two feet deep. "The wheels hit, the nose hit, and we just flipped over and landed on the top of the plane. Everything went through the wind-shield, and we ended up hanging upside-down." But Zach was in a carrier in front of her. And, because Carolyn had been a little wary of the landing, she had covered him with her parka before touchdown. Everyone got a jolt, but everyone was fine. George mushed to Coal Creek and radioed for a helicopter in Circle to come and flip the plane right-side-up. The pilot took off the prop, bent it more or less straight, and flew back to Fairbanks. Just in time, as it turned out. Within a couple of hours, Sam Creek went out, and the landing area became moving water and ice.

The family spent the summer at Slaven's Roadhouse at the mouth of Coal Creek and another winter at the Sam Creek cabin. They finished the Andrew Creek cabin in the fall of 1980 and lived there for four years. At eleven by fourteen feet, it was the biggest cabin they'd lived in to that point, but now there were three people in the space. George was away much of the time, either building a trapline cabin or check-ing his line, which took five or six days. Meanwhile, Carolyn watched the baby, and when he was asleep, she'd wash the diapers out by hand. Cooking took a lot more time out there too, she says. To cook, she had first to cut and split wood and build a fire. For water, she had to chip and haul ice from the creek and melt it on the stove. And she had to grind the grain to make the flour to make and bake the bread.

"A friend of ours said once that the men were the lucky ones be-cause they got to go out and do all the fun things, and the women had to do all the work. And, you know, that's partly true because when you had a family it seemed it broke out that way. Because the men were more likely to be the ones to go do the hunting and trap-ping and fishing, and you stayed home with the child or children," says Carolyn. If the women were cabin-bound, the whole family was river-bound. "You just can't pick up and go. It always seemed we were tied to the seasons and the river. You didn't ever want to leave during king fishing or chum fishing. And you never wanted to leave—you couldn't afford to leave—during trapping. And you certainly weren't going to leave during moose hunting season. And you *couldn't* leave at breakup or freeze-up. When you figure the windows there, there weren't that many." And then they had to find someone to feed the dogs. The upshot was a once-a-year, five-day shopping trip into Fairbanks in early June—a short span of time after breakup, but before one can quite get out on the river, and a time when the bugs are especially bad. In the fall they would get away for a short boat trip up the Yukon twenty miles to visit Jean Trainor and Larry Ricketts at the mouth of the Kandik.

Eventually, Carolyn went a bit stir-crazy. She wanted to spend more time around people. "I started missing seeing other women. Because I'd go for months, I mean for the whole winter, without seeing another woman or having another woman to talk to. I think that probably was the thing that got to me most." At the same time, Zach wanted to be around kids. In fact, a number of things were stacking up on the same side of the scale. Carolyn's mother died, and it is hard to be out of contact when something like that happens. Andrew Flats flooded during the breakup of 1982. Fourteen feet of water floated the cabin off its foundation, and it settled back down a little cockeyed. As Zach grew, the cabin shrank. Once, Zach got sick and had to be flown out. The illness cleared up, but doubts about risks and parental responsibilities remained. At this time too, the Park Service arrived. "The final straw for me, personally, was that summer the Park Service showed up," she says. "Up until the time the Park Service came down there, we saw very little river traffic. It was real quiet. And once Park Service came down, they had boats up and down the river constantly, and there was a lot of traffic and a lot of noise because they had boats and they had helicopters."

Now there were people streaking through their country, right past their doorstep, who may have left Eagle that morning after a ham-and-eggs breakfast at the cafe. Or they may be zipping back up to Eagle, contemplating a shower and TV before bed. "It suddenly seemed like a joke to me," says Carolyn, "that we were going to all this work to be down here and do things the way we were doing them, when there was all this stuff happening right there."

Carolyn had always considered herself a conservationist, had been a member of the Sierra Club, had even testified in favor of the Alaska land withdrawals leading up to the creation of such park lands as Yukon-Charley under ANILCA. But she had in mind that Alaska parks should not degrade the thing being preserved. "It always was available for public use. And the people who would come and use it were the people who had the gumption to get there and could take care of themselves," she says. She didn't want to see it "turning into a Yosemite or something," and felt that there should be some places where "somebody's got to work to get to, and want to go there, and not want to have somebody in a uniform greeting them."

If it was bad when the rangers sped by, it was worse when they stopped. "They would stop, and they wanted plans of all our cabins. And they wanted this, and they wanted that, and they wanted to issue permits for everything. And it just seemed like that wasn't why I was out there." The big question, given all of this, was should the couple invest the effort in a new cabin if they might be kicked out, or should they just move on? They moved on. To Eagle in 1984, then later to Fairbanks.

Carolyn acknowledges that she and George always knew that "at some point we would have to leave or we would want to leave." They knew they "weren't going to be in that spot forever." Still, the way their departure was hastened by the presence of the Park Service bothered her. "At the time, I was angry," Carolyn says. "And I guess I still am angry in some respects." But she treasures the experience that allowed her to grow in significant ways. "I was never a very self-confident person," she says. "My dad died when I was young, and I'd never even been camping or anything. I never had to take care of myself in the true sense of the word." It took moving back to town for Carolyn to realize how much the bush life had changed her. "I developed self-confidence. Because things happened. I got in situations where I had to take care of myself, had to take care of Zach. . . . It was so good for me," she says. "I think other people should be able to do that if they want to." She, herself, doesn't want to live out there any more. "I mean, now my life has changed." But, says Carolyn Kelly, it is important that some other young woman or man "right now, today, have the same opportunity that I had."

AT PRESENT, THE SAM CREEK CABIN tentatively has been determined to be eligible for inclusion on the National Register of Historic Places. The rough attention of whoever put on the tin roofing and an old brace on the far gable wall are probably the only reason the cabin still stands. The log ends are beginning to rot. The biggest contributor to a cabin's demise is water, and water is getting in at the ridge and where the tin doesn't lap properly. Sooner, rather than later, the cabin will go. I ask the Park Service managers what's wrong with simply putting a tarp over the roof against the day that somebody might want to save it. For twenty bucks, I tell them, you can retain for years the option to fix up the oldest structure in your park. The reply is so prolix and discursive, I honestly am at a loss to paraphrase it.

Slaven's Roadhouse, Coal Creek

You can't miss Slaven's Roadhouse at the mouth of Coal Creek. In a country nearly empty of visible buildings, a two-story structure in a clearing on a high bank looks enormous from a mile away. Only when you climb the bank to have a look do you see it is about the size of a smallish house (thirty-seven by twenty-one feet). Still, that's big by local standards. As big as Frank Slaven was little. From the old photos, he looks a rugged little Irishman, with big mitts on him and a nose that probably had been flattened a time or two by fists. Slaven had stampeded to Dawson, then moved on to Coal Creek, where he'd staked ground by 1905. Thirty years later, he sold his claims to Gold Placers, Inc., which had brought in a dredge. It is known that Slaven had a crew building the roadhouse in 1932, though that work might have been an expansion to an existing structure. Helping Slaven in 1932 were four miners from the area, including Sandy Johnson, who built the mail trail way station and Sam Creek cabin. The roadhouse is a fine example of log work. The crew cut big spruce logs on the Kandik River and floated them down to Coal Creek. They are expertly hewn to give flat wall surfaces on the interior. The milled lumber came from abandoned buildings at Fort Egbert in Eagle. The Park Service did a nice job restoring the building in the early 1990s, including a new foundation and new bottom logs to replace those that had rotted. It's now listed on the National Register of Historic Places. To my mind, it's a shining example of the good work the Park Service can do. Volunteers from the States stay here in the summer and keep track of such things as the number of floaters on the river and the number of dog-fighting Air Force jets overhead (fifty-four in a busy week the month before I arrived). And in winter, Park Service people come in and prepare the roadhouse as an unofficial checkpoint of the Yukon Quest International Sled Dog Race that runs between Whitehorse, Yukon Territory, and Fairbanks, Alaska. They stomp around the yard on snowshoes, packing the snow so the mushers have a firm parking lot where they can stake out their teams. With snowmachines, they pack down an airstrip on the frozen Yukon River so that Quest officials and the veterinarians can fly in. They chop a hole in the Yukon River ice to use as a water hole, split firewood, fill the lamps, and keep big pots of moose stew or moose chili simmering on the woodstove. I came in with them one year, and it is wonderful to see the old roadhouse lit up in lantern light and people talking about dogs around the stove, just as it ever was. When the mushers arrive, they are treated like celebrities, just as the mail carriers were. They are directed to a seat near the stove. A bowl of stew and a stack of pilot bread crackers are pressed on them. Room is made on the few nails above the stove for the musher to dry mitts and hat and parka.

Before the first dog driver arrived, I had noticed an odd lack of advantageously located nails above the woodstove, the most logical place to hang a hat or mits. Intending to be helpful, I instead set off a minor alarm by saying I was going to go look for a hammer so I could pull and reposition some of the nails. The nails, I was told, are regarded as historic and may not be moved. Nor could new ones be added. The staff laughed about the rule but said we had to observe it. They told about the time when the gravel road that runs up Coal Creek to the mining camp washed out. The obvious solution was to repair the road with some of the dredge tailings, the cobbley waste rock that covers the entire valley floor for about seven miles. But a Park Service historian said it was "historic gravel" and not to be moved. Of course, if any of the miners were still operating here, that is exactly how they would have fixed the road. I figured the nails weren't just as Frank Slaven had left them in 1939 when he moved down to the States; they were as Carolyn Kelly and Ole the Swede and any number of other people who stayed here in the 1970s had left them. But it's good to see that the Park Service cares about the old place.

Coal Creek Dredge and Camp

A mile up a little road along Coal Creek sits the dredge that operated here from 1936 to 1957. It was built in San Francisco for Gold Placers, Inc., the firm that had bought up all the claims on Coal Creek. Once built, the dredge was taken apart and shipped in pieces by steamer to Skagway in the summer of 1935. From there, the four hundred tons of steel parts were carried aboard the White Pass and Yukon Railroad to Whitehorse. Ernest Patty, who ran the mining operation at Coal Creek, said the railroad tunnels were measured and the dredge parts sized to fit through them. A sternwheeler and barge carried the materials six hundred miles downriver from Whitehorse to the mouth of Coal Creek, where they were offloaded. In October, when the ground was frozen hard, bulldozers skidded the dredge parts up the creek on sleds. (Today's prospectors have an easier time transporting in their excavation equipment within the preserve because by regulation the only digging tool allowed these days is a tablespoon.)

The assembly site for the dredge was six and a half miles up Coal Creek. During the summer, crews had been stripping off the overburden there to get down to the gold-bearing gravels. First a dozer pushed off the trees and brush and sod, then hydraulic "giants" washed away the "muck," or silty material. The muck ran to a depth of between six and twenty-six feet, and all of this material the giants washed down Coal Creek and out into the Yukon, blackening them both. The next spring, in April of 1936, a crew began putting the dredge together on the frozen surface of a pond created for that purpose. In mid-June, the two diesel engines chugged to life for trial runs, and on July 1, the bucket line began to turn and bite into pay dirt. "It was a great moment," wrote Ernest Patty, who ran the mine, "to hear the thump of the first gravel falling into the hopper."

A dredge looks something like an angular mollusk with corrugated tin siding and windows for eyes. A great radula extends out from the head of the floating building, and an excretory appendage projects from the other end. A chain of sixty-two buckets scoops gravel and tosses the stuff into a great maw. Thence it slides into a digestive organ called the trommel. It's a huge rotating steel drum, perforated with holes of graduated size. Rocks larger than these holes bounce straight through the trommel and out a conveyor belt that juts rearward (the stacker) and dumps the rock astern of the dredge. Smaller rocks and sand pass through the screen, aided by jets of water, and are sorted by size. This material drops onto sluices and is moved along by moving water, except for the gold, which is caught in riffles. The miners added mercury to the sluices where the finest material was processed because mercury binds with gold fines and makes recovery easier. The waste rock, or tailings, end up in fan-shaped windrows (linear heaps) behind the dredge—fan-shaped because the whole dredge pivoted on a massive spike at the stern called the "spud." As the bucket chain swung right, the stacker swung left. Two big diesel engines provided power. An Atlas drove a big twelve-inch main belt that moved the digging ladder and turned the trommel, and a Cat engine ran the water pumps and the belt for the stacker. Roaring and clanking, the dredge proceeded up the valley. It could process with a single revolution of the bucket chain the volume of material that nine pick-and-shovel miners could move in a day. It moved in a day the material a single miner could move in about ten years. In its first season of operation (which was only eighty days) the Coal Creek dredge produced about three thousand five hundred ounces of gold, with a 1936 value of around one hundred twenty thousand dollars (an August 2005, value of $1,529,500). By the time Gold Placers, Inc., shut down its operations here, they had taken more than three million dollars out of the creek.

Today the Park Service embraces the mine as an important record of capital-intensive mining, to date directing at least a million dollars (local people say "millions") to restoration and interpretation of the dredge and camp. The agency flew in a restoration carpenter for four months to redo all the windows and doors on the dredge, including fabricating mullions to match the old style. They spent another eight hundred thousand dollars cleaning up the miners' mess (though it is not clear which of several mining companies left it). Before the cleanup work began, I remember seeing a display at the dredge offering colorful anecdotes about the heyday of its operations. But nothing at the site, except the still-remaining junk piles of twisted scrap metal and the rusting drums leaching God-knows-what fluids into the shallow water table, suggested the extreme irony of a parks agency celebrating a machine that ate its way through this pretty little creek valley excreting uniform rows of barren rock. Meanwhile, the same managers pointedly overlooked the historical worth of folks like Dave Evans, whose developments were, as McPhee noted, essentially biodegradable. During the environmental remediation, crews here removed mercury, blasting caps, dynamite, pesticides, acids, spilled petroleum products, and of course a scattering of fifty-five-gallon drums. Recent interpretive work includes a book by a Park Service historian that gives a lot of wonderful details about the old prospectors who lived in the area. It's called *The World Turned Upside Down: A History of Mining on Coal Creek and Woodchopper Creek, Yukon-Charley Rivers National Preserve, Alaska*. It is so detailed that it contains tables listing the employment dates of every employee. There's room even for a page on the camp cat (Bozo, who, we are told, used to leap onto the backs of wolves and ride them around the camp). But the book does not budget so much as a paragraph to mention pollution so extensive that it cost eight hundred thousand dollars to remediate.

The book stops where the Patty family's involvement with the two creeks ends. The final passage in the body of the text features a quote from Ernest Patty's son, Dale, who was the last superintendent at the mine. He says that when his company shut down the dredges on Coal Creek in 1957 and at Woodchopper Creek next door in 1960, that that was "the last time the dredges have ever run to the best of my knowledge." As the Park Service knows, however, after Gold Placers, Inc., closed up shop, others took over and ran the dredge. Ted Matthews ran the operation in the early 1960s, followed by Ernest Wolfe and Dan Colben from Fairbanks. It's too bad the Park Service excludes from history the events of the 1960s, because interesting things were happening. For example, to get the dredge running again, Wolfe and Colben brought in a few aging miners who had worked on dredges decades earlier, including Joe Bayless from Circle. With wrenches and torches, the resourceful old-timers performed CPR on the dormant behemoth until it sputtered to life. Some local new-timers, like Charlie Kidd and Ole Beckloff, worked on the dredge too, as did Richard Smith from down near Eureka Creek. Kidd says that Bayless knew just how much coaxing the old dredge could take. He'd nurse her along, running at one-third power, unless he got an order to speed up from one of the bosses. "[A boss] would get on the dredge [and say], 'Bayless, you can run more dirt than that.' Every time he did, everything just slowed down and stopped." Wolfe and Colben sold out to AU Placer, a Texas outfit that had the dredge running in 1977. It's hard to tell if these enterprises produced much gold, or just how long the dredge ran, because this part of the history is not included in Park Service interpretive work.

The camp itself is about four miles up from the mouth of Coal Creek. There are twenty-six buildings there, including a mess hall, bunkhouses, a bathhouse, and a machine shop. Of the million or so dollars spent by the Park Service on the Coal Creek mining operations, much of it has gone to rehabilitate the buildings and to map, describe, and photograph the industrial leavings. The camp and the dredge area is now a designated National Historic Mining District. Today the Park Service maintains the air strip and camp as an "administrative site," a place where agency personnel and VIPs can gather for overnight retreats and various functions. In large part because of this use, the camp is one of the few sites in the whole preserve that is assigned the highest level of fire protection: "critical."

Woodchopper Roadhouse

Six miles below Coal Creek, on the same side of the Yukon, a companion creek called Woodchopper slices through the same gold-bearing formation. The pair of creeks parallel each other, hooking from the northwest to the southwest, as if God had used two fingers to scratch quotation marks in the sand. By 1917, a fellow known as Woodchopper Smith had built a large, two-story roadhouse here with the help of Fred Brentlinger. After World War I, Smith sold out to Brentlinger and bought an orange grove in California. When Brentlinger died, his widow, Flora, sold it to Jack Welch and his wife Kate. According to Ernest Patty, the Welches were old and rheumatic by the early 1940s when the ice jammed one spring right here in Woodchopper Canyon. The Yukon backed up and rose over the banks, and the Welches awoke in their second-story bedroom to the sound of massive ice cakes banging dangerously against the walls. Jack stood at the window with a pike pole deflecting some of the oncoming icebergs that were swirling around the cabin in the dark. The terrifying night left Jack mentally unbalanced thereafter, and his wife became bedridden. Perhaps it was the next winter that Jack became seriously delusional and one night told his wife that he knew what was wrong: he was losing his mind. He got out of bed, went outside, and shot himself. Kate Welch managed to get her wounded husband into bed, then, supported by two canes, she staggered a couple miles up the winter trail to George McGregor's cabin. McGregor loaded both the old people into his dogsled and hauled them up to Coal Creek, where the watchman radioed for an airplane from Fairbanks. The ordeal proved to be Kate's undoing. As Jack recovered, she passed away. Patty tells of Jack wandering up to the mining camp and asking, "Have you seen my wife? I can't find her. She's hiding from me." The men tried, gently, to explain, but Jack could not accept that his old companion was gone forever. The next day Jack and his boat disappeared. According to Patty, reports filtered back to the camp from villages far downriver of a man alone in a boat, drifting all the way down the Yukon and into Bering Sea.

The Woodchopper Roadhouse was salvageable when Melody Webb surveyed it for the Park Service in 1976. As the largest structure in the preserve to still have its roof on, she recommended it be "restored if a lodge is ever needed for the park. A National Register would give added protection." But by 2003, the roadhouse lay "in ruins, the roof caved and the upper story fallen in," according to a Park Service pamphlet.

Woodchopper Creek/Joe Vogler

After their initial success on Coal Creek, Ernest Patty's company bought out the small-scale miners on Woodchopper Creek and set up another dredge here. In his book, *North Country Challenge*, Patty recalls an old-timer named Frank Bennett who had come into the country around 1890 and had mined on the Fortymile before the Klondike discovery. He had already been on Woodchopper Creek for twenty years before Patty optioned his ground in the 1930s. Bennett was youthful looking, with bright blue eyes, white hair, and cheeks "pink as a baby's." The cabin was spick-and-span, with gingham curtains on the cupboards, a polished cook stove and a scrubbed floor. He was a kindly man, dignified and cultivated, according to Patty. He spoke well and had a shelf of quality books, including poetry. Eventually, Patty's crew finished their test holes on Bennett's claims, exercised their option, and bought the ground. Workers began stripping off the overburden with hydraulic giants, but Bennett kept finding reasons to forestall moving out of his cabin and into another one the dredge crew had set up for him. Pretty soon the giants had washed away all the ground except Bennett's cabin site, which now stood alone on a little "mesa-like island" above the gravels. When Patty finally got him to climb aboard a truck with his belongings, a bulldozer standing by, Bennett said, "Please don't knock it down until I get out of sight." In a little while, even the spot where it used to be ceased to exist. Frank Bennett lived out his life on Woodchopper Creek, and when he died, no one knew if he had any family to contact. He hadn't spoken about his past, left no papers, no letters, "not so much as a faded snapshot," writes Patty.

BY THE 1970s, the most visible claim holder at Woodchopper Creek was a Fairbanks character named Joe Vogler, who had bought the Woodchopper dredge and some acreage from Patty's company. Maybe "most audible" would be the better phrase. Vogler's mouth produced fiery salvoes at about the rate of a Roman candle. He could work himself into a great froth over the environmentalists, or "posy sniffers," as he called them. And when he finally tangled head-on with the Park Service in the 1980s, it was a battle royal. Frank Bennett and Joe Vogler were both Woodchopper miners—in the same way that Mother Theresa and Jessie Ventura were both cultural figures.

Joseph E. Vogler was born April 24, 1913, in Barnes, Kansas. He must have been a precocious child, as he entered the University of Kansas at sixteen, and emerged five years later with a law degree. He passed the Kansas bar, but the Depression came along and limited Joe's chances of practicing law. It seems like he became a bitter old man while still in his twenties. He famously told McPhee he was fired from one job for calling President Roosevelt "a dirty rotten son of a bitch Communist traitor." Vogler moved to Alaska in 1942 to work construction on military bases, but his wife did not like the country even a little and left with the two kids. Joe diddled at mining here on Woodchopper Creek, but it seems to have been more a hobby interest. One local person told me, "Oh, he really didn't do a whole lot. He couldn't really get it together himself. Messed around a little bit." Maybe he valued more the job title "gold miner" than he did the actual job of producing gold. Joe made his money subdividing his land in Fairbanks. He was well known for the covenant he insisted every buyer accept: a legally binding promise to cut down every aspen tree on the property. Joe considered them "arboreal weeds" and had no problem suing eight of his new neighbors to see that they obeyed the covenant.

JOE LOVED TO MINE, he just didn't do all that much of it. On the other hand, he "detested" politics, he said, but did a lot of it. "A couple of us got a belly full one Sunday afternoon in the spring of 1973 up in my shop," Joe said in a videotaped talk at the University of Alaska, Fairbanks. "We started the Alaska Independence movement." He drafted a petition asking for a vote of the people on whether or not Alaskans wanted to remain in the union. His own view was clear enough: "I'm an Alaskan, not an American. I've got no use for America and her damned institutions." Anger became something of a trademark for Joe and he built upon it in his first run for governor, as an independent, in 1974. That year's election was decided by two-hundred-odd votes, while the renegade Vogler pulled in four thousand seven hundred and seventy. His five percent of the vote determined the outcome. Four years later, from the nucleus of a lunch group that called itself the "Cuss and Discuss Club," Joe founded Alaskans for Independence, a nonpartisan organization devoted to pressing the issue of an "Independent Nation of Alaska." The same year, 1978, Vogler and pals launched the Alaska Independence Party (AIP), and he ran for lieutenant governor under its banner. Next election cycle, 1982, Vogler was back at the top of the AIP ticket. I remember hearing him in debate with the major party candidates at the fairgrounds in Fairbanks. Although his voice was loud, it squeezed through a constricted throat until it came out high-pitched and thin. But Joe was a gifted orator. He was a flinty-eyed hellion with a hard mouth, and he didn't use weasel words. The Fairbanks crowd loved him. Vogler did well enough—after a court challenge of the state's rules—to earn the AIP official recognition as Alaska's third political party. The Alaska Independence Party would be printed on future ballots alongside the Democratic and Republican Parties. As the AIP gubernatorial candidate in 1986, Joe pulled in more than ten thousand votes statewide, or 5.6 percent of the vote, including nearly twenty percent in feisty Fairbanks. The

Republican candidate lost to the Democrat by about seven thousand votes, so it looked like Joe was the kingmaker again. All this set the stage for the election of 1990, when the Alaska Independence Party candidate didn't just influence the governor's race but stole it.

It was a brilliant switcharoo. With Joe declining to be nominated again, the AIP put up a dubious but eminently available character named John Lindauer. Seven weeks before the election, Lindauer and his running mate dropped out of the race, implausibly citing Lindauer's wife's illness. Joe Vogler, as chairman of the AIP, promptly announced that two long-time (not to say old) Republicans were the new candidates: Walter Hickel in the top spot, and Jack Coghill riding shotgun. Hickel had served half a term as governor of Alaska in the 1960s, before leaving to become President Nixon's secretary of the interior. After that early prominence, Wally had spent millions of his own money (made as a shopping mall developer) in repeated and failed attempts to recapture the governor's mansion (1974, 1978, and 1986). Coghill, to make matters really interesting, accepted the AIP lieutenant governor nomination even though he had just won the Republican primary for the same job and was on the Republican ticket. Hickel and Coghill switched parties and filed their candidacy papers minutes before the deadline, leaving the Republican gubernatorial nominee that long to find a replacement for Backstabbing Jack.

So, two lifelong Republicans had just trashed their Republican allies and split the vote in order to join the one percent of registered voters who thought Alaska should be an independent nation. For the Democrat, it looked like a cakewalk. But Hickel put his fortune behind the campaign, and his ads had a polished look. There wasn't much time for him to produce detailed position papers, let alone for anyone to analyze them. On election day, it wasn't the Republican vote that got split, it was the sanity vote. With 38.9 percent, Hickel-Coghill won. Joe Vogler had just pulled off an astonishing coup. Only six times in U.S. history had a third-party candidate won a governor's race. And *this* third party was advocating secession from the United States.

During his single term, Wally Hickel was not particularly interested in secession, and some AIP members were miffed at the way he had rented the party. They and others launched a recall initiative, charging Hickel was mentally unfit. Vogler thought the interference showed every sign of being the work of the "damned, dirty, filthy hands" of the CIA. With Joe Vogler's help, Hickel served out his term and, in fact, proved to be a moderating force in Alaska politics. Hickel managed to hold in check a Republican-controlled legislature that was, believe it or not, more radical still.

IF JOE VOGLER WAS CRANKY with mainstream Republicans and renegade secessionists, he was notably crankier with people he didn't like, for instance representatives of the National Park Service. One day in the summer of 1984, Joe was driving some equipment over an old trail from the Steese Highway to his claims on Woodchopper Creek. He had a Caterpillar tractor and a monstrous wheeled vehicle with six-foot-tall rubber tires. Just as he was crossing some boggy ground around Webber Creek a black helicopter swooped down on him, and six armed federal agents leapt out to cut him off. It was either Joe's worst nightmare or a supreme validation of all that he suspected was true. He was on Park Service land, the agents told him. He didn't have a permit to walk a Cat across boggy ground in summertime, they said, and his equipment wasn't going any farther. Walter Roman, who carried the mail by dogsled from 1934 to 1940, has said the government cut that trail for the mail carriers in 1900. Vogler knew that even backcountry trails could fall within the definition of "highway" under an 1866 law called RS 2477. "That's a public highway," he said. "I don't have to get a permit to get out here on the public highway." The law was repealed in 1976, but "highway rights of way already established may still be valid," said Vogler, the nonpracticing lawyer.

The Park Service pointed out that when people drive bulldozers across tundra trails in the summer, they destroy the plant cover that insulates the permafrost below. That causes the permafrost to melt and turns the trail into something like a canal of chocolate pudding. The next driver through avoids the muck and drives his Cat alongside the earlier track, making a new mud rut. The Park Service was finding trails sixteen, seventeen, even eighteen tracks wide. The scars can take generations to heal. Or erosion can accelerate thawing and carve canyons or turn the whole area into a quagmire. That's why the Park Service asks people to use *winter* trails in the *winter*time. Then the ground is frozen hard and the snow protects the plants. A permit ensures that it happens. Reasonable people can see that. "Well, I'll tell you one thing," said Joe to all that. "That Cat will either move out of here without any permits, without any red tape, or it'll set here and rust into the ground."

By the time Joe was being interviewed on the subject for an Alaska public television documentary called *Battle at Webber Creek*, it was winter. The ground was now frozen, snow-covered. Dave Mahalic, then superintendent of Yukon-Charley preserve, said, "You know, if Mr. Vogler came in here this morning and asked me for a permit, he could be driving that Cat to his mine this afternoon." To which Joe replied, "They can go straight to hell! And hell will be frozen over before I'll do that! There's no compromise!" Amplifying, he said, "I don't know the word 'compromise,' because I'm right, they're wrong." It was a fight Joe was ready to carry on to his last breath. And beyond. "If I'm wrong in my belief that the federal government cannot retain sovereignty here, my bones won't rot under the American flag! I'll tell you, I'm going to Whitehorse. I'm going to buy a burial plot. And if I do not win this lawsuit lock, stock, and barrel, if I'm wrong in my concept of what America meant when it started out, I don't want to lie under their flag."

With a phalanx of government and environmental lawyers arrayed against him, Joe fought the case all the way to the Ninth U.S. Circuit Court of Appeals, losing all the way. He appealed to the U.S. Supreme Court, but that body refused to review it. He said he was "going to take it to the bitter end." As things turned out, Joe's bitter end came not from the federal government but from a firebrand like himself.

IN MID-APRIL 1993, Joe Vogler turned eighty, and friends gathered for a big birthday party. That was the last time most of his friends saw him. Two weeks later, sometime over the Memorial Day weekend, he disappeared. A friend found his four dogs locked in Joe's large log home. His wallet and heart medicine were on the table, but his trademark fedora was gone, as was his "belly gun," a .32 caliber handgun he liked to carry. Things didn't look right, especially to Joe's inner circle. They thought that the government had reason enough, and was sinister enough, to murder Joe. The authorities declined to investigate the disappearance as a crime, which only added to the growing outrage and suspicion. The troopers suggested Joe had gone for a walk and gotten lost. After all, they pointed out, he was eighty. Or maybe he was despondent over his wife Doris's death from cancer a year earlier, they said. Or maybe he'd gone over to Dawson City to visit her grave. But he might have his vehicles were in the driveway, and Air North had no record of him boarding a flight to Dawson. Besides, he would have arranged for the care of his dogs. And, eighty or no, Joe Vogler had all his marbles. (Well, he had all the marbles he'd ever had.) The Alaska state troopers said they could find no evidence of foul play. Only after "five days of mass call-ins to the governor's office," as an AIP account says, was a specialist finally assigned to examine the house.

The house was clean as a whistle. No leads. The search for Joe Vogler continued through that summer and into the winter. Alaska Independence Party members raised money to fund their own search and hired a private investigator. The group had posters printed asking "Where's Joe?" It featured a mug shot of Himself, hard eyes staring from under the brim of his fedora, looking far more like a crime perpetrator than a crime victim. The signs were everywhere in Fairbanks, even stapled to stakes and jammed in the snow. But no trace of Joe turned up.

IN THE SPRING OF 1993, thirty-eight-year-old Manfried "Fred" West was living (at the insistence of the courts) in a residential alcohol treatment center in Fairbanks. He had violated probation on an earlier burglary conviction and presently faced sentencing for passing seventeen bad checks drawn on the bank account of his son's grandmother. For the moment, said the court, Fred's options were two: treatment or jail. Eventually, he was kicked out of the treatment center for a breach of the rules. It wasn't a lockdown facility, and he was simply told to pack up his stuff and go. Out of treatment, West had to go back to jail. He says he called the jail to arrange serving his time but was told to call back the next day. Eight days later, troopers learned that he was hiding out in his stepbrother's cabin on the outskirts of town. By now the troopers wanted to talk to him for more than serving his time for parole violations. They had reason to believe Fred knew something about the Vogler disappearance. On May 27, 1993, shortly after 7:00 P.M., they surrounded the hideout cabin and called in a helicopter. Using a cell phone, trooper Jim McCann phoned West in the house and tried to get him to surrender. West told McCann that he was armed and had dynamite in the cabin. He threatened to blow the place up. But he alternated between threatening violence and discussing favorable terms of surrender. One of the things he dangled in front of McCann was a story of how he had shot and killed Joe Vogler. The call lasted more than three hours, and an on-the-ball news photographer named Genezaret Barron caught the exchange on a radio scanner:

West: Let's talk about what me and Joe talked about the first time we met. I was supposed to get some plastic C–4 . . . but I didn't know where it was. I had no idea where it was. I told him I'd bring it up to him the next night. I didn't have it when I went up there, and that's what started the whole thing. Hell, I was "a no-good son of a bitch." I was not a man of my word.

McCann: What's this got to do with it?

West: Well, I'm getting to the story. There's more to the story than just a robbery. You want to hear what happened, or not?

McCann: Yeah, yeah.

West: So, I go back and try to do the best I can . . . to get the whole fucking situation straightened out. He gets mad. I've got the fucking C–4. I get out and go to open the back of the truck. He gets all pissed off, fires a shot, apparently up in the air, and says, "I told you to get the fuck out of here, and the next one, I'm blowing your head off." I remember the words almost exactly the way he said them. You can believe me or not.

McCann: I believe it.

West: So, I get in the truck, and he says something about, "For further reference," and then he shot the truck. I thought I was shot. I really did. But I wasn't. But I thought I was. And it pissed me off. I grabbed my little brat .22 that I stole from a house. . . .

And anyways, I shot it [*sic*] with a .22. He apparently only had two shots in his gun. I don't really recall what was going on. All I know is that he turned once. He looked like he was getting ready to reload, and I pulled out the .22, aimed at him, fired, missed, fired again, and he turned around and ran for the house. And I hit him again. . . .

McCann: Where'd you bury him? Or do you even know?

West: Well, I know.

McCann: We're all going there?

West: I put him in a tarp and I dug a hole about three feet deep . . . I laid enough stuff on him, wrapped him up in a tarp, duct-taped it together numerous times so it could stop the swelling. . . .

McCann: Where is he? Where is he, Fred?

West: It's all over, bud . . . this place is gonna blow . . . the best you could do . . . is get the hell out of here . . . the dynamite is in the living room, [garbled] and dynamite toward the back of the garage is going to blow when it hits the fuses.

McCann: You gonna take this with you, huh? You gonna take this with you? That's not the way to do it, Freddie. That's the coward . . . [Explosion].

The troopers heard a blast and saw smoke billowing, then flames burst out of the windows. In a few minutes, the whole cabin was engulfed in smoke and flames. A propane tank exploded. Ammunition began to go off like popcorn. Firefighters responded but had to stand by, only moving in after the roof collapsed. The cabin burned almost to the ground, with all of West's stepbrother's possessions in it. After firefighters put out the flames, the troopers moved in to search for the body. When they found it under a toppled concrete block wall, they thought he was dead. But his hands were shaking. The firefighters had been pumping frigid water on the building. In the midst of an inferno, the hapless arsonist was nearly hypothermic.

THE CONFESSED KILLER was in jail, but for Joe's friends in the Alaska Independence Party that explanation was too simple. "Joe wouldn't have done business with [West]," Lynette Clark, the AIP secretary, told the Fairbanks newspaper. "If Joe wanted dynamite, he knows reputable members in the blasting community." It was a good point. Joe would have only been inclined to deal with *reputable* government-hating, secessionist dynamiters. (Still, the reference to a Fairbanks "blasting community" leaves me uneasy.) For Clark, it was more likely that Joe was the target of an assassination by a government hit man. "I don't think it's far fetched at all to think that the government would want to eliminate Joe Vogler," she said.

ONCE A WEEK for seventeen months, volunteers with sniffer dogs had looked for Joe in ten different locations (the same dogs had looked for Dick Cook). On October 12, 1994, a couple of inches of snow were on the ground, mixed in with recently fallen leaves, and searchers were looking at yet another site. But, there was a strong sense of anticipation this day at a gravel pit off twenty-five mile Chena Hot Springs Road, about thirty miles from Fairbanks. The spot had been suggested by a jailhouse snitch. Five hundred yards north of the road, down a little track into a lightly wooded area, in a depression that had been scraped with a dozer some years earlier, a Bouvier named Maya stopped and pointed. Tanna, a golden retriever, joined Maya and began to dig frantically. Two troopers began the excavation with shovels. As they did so, Trooper Jim McCann was saying to himself, "Give me some tarp—blue tarp and duct tape—and I'll know he's there."

Three and a half feet down, the tarp began to show. The body was wrapped up and sealed with duct tape. The seventeen-month-long search was over, as dental records and fingerprints later confirmed. In the matter of his burial, Joe had been wrong about one thing and right about another. Wrong in that he *was* buried under the American flag. Right in that his bones would not rest peacefully there. For Trooper McCann, the tarp meant the case was solved and that he already had the murderer in jail. "I don't see any other plot than the simple one," McCann said. "People don't want to hear that."

A blue tarp and duct tape. Archetypal implements of Alaskan culture. Joe, the Alaskan patriot, was wrapped in a kind of unofficial Alaska flag, buried in a gravel mine. Maybe this quintessentially Alaskan paraphernalia inoculated Joe from the objectionable influences of American dominion, like a necklace of garlic warding off vampires. But soon, according to his wish, he was buried next to his wife Doris in Dawson City, Yukon Territory, Canada. The grave is regularly visited and tended by Joe's admirers. Several Alaskan flags flutter inside the white picket fence, like a little stockade of Alaskan nationalism amid all the Canadians. Inside it is a block of granite, looking hard, immovable.

DRIFTING BELOW WOODCHOPPER, I think about the small-scale miners like Frank Bennett, the industrial-scale miners like Ernest Patty, and the intensely dedicated but somehow not quite real miners like Joe Vogler. I have no unified theory. The idea of taking wealth out of the ground, from the earth directly to your pocket, without a lot of intermediary fuss, is appealing. There is freedom in that. I can understand it. But there is a real environmental cost too. Ken Ross gets at it in *Environmental Conflict in Alaska*: "A placer operation typically disrupted a valley by changing the landforms, altering surface and groundwater flows, removing streamside vegetation and topsoil, silting fish habitat, reducing natural food supplies, and rendering the floodplain nonfunctional. Impacts could be lasting, and 'many, if not most, miners and regulators believed that once a stream was disturbed, it could not be reclaimed to a stable state.'" Maybe we should pay that cost, if the result is important enough.

To me it's reminiscent of the plot line of the film *The Misfits,* based on a screenplay by Arthur Miller. Nevada cowboys had been rounding up wild mustangs for generations, productively breeding the wild stock into the quarterhorse. And the tradition of the roundup was important social glue. It kept people connected with the land and preserved certain skills. But now (the 1950s) the techniques had changed. Instead of horses, the cowboys started mounting aircraft and pickup trucks to herd the mustangs. More than that, the purpose of the enterprise had changed. Quarterhorses weren't in great demand on ranches any more. The mustangs were still chased, corralled, and transported. But they were not taken to ranches for breeding, they were trucked to factories to be ground into dog food. Maybe it was time, Miller seemed to say, for Nevada outdoorsmen to connect with the land in some other way.

Gold is put to important uses, for example in electronics. But this use accounts for only about seven percent of gold production. Use in dentistry is three percent. Add up all industrial applications, and you have a use for twelve to fifteen percent of the gold we mine. Eighty-five percent of gold mined in the United States is used for jewelry and ornamentation, and the number-one retailer of jewelry is Wal-Mart. The Worldwatch Institute calculates a single ring (.33 ounce, eighteen karat) leaves behind eighteen tons of mine waste. As student activists across the country have suggested, maybe we don't need to turn creek valleys upside down in Alaska for school rings. Maybe, they say, we should make class rings out of something else, like recycled metals. And maybe, like the Nevada cowboys, Alaska gold miners should throw the dozer into neutral for a minute and think about just exactly what this endeavor has morphed into in the modern era.

WHEREFORE TRAPPING, in light of all this? Brad Snow told John McPhee he wouldn't kill wild animals just "to clothe fat whores in New York." Others have reached the same conclusion. Of course, fur can be made into more than fashion apparel. Marten hats, beaver mitts, and wolverine ruffs are still unsurpassed as winter wear in this part of North America. But there aren't too many people walking around Fairbanks in lynx clothing, for example. And I know trappers who have sold lynx pelts for as little as thirty-five dollars. It ought to give a person pause to take such an animal out of the wild for thirty-five bucks. But here's the flip side, the part that makes this screenplay complex. Trapping is one of the few sources of cash for rural subsistence people. In other words, it is very important. And in the villages of bush Alaska, trapping's demise cancels one of the reasons to maintain a dog team. In turn, eliminating a dog team takes away one reason to run a fishwheel. If you aren't fishing, there isn't much of a need to own a boat. And as village life ceases to revolve around these vigorous outdoor activities, it will more and more settle on the four prongs of a cultural pitchfork: welfare, TV, junk food, and alcohol.

I HAVE FRIENDS who can retain for years precise recollections of the taste of a particular bottle of wine. My brother-in-law can whistle a melody he heard once six months before. I cannot hold these things in my mind. But I do store away, like a tray of special slides, scenes from trips along this river. I can put myself back in those scenes and sit again by the fire and feel the breeze. I can watch as the most amazing colors light up the world, including, somehow, the inside of me. I am a lone person among billions. On a world among billions. And, for a brief moment, I am aware of it.

The sun is sliding into the north now, and the sky glows with gold. A little breeze makes the river sparkle with white light, flashing like a handful of diamonds scattered across the water. I am a miner too, I'm thinking. This is what I mine.

Eureka Creek/The Other Fortymile

On the right bank, forty miles above Circle, beneath a handsome bluff, is Richard Smith's cabin. I remember the time I stopped in to meet him, and he told me his bear story. After hearing it, I was glad that I was within striking distance of Circle. For the previous ten days I had been camping on gravel bars along the Yukon, but as Richard says, "After you hear a story like that, you don't want to camp on the river for a couple of nights."

Richard came into the country as a ten-year-old in 1968 when his mother and stepfather, Ray and Arlene Bell, converted a school bus to a motor home and drove with their five boys from Grand Rapids, Michigan, to Alaska. Five miles out of Central, on the way to Circle, they pulled the bus off the road to spend the night. In the morning they found that the bus was stuck, so Ray set out for Fairbanks, where he filed for a homestead on the land surrounding the vehicle. The bus stayed put, while the family cut logs right on the property and built a twenty-two-by-twenty-four-foot cabin. About half the five hundred twenty-eight square feet was devoted to kitchen-dining-living room. Of the remaining space, about half was partitioned off as master bed-room, and half accommodated the five boys.

The family had been living on the homestead for three years when Richard's stepfather took a notion to spend a year in the woods. He was friendly with Gordon Bertoson, a bachelor sourdough, who had trapped and fished at this place, known locally as Fortymile (not to be confused with the town of Forty Mile, one hundred sixty-five miles up-river in Canada). Bertoson had occupied the site since 1960, but he was getting pretty old for the heavy work of living in the woods. Once, he hurt his back while working on his fishwheel and lay in his bed for two weeks before a friend from Fairbanks visited. Then in 1971, around breakup, the time when the river ice begins to move, Bertoson's cabin mysteriously burned down while he was away in Circle. "I'm all done with it now," said Bertoson, according to Ray Bell. The old trap-per allowed Bell to take over the site, together with the trapline trails and the fishwheel spot, which was just upstream of the cabin. Richard, then thirteen, and his brothers helped their stepfather build an eighteen-by-twenty-foot, one-room cabin at the site. It was ready by fall, and the family moved upriver.

Richard's family fixed up the cabin and filled their days with chores. They hauled water from a nearby creek in summer and from the Yukon in the winter, when it runs clear. They cut firewood from driftwood piles on the islands in the Yukon. Ray and the boys learned to trap and skin fur. They cut, hung, or canned salmon in the summer and tended a huge vegetable garden. In the fall, they hunted and put up meat. Arlene taught her kids from correspondence materials. When Richard was seventeen, his parents moved upriver to work for wages at mining claims, first at Woodchopper, then at Coal Creek. Richard kept the place at Fortymile, though sometimes he'd work a summer "running Cat" at the mines.

One day in the summer of 1979, Faye Chamberlain, a pretty, dark-haired young woman from Canada, floated down the river and into Richard's life. Faye was twenty-two and had been in the Dawson area for a few years, living out of town in a cabin. In the summers, she worked for wages bartending and at mining camps. She had dabbled a bit at trapping and was keen to get her own trapline. The local conservation officer, however, seemed hostile to the young people moving into the country wanting to trap, especially to the idea of a woman trapping. She heard that things were less regulated in Alaska, and one summer day she packed up her canoe to see what opportunity might await downriver, across the border. At the last minute, a girlfriend decided to join her. It was a great vacation as they visited with people along the river. When they stopped in for a while at Glenn Creek, Faye remembers, all the river people were totally naked. "My girlfriend and I took off our tops, but that's all we felt comfortable with." Downriver at Fortymile Bluff, they saw smoke coming out of a smokehouse and pulled the canoe over to see who lived there. When they crested the bank, they saw, standing on the porch on either side of the door, two long-haired, rugged young men, Richard Smith and Charlie Kidd. Kidd was wearing a bear hide vest and a marten-fur headband. Both were holding jars of homebrew, and marijuana plants were all around (it was legal to grow pot in Alaska in those days). If a cartoonist had drawn the encounter, he would have all four bug-eyed and sharing the same thought balloon: "Oh, my *God*! I must be in heaven." "We ended up spending three days," says Faye, "playing crib—nothing serious." But she and Richard spent hours talking beside the campfire about life in the bush and how much they both liked it. She told him about how much more regulated Yukon Territory was becoming, that she wanted a trapline and to mush dogs. He understood. "And towards the end of our visit, that's when he invited me down to trap for the winter. As I left, I told him there was a fifty-fifty chance that I'd show up in the fall."

Faye and her girlfriend continued on down to Circle and back to Dawson. In September, Faye made up her mind. Into her leaky canoe she packed her wall tent, rifles, miscellaneous gear, garden gleanings, and a sack of salmon strips. Alone, she paddled two hundred sixteen miles downriver to Richard Smith's cabin at Eureka Creek. They hit it off well, trapping in the winter and fishing in the summer. They would run the traplines together, with Richard letting Faye take his three-dog team, while he walked. Later, she had her own team of three big dogs. In places, they had branch lines, and each would take a branch, covering those separately. They stayed together for five years, and when they split up, Faye moved on to her own trapline. One day, she remembers, she joined a few of the boys who were gathered out in back of the Carrolls' place in Circle, drinking beer and talking trapping in a little shack among the derelict vehicles. "How many marten you catch?" said one guy to another. It was November, still early in the season.

"Oh, five, I guess. How about you?"

"I got fifteen." And so on around the group, fifteen being tops. Finally, someone asked Faye, jokingly, how she was doing.

"Twenty-five," she said, quietly.

"Five?" someone asked.

"Twenty-five," she said again. And the whole group burst out laughing at being shown up. Guys were rolling on the floor, she says, but they were also probably calculating their chances of connecting, or reconnecting, with the hottest trapper in the country.

IN AUGUST 1981, when Richard and Faye had been together for a couple of years, they took a boat trip upriver to Dawson to visit friends. On the way back, twenty or so miles below Dawson, they saw at the water's edge a sow grizzly bear and three good-sized cubs. Grizzlies are larger than the more common black bears, and they can be aggressive. A traveler might not even mention having seen a black bear, but spotting four grizzlies is always a notable occurrence. Richard, who had seen a lot of bears over the years, decided the cubs were bigger than any black bear he had ever seen, and that the sow was the biggest grizzly he had ever seen. The cubs ran up the bank, but the towering sow stood up. "She stood there," says Richard, "and gave me a look in the eye that I've never seen from anything. Like, 'I'll remember you. I'm going to get you.' It was that kind of look, you know."

A mile downriver, Richard and Faye stopped to spend the night with some friends at their fish camp at the mouth of Fifteenmile River. There were two couples there, each with two kids, and a big dog. Richard mentioned seeing the bears. Their friends said, yes, they had seen some bears in the area. No one said much more about it, and after a bit of visiting, everyone got ready for bed. There were two canvas wall tents housing the families, with a picnic table in between. Richard and Faye, traveling light, had no tent and only one sleeping bag, which they threw out near the picnic table. Everyone fell asleep.

About 1:00 or 2:00 in the morning, the dog began to bark, says Richard, piecing the story together from everyone's account. Faye sat up, "And right there's that grizzly bear. The sow. And it only took"— he snapped his fingers—"like that. I mean Faye tried to turn over on her stomach, you know, hide her face, but before she could do that, that bear jumped around that picnic table and got her by the head. Drug her out of her sleeping bag."

Perhaps because he grew up with six other people in a one-room cabin, Richard has developed the ability to sleep through a fair bit of commotion. While the bear continued to attack Faye, Richard continued to sleep. One of the women, however, heard the ruckus and woke up her man, who opened the tent flap. The bear at once dropped Faye and charged the tent, says Richard. "He's standing there and sees this thing come charging at him and the only thing he can do is close the tent flaps and pray to God that thing didn't get him." With one swipe, the rampaging bear brought down the wall tent, then clamped her jaws on the man's leg and "shook him like a rag doll." There was only one gun in the camp; it was in the other tent, in the custody of the third man, who happened to be another deep sleeper.

Richard finally awoke, but he was disoriented. "When I woke up I was standing up. And I had this really weird feeling, like doomsday, you know. I didn't know what was happening yet, and I look down and I see Faye laying there, just all chewed up and blood everywhere. And my back was to Zeke and the bear. Zeke was the guy getting mauled at the moment. Well, when I stood up the bear saw me and dropped Zeke and came over and stood up behind me." As Richard turned, he became fully awake. He knew he couldn't run. Playing dead was no option. "So I start slugging it . . . I was yelling at it, you know. I was freaked out, you know . . . it let me hit it a few times." Then the bear gave a swat that Richard reenacts as an effortless forehand, as if shooing a fly. "I was airborne. Just flying." As soon as he hit the ground, the bear was on top of him. "Its teeth kind of raked across my skull, split it, tore it wide open, tore my scalp off. Started chewing me up and down the back."

Zeke got up, hoping to crawl under the fallen tent, but now the bear saw him and dropped Richard. Zeke ran once around the picnic table with the bear on his heels, then dove under it. The bear kept running. Straight back to Richard. Meanwhile people were beginning to shout and scream, and the dog was going berserk. The grizzly stopped for Richard, clamping her enormous jaws around his midriff, stopped again for Faye, gathering her up under one arm, and ran off into the woods with both of them.

All of this took just a minute or two, Richard thinks.

About thirty feet down the trail out of camp, the bear dropped or lost her grip on Faye. She fell into the bushes, but the bear continued on with Richard in its mouth. The trail led to a deadfall tree, and as the bear sailed over it, Richard remembers having a clear vision of his fate. "Well, when she jumped, I'm hanging there and I'm seeing what's all going on, you know. I'm going, 'God, this thing's taking me out to its cubs!'"

But the deadfall saved his life, he thinks. "She probably figured she couldn't make it over with me in her mouth. As we're sailing through the air, she dropped me right on top of it and kept sailing over it."

It took a couple hours for the badly injured friends to reach Dawson by riverboat. There was no hospital there, no doctor. The little nursing station was unable to do much of anything for them, other than to call for a chartered plane from Whitehorse, the territorial capital, two hundred seventy miles away. It was ten hours from the mauling to the time they were on the operating table in Whitehorse. "I don't know how you guys are alive," Richard remembers the doctor saying, "you ain't got no blood left."

At about the same time that Richard and Faye and Zeke were being stitched back together, some well-armed Dawson people motored down to the camp at Fifteenmile River. By then the bear had returned and gone. The camp was destroyed. She had knocked over the picnic table, staved in the shelves in the cooking area, and sliced to ribbons the tent that had been left standing.

DURING BREAKUP ONE YEAR, when Richard was away at Circle, Yukon River ice jammed below Fortymile, and the river rose until Richard's cabin began to float. It floated right out into the river. A pilot friend had flown over the area after the water dropped and reported that the cabin was sitting on ice floes out on the edge of the Yukon's channel. But then the water—and the cabin—rose again. Somehow the river floated the cabin back into Richard's yard and set it down near its original spot. The building was plenty worse for wear, and by the time I visited Fortymile late that same summer, Richard was about seven rounds up on a new cabin. "It really ain't mine," though, he said. Park Service people had visited Smith after the preserve was created and noted that he had not filed for a homestead during the many years when it was possible to do so. According to the law, they said, he had "no possessory interest" in the place. He was a trespasser on public land.

It was true that Richard Smith hadn't done the paperwork necessary to get legal title to the site. Neither had his mother and stepfather. Nor had Gordon Bertoson, who lived there before them. Nor had Phil Berail, who was there before him; nor Walter Roman before him; nor John Nathaniel, nor Hank Connette, nor Charlie Moon, and so on going back a very long time. In those days, title to the land might have been easily obtained. The federal government even ran advertisements in stateside newspapers promoting the colonization of Alaska through homesteading and other programs. But the old-timers didn't always bother with the legalities. Many say they always thought they'd be let alone, that they didn't need to own the land anyway, just wanted to use it. Besides, respect for each other's rights to cabin, trapline, and fishing site was an unwritten law here. By any moral standard, they felt, they owned the modest bit of material culture they'd wrestled from a tough country: a log cabin, a cache, an outhouse.

The park managers explained the new law and told Richard that he could apply for a five-year, renewable permit to stay in his family's cabin. "But when the permit finally came in the mail, they put in there that I had to sign over all rights to the buildings and the land and everything. And that kind of stumped me there for a while. So, I don't own the cabins. I don't own any of the buildings I built around here or nothing. It's all Park Service. And I don't know what to make of it. It wasn't the way I understood it at first."

A lot of people on the river "get up in arms about it," says Richard. But he, himself, takes a live-and-let-live view: "Well, I just figure, you know, I'll just live here and do what I've been doing. If they decide to kick me out, well, that's my tough luck. I can't worry about it. . . . I'm building this new house here. I'm not worrying about all the time and effort and money I'm spending on it. I've got to have a house to live in. So, I just do like I would have done back in the old days. Just go ahead and do it and hope that nothing will ever happen where they'll phase me out."

Richard said that the Park Service people he had met, the ones who signed his permit, were nice guys. But considering that the permit had to be renewed every five years, and that the average length of a super-intendent's stay at Yukon-Charley was running about three years at the time, Richard's domestic security was nil. "Maybe the next guy who gets the job there, he might not like me. It's up to them, you know. And that's kind of scary. To me it is. But I been getting along with them. But there's always that to think about." Richard Smith is wary. Not afraid, not bitter. It's a bit like his view of the other large omnivore that claims these woods: the bear. "I still get the jitters every time I think about it. But, as far as bears go, it don't bother me to have bears around. I don't go shooting every one I see."

Since I saw him that time, Richard has married and moved away. He was the last person to hold a permit to live in a cabin within the Yukon-Charley preserve.

Falcons and Jaguars

From my chair, from my camp, on an island a couple of miles below Eureka Creek, I look back upriver at the bluff above Richard Smith's cabin. I've taken my seat for the evening's entertainment. Tonight it is the deepening peach in a horizontal band behind the hill. The clouds are as dense and dark as the bluing on a rifle barrel. But beneath these an orange wash, pale and delicate, claims a good bit of the horizon to the northeast. It's as if somebody's fingers are on a board of rheostats, muting this hue, boosting that, dialing up the intensities. And all the while, imperceptibly fading to black. The old-timers, I'm thinking, they didn't see in sepia. They saw these colors too. The streak of peach and patches of baby blue. Skookum Jim and Chief Charley. McQuestin and Harper. Phonograph Nelson and the Fish boys. De-Wolfe, Adney, and Stuck. They too sprawled under these quilty covers, this comforting blanket I would pull all around me, in the bosom of the same mother.

And now the hills go from green to green-black. The rugged, tan face of the bluff experiments with a softening rose. And the river carries all of these colors, and shines silver too.

IN THE MORNING I am back in my chair, almost unable to move, with the flowing water charming me into a stupor. The start of the last week in August. The start of my last day on the river. I am sitting by a pleasant fire, drinking coffee and listening intently to the absence of sound. I think I could hear the footfall of a moose a mile away. But there is no moose. The tree did not fall in the forest, and I was there to notice. The stillness suggests emptiness on a continental scale, as if I were the first man to cross the land bridge, the first to discover an entire hemisphere of the world. The interior of Alaska and some of Yukon Territory remained unglaciated during the last Ice Age, except for alpine glaciers in the high country. Hence, it served as a refugium for animal and plant species that the ice cap displaced or destroyed elsewhere. Some south-facing slopes along the Yukon River contain rare plants associated with an Arctic steppe community, a holdover from the Ice Age. During this period, with the land bridge emergent, but with the ice sheet cutting off access to the south, some of the first Americans may have settled here. When it began to warm again, and the glaciers retreated up into the mountains, the people may have followed along the Yukon River valley, using it as a migratory corridor in their expansion southward.

But this country between the Kandik River and Circle City is not always so quiet and empty as it seems today. In fact, it is home to noises that boom louder than thunder and shriek wilder than any animal.

My friend Skip Ambrose is the man to tell the story. I was sitting on a sandbar not far from here earlier this summer with Skip and his colleague and wife Chris Florian. Skip is a little older than I, but he looks much younger. He has a sort of modified punk haircut. It's not exactly spiky, but every hair on his head seems to stand perpendicular to a point at the center of his head. He is tall and lean and tan. He looks cool and relaxed in a powder blue polo shirt, gray nylon pants, and wraparound shades. He is an outdoorsman, but he looks like he just stepped out of an air-conditioned clubhouse on a golf course in Charleston. His face shows a perpetual half-smile, as if he is constantly taking in folly and converting it to mild entertainment. When he shrugs and smirks and his eyebrows invert and suggest a helpless resignation to the fates, look out, because he's about to launch a zinger. Half the time I do not hear what Skip is telling me because I am too caught up in his South Carolina accent, saying over in my mind words like "bucawz." The accent has not been much attenuated by thirty years in Alaska. Chris, who can identify the calls of two hundred birds, is much younger than we are and constitutionally quiet. Her blond-streaked ponytail pokes through the crescent in the back of her baseball cap. Her wide eyes absorb everything, miss nothing.

We have finished breakfast and are all three glassing a bluff across the river, keeping an eye on the peregrine falcons. Presently, Skip says, "Well, I guess it's about time for the morning war." We fold up our chairs, jump in the riverboat, and skim over the placid river for a few miles to a spot he thinks will offer good viewing. We set up our chairs again, and Skip scans the sky. It isn't long before he zeroes in on an area just above the hills to the north. "See them?" he asks. I see nothing. "C-130s," he says. Finally, I focus on three specks just above the horizon. They are no more than specks. His binoculars are no more powerful than mine. In minutes, they grow into transport planes with one hundred thirty-two-foot wingspans that can haul Caterpillar tractors. They roar over us, disappearing over the horizon to the south.

"Toranado," says Skip, now looking back to the north. "It's British." I look where he is looking. I see a speck and a smudge. "A-10 Warthogs." Slightly blobbier specks. I happen to know what an A-10 looks like, but I certainly can't see these dots—about the size of a period on this page—well enough to identify them as A-10s. "Jaguar," he says. "Also British." I've known him for thirty years, but I didn't know he possessed these talents.

Skip came to Alaska in 1973 after service in the army, but he had grown up on air force bases. He came up here because his father was the base commander at Eielson Air Force Base, just south of Fairbanks. As a kid, he learned about airplanes the way I learned the stats on baseball cards. The blue sky is now streaked with white contrails. They diffuse into fat lines, as if they were made with the flat side of the chalk. Soon, they waver like the tentacles of a jelly fish. An invading jelly fish from Jupiter. The planes will make a turn, Skip says, and re-cross the Yukon. He has an idea where, so we climb in the boat again and shove off. "I don't know when they'll figure out that they should just put a transmitter on my boat," he laughs.

Skip is spying on NATO war games because he is a peregrine falcon biologist, formerly of the U.S. Fish and Wildlife Service. He has returned here to the bluffs along the Yukon River between Eagle and Circle to look for peregrine aeries every year since 1973. In that year, the Fish and Wildlife Service added the American peregrine (*Falco peregrinus anatum*) to the endangered species list. Thanks to industrial pollution, especially the widespread use of DDT, the American peregrine falcon experienced reproductive failure. When use of the insecticide was restricted in the United States, the birds gradually rebounded. Skip thinks that after the 1947 introduction of DDT, peregrine populations along the Upper Yukon declined to perhaps twenty to twenty-five percent of their earlier levels. By 1973, only eleven pairs could be found between Eagle and Circle. With the ban of DDT in 1972, the birds have steadily recovered until this stretch of river seems to be nearing saturation, and territorial disputes are increasing. Now at about fifty pairs, this is one of the densest populations of nesting peregrines in North America.

But as DDT's presence in the environment declined, military training activity increased. In the early 1990s, Alaskan politicians and captains of commerce saw dollar signs in the war games and suggested that their state should become "the military training capital of the free world." And that is exactly what happened. Foreign nations, delighted not to be dropping bombs on their own landscapes, now come to interior Alaska, where they are welcomed by civic boosters and a fawning Fairbanks press. Besides NATO forces, countries that have come to rain bombs on Alaska, or to participate as observers, include Canada, Great Britain, France, Germany, Japan, South Korea, New Zealand, Australia, Philippines, Singapore, Thailand, Malaysia, Brunei, Indonesia, China, India, and Bangladesh.

Big chunks of Alaska's land and air space have been given over to this training. One military officer enthused, as if he couldn't believe his luck, "They can fly their missions over something like the size of Kansas!" And vast stretches of Alaska land have been appropriated for bombardment, such as the "live-fire exercises" that take place in the Tanana Flats just south of Fairbanks. Much of this new training involves very low-level, high-speed flights. Screaming jets may come upon a dog musher or canoeist without prelude and at treetop level. Multiple, sudden sonic booms are now daily events on hunting, fishing, or canoe trips in many parts of Alaska—even along streams officially designated Wild and Scenic Rivers and in national preserves. Here in Yukon-Charley Rivers National Preserve, the air force is authorized to fly jets one hundred feet above the ground at nearly the speed of sound. A hundred feet is about the height of a mature spruce tree. The jets may break out over a hill and streak across the sky at low levels above calving caribou or lambing Dall sheep. The pregnant or postparturient females are said to be somewhat less startled than if a wolf were charging them, according to studies, but the long-term effects of this sort of disturbance are not known. Skip worries that sonic booms, or just the sudden, unexpected roar of a low-flying jet, may disturb the falcons during the critical nesting time. Largely because of his efforts, the military has been constrained to fly no lower than two thousand feet above ground level in a corridor that follows the Yukon River and extends for two miles on each side. A similar corridor restricts low-level flights over the Kandik and Charley Rivers. So, where "ground level" behind a bluff is at two thousand feet, the planes are supposed to be no lower than four thousand feet.

WE SET UP OUR CHAIRS across the river from a bluff near Wood-chopper Creek and scope the face of it, looking for the nesting pair. A C-130 transport plane flies over. He is clearly not two thousand feet above the height of the bluff. Four more follow in formation. It is less certain, but they appear to be flying too low as well. Skip says he doesn't want to bust the pilots, he just wants them to stay out of the restricted area. He doesn't like reporting the violations to the colonel, but he likes it less if he is treated patronizingly, as he was at first. A colonel told him once, "Well, you know, Skip, it's pretty darned hard to estimate heights from the ground. Unless you're pretty experienced, it's easy to be off by hundreds of feet." Skip replied, "Yup. But when I'm standing on a bluff that the USGS shows to be 1,500 feet high, and I am looking down on an airplane flying along the Yukon River, I'm pretty confident that he's less than 2,000 feet above ground level."

Once the Air Force got a better idea who they were dealing with, they moved to work with rather than against Skip, to the point where they funded his peregrine monitoring. Most of Skip and Chris's time is now spent climbing the cliffs into the aeries and adding to their incredible data set, now more than thirty years old.

AS IT HAPPENS, I am not overly fond of heights, but Skip prevails in arguing that I'll have no problem climbing up to an aerie. Then, too, I must "get the story." When our riverboat is still most of a mile away from the bluff where a pair of peregrines are nesting, the birds start squawking. We can't hear this from a mile off, of course, but Skip has observed the birds' reaction a couple of times when he has been on the ground below and his boat was being operated by someone else. Skip's boat will occasion a ruckus every time, while the appearance of other boats elicits no reaction. The falcons can distinguish his boat from others, and they can do it from such a great distance that the boat would appear to us as little more than a speck. The falcons are detecting Skip the way he is detecting Jaguars and Warthogs.

The pair of falcons is circling and kak-kaking as we start up a steep three-hundred-foot scree slope. I am wondering if one of them might rake my T-shirted back, laying it open with a talon. But Skip isn't watching or ducking, so I figure, "no problem." Later, when I ask him about it, he tells me about a time when a friend got his scalp sliced open. "There was blood all over," he says. And once a diving bird nailed Skip with his balled-up foot. "It felt like getting hit by a small ball peen hammer." For the moment, I do not worry about being attacked by razor-footed missiles that can dive at over two hundred miles per hour. I am busy worrying about falling to my death.

Accepting the age-old wisdom, I do not look down until we are at the aerie. It makes me dizzy to notice, but I notice: what a spectacular site. A sweeping view of a very big river in a very big country. It would be consciousness-transforming for a human to be reared with this million-dollar vista. The sun streams in. The breezes sift through the sage plants, scenting the air in a salubrious way. Consciousness would expand another notch if one could live here without walls, as these birds do. Amazingly, peregrines do not build nests. Falcons are one of the only birds not to. They simply lay their eggs on a little shelf, totally unprotected from above and from the sides. There are no nesting materials whatever where these four little birds huddle. Their white, fuzzy plumage is just beginning to yield to dark gray and orange feathers. They have sunken chests, scrawny necks, and pot bellies. Their Barney Google eyes bug, and their mouths stand agape, ready to snap at us, I figure. But Skip says they are not programmed to fight with their beaks. You can grab one from behind, keeping the talons away from you, but it's good to wear leather gloves for backup.

Massive, black thunderclouds are rolling in fast, and we leave the foursome to their tiny ledge. That's the downside to the no-walls plan. The little birds are totally exposed to driving wind and icy rain. And that appears to be the biggest cause of mortality. If it is a cold, wet May, Skip says, many of the young do not survive. The summer of 2000 was unusually rainy and cold, and only thirty-eight percent of the breeding pairs raised a fledgling. This year, with a pretty rainy June and local hail storms, forty-nine percent have raised young. Another downside—for me—is getting down off this cliff. Skip tells me not to be tempted to lean into the hill, as intuition would suggest, but to lean *away* from it so as to stand more vertically. That way you are less likely to lose traction and go into a slide that might not end until you are in the Yukon River. So, I lean into space and follow Skip, half loping, half surfing on the loose scree.

AT ANOTHER SPOT on the right bank of the Yukon, we climb a wooded slope upstream of a cliff face and make our way to a point above a nest. I'm watching Skip tie a climbing rope to the base of a spruce tree when suddenly he flings it into space. Oh, no, I'm thinking. It's only about eight feet down to a little scrap of ledge, but below that it is maybe a thousand feet almost straight down to the river. I look, in order, at the stoutness of the rope, the knot, the tree. It all looks strong enough, though I could wish for a thicker rope to make gripping it easier. Over we go, first he, then I. Ignoring all the hard-wired warning lights flashing "PERIL, PERIL," I follow another bit of Skip's counter-intuitive advice and lean outward into the void, walking backward down the face of the cliff. There is one egg here, and it is too late for it to hatch now, says Skip. No young for this pair this year. The adults are likely nearby, but Skip says they will not defend a nest where there is no young. They will defend the ledge from other falcons, however, to protect their property rights for next year.

It's especially disappointing to have no young falcons at this nest because it is one where Skip has installed a camera. It's about the size of one of those little flashlights sized for two AA batteries. A cord trails up the cliff to a transmitter wired onto a tree and pointing out over the river. A deep-cycle twelve-volt battery at the base of the tree powers the transmitter, and a solar collector keeps the battery charged. The signal beams out toward an island in the river. In a few minutes we are at that island and bushwhack through the willows to a little clearing Skip and Chris had found earlier. Taped to a willow is a receiver positioned to pick up the signal from the transmitter on the hill across the channel. A cord from this receiver sends the signal on to a laptop computer inside a weather-tight hard case. Five twelve-volt deep-cycle batteries power the computer, and they in turn are charged by a large solar panel. On a stand is a microphone with a wind screen. The microphone is wired to a sound-level meter, which is plugged into the computer.

All this gadgetry is, in a sense, aimed at air force jets. The video signal from the nest is constantly streaming into the computer, and the microphone is continuously picking up all sorts of sounds, from bird calls to wind and rain. But the computer can exclude the extraneous events. The sound meter takes a reading every second, and it sends that information, expressed in decibels, to the computer. The computer saves, but soon deletes, all sounds and all video images unless a sound threshold is reached, namely fifty decibels. As soon as the noise reaches that level, the computer saves the audio and video files beginning ten seconds before the onset of the noise event to ten seconds after its cessation. When a jet roars overhead, the computer saves both the audio of the jet and the video of the birds' reactions. Back at home, Skip mixes the two together, and he and Chris can watch the falcons on their TV.

He was still in the early stages of this study when I was with him, but what Skip was noticing at the several sites where he has installed this array of instruments is that the birds often jump at the onset of a loud, sudden noise, like a sonic boom. But they show less of a response when the sound of an approaching jet increased gradually. Skip hasn't documented it yet, but he worries that, apart from whatever stress-induced effects there may be, sudden, unexpected sounds may startle the peregrines enough that they dart out into flight and some eggs or nestlings could be knocked off the ledges.

AFTER MANY YEARS with the Fish and Wildlife Service, Skip was lured away by the Park Service. The agency was interested in his studies of jet noise, and now they have him leading noise studies in many park lands throughout the western United States. But he has made it part of the deal that he be allowed to return in the summer to the Yukon to monitor these birds. He still pesters the air force, as necessary, as well as the Park Service's Yukon-Charley administrators. When the preserve was established, there were two MOAs, or military operating areas, already in existence, covering the western half of the preserve. In the mid-1980s, the air force successfully applied for additional temporary MOAs that would overlap every bit of the preserve. In the 1990s they proposed to make those MOAs permanent. These changes would permit warplanes to streak over the landscape, as low as one hundred feet above the ground, over the entire preserve. In each case, in the 1980s and the 1990s, the Yukon-Charley superintendents (a different superintendent in each case) chose not to object to the plan to make the entire preserve a training area. Once, Skip says, he confronted an air force officer, saying the air force did not need, for example, to fly at one hundred feet over the Kandik River. He says the officer replied, "We don't need it, but as long as the Park Service wasn't going to object, we took it." Skip shakes his head. "I think there should be some place in a national preserve such as this one where the military cannot fly, where they cannot fly at near-supersonic speeds a hundred feet off the ground." Warming to the topic, he says, "Everybody thinks it's great that the Park Service got the entire Charley River drainage to 'preserve in its wilderness state,' as the enabling legislation directs NPS to do. But then for NPS not to object to military jets roaring through on war game sorties, at a hundred feet above the ground anywhere in the preserve, just does not make sense."

The jets sometimes drop chaff and flares. The chaff is a kind of jettisoned litter that is picked up by radar and is intended to confuse radar-guided antiaircraft missiles. The flares are used to foil heat-seeking air-to-air missiles. In real combat, the chaff and flares confuse real missiles; in these war games, the chaff and flares confuse electronic missiles. Flares dropped by dog-fighting jets in June 1991 started a forest fire in the heart of the Charley River drainage that torched about forty thousand acres in one week, including Charlie Kidd's trapline. Skip was working for the U.S. Fish and Wildlife Service at the time of the MOA expansion, but his main area of professional interest was in Yukon-Charley, studying the peregrines along the rivers. He couldn't believe how easily the Park Service caved to the military. "It's like the NPS just didn't care about Yukon-Charley, as they did for the other parks in Alaska—like Denali, Lake Clark, and others—where they got the air force to exclude areas of the parks from the new MOAs. But they never even *objected* to the air force's plans in Yukon-Charley."

Shahnyaati'

About twenty-five miles below Richard Smith's cabin, and fourteen miles above Circle City, I pass over the invisible boundary of the preserve and see immediately a white rail fence and a large white cross among birch and spruce trees on a grassy hillside on the right bank. This is said to be the grave of Shahnyaati', a famous Gwech'in Indian chief. The last of the trading chiefs, Shahnyaati' lived during the later stages of the Hudson's Bay Company's presence on the Yukon and the early part of the American period. The Hudson's Bay people preferred to do their trading with the top man, and a chief's stature with both the whites and his own people grew in consequence. Shahnyaati' presented his people's furs and meat at the post, and he divided up the acquired ammunition, matches, flour, tea, blankets, and knives.

His band moved around within the Yukon Flats, up the Porcupine River, and into the Brooks Range. People in Circle and Fort Yukon, many of whom are related to Shahnyaati', say the chief was such a great provider that he had seventeen wives and twenty-four children, though some of the wives were widows he took in, and some of the children orphans. Maybe this was over the course of many years, but if the entire household customarily gathered for the evening meal, that would mean dinner for forty-two every night.

Several early adventurers met Shahnyaati'. Alexander Murray, a Canadian explorer who came through this region in 1847, was impressed with the chief: "This Indian never saw Whites before we arrived. He has given us more fur and more meat than any other, was our Fort Hunter this spring, has great influence with his band, and is the person for whom the Red Coat is intended." Robert Kennicott called him "Old Thunder" and says he had five wives. Frederick Schwatka magisterially describes him as "a savage of more than ordinary authority and determination." Francois Mercier says he knew Shahnyaati' well. "He was a man of extraordinary stature and strength, of braveness or more than that, ferocity, and duplicity which one rarely encounters even among the savages. He was not only the terror of the people of his tribe, but above all the other neighboring tribes, whom he rarely left in peace, and whom he massacred each in their turn for the least reason, or for only the love of carnage."

Mercier relates an Indian story that he says he heard many times. Shahnyaati' was camped with some of his men at the head of the Rapids, about forty-five miles above Tanana, while several men from another regional tribe were fishing at the foot. "Senate [Mercier's spelling] made each of his men take two knives, of which one was in sight in a sheath hung from a shoulder belt, as is the custom among all the savages of the Youkon, and the other knife hidden in their clothing. This done, he sent two of his men in advance to announce to these poor fishermen that they should not be alarmed to soon see him arrive with his men, that he came in friendship, desiring for a long time to make peace with them. Believing that they were on a mission of peace, the poor Gen du Large received Senate and his men with open arms, and, as is the custom on such occasions, they sang, feasted, danced, and exchanged presents, etc., etc. And as it is also the custom among all the savages of the Youkon to wrestle when they meet with each other, Senate proposed then to the Gen du Large that they wrestle together, but he said, 'Is it not possible that on wrestling with our knives someone would become angry?' All disarmed themselves of their knives, and when they were all held around the waste, at a signal from Senate, each of his men pulled out his knife which had been hidden, and each killed his man."

Oral tradition among the people of Circle and Fort Yukon say that Shahnyaati' died an old man at Circle in 1894. It is said that all throughout the area, other men with strong medicine knew at once that someone of importance had died. Shahnyaati' was placed on a scaffold until a sign should appear indicating where he should be buried. When a rainbow shone on this hillside, the chief was brought here. For many years, travelers on the river would shoot their guns as they passed this place, and the sternwheeler captains would blow the boat's whistle, in salute to Shahnyaati'.

Into Circle City

The Yukon begins to braid out into vast flats just before Circle, and the distances are immense. I keep to the left channels until I see a blue oil drum on the bank and know it as a sign: Welcome to Circle. It is almost impossible to conceive that all this vast land was intended to be flooded, especially by a dam so far away. But in 1959, the Army Corps of Engineers hoped to build the largest dam in the world at Rampart Canyon, three hundred miles downriver. The impoundment would have been larger than Lake Erie, and more than ten thousand square miles of wild land would have been lost. Alaska's Senator Ernest Gruening, the dam's chief proponent, didn't think the loss amounted to much. He said, "Scenically it is zero. In fact it is one of the few ugly areas in a land prodigal with sensational beauty." The Yukon Flats, he said, was "nothing but a vast wasteland."

Gruening's chief of staff, George Sundborg, who had been the editor of the *Fairbanks Daily News-Miner*, said, "Those who know it best say the kindest and best thing one could do for the place . . . is put it under four hundred feet of water." "Those who know it best" were not the residents of the seven Athabascan villages that would have been inundated, but apparently the Corps of Engineers. Sundborg also helpfully pointed out that the whole area contained "not more than ten flush toilets." I always thought that an interesting way to objectify the value of a culture. (It's probably just as well Sundborg doesn't control the fate of Mayan temples.)

You don't see it much these days, but the biologists working for the U.S. Fish and Wildlife Service in the 1960s bravely confronted the politicians and the boosters with the blunt facts: "Nowhere in the history of water development in North America have the fish and wildlife losses anticipated to result from a single project been so overwhelming." The Yukon Flats is an Arctic solar basin, gathering in twenty to twenty-four hours of sunlight each summer day. The elevation is low (less than six hundred feet), and the area is both far from the cool coast and protected from Arctic weather by hills. Temperatures here can reach one hundred degrees, higher than any place in Alaska. Minnesota may be the Land of Ten Thousand Lakes, but the Yukon Flats encompasses thirty-six thousand lakes and ponds. And all this adds up to abundant food and superb nesting habitat for ducks.

In response to the Rampart Dam proposal, Fish and Wildlife Service personnel launched a crash program to band ducks in the Yukon Flats in the summers of 1960 and 1961. "They knew that damming the Yukon was a serious threat to the wildlife to whose protection they had dedicated much of their lives," says Jim King, a retired Fish and Wildlife Service biologist. "The banding project was their chance to do something about it. Getting the job done in two seasons was a major challenge. We hit the road running." Actually, they hit the lakes in float planes. During the molting period, when the ducks shed their flight feathers and grow new ones, there is a three- or four-week period when they cannot fly. King and his colleagues landed on lakes where molting ducks gathered in large numbers. They constructed corrals and herded the flightless birds into them. In two seasons, they fitted eighteen thousand ducks of fifteen species with metal leg bands. And shortly after that, but continuing for twenty years, hunters from forty-five of the forty-nine lower states turned in the bands. Eventually, with improved counting techniques, the biologists determined that 2.4 million ducks fly out of the Yukon Flats each fall. Today, the nine-million-acre Yukon Flats National Wildlife Refuge is considered "the premier duck nesting refuge in the world," says King.

Rampart Dam died because, as a financial proposition, it was a gigantic white elephant, and the federal government had no inclination to underwrite it. Still, the Bureau of Land Management continued to classify the area as a power site until 1990. Woodchopper Canyon was also investigated as a dam site. And those who liked big water projects loved one called NAWAPA. Conceived in the 1960s, the North American Water and Power Alliance proposed reversing the flow of the Yukon and Tanana Rivers, sending them south to the desert states of the American southwest via a system of dams and canals, some excavated with nuclear explosions. Occasional presidential candidate Lyndon LaRouche periodically resuscitates the idea, sometimes from a jail cell. Yet there are serious thinkers who maintain that, with NAWAPA, it's not "if," but "when." The Yukon Flats National Wildlife Refuge, as well as Yukon-Charley Rivers National Preserve, stand as the best deterrents to the revival of these visionary propositions.

Another once and future project that the existence of the Yukon-Charley preserve so far has impeded is the construction of a road along the Yukon River between Circle and Eagle. Boosters and business people who cater to tourism like the idea of a loop where today there are two dead-end roads. Then, to the experience of floating the stretch of river I've just descended, a traveler might add traffic noise, dust clouds, motor homes, Jet Skis, boom boxes, generators, satellite TV dishes, awnings, Astroturf, and barbecues.

ON NEARLY THE LAST PAGE of his book, and in a rare first-person appearance, McPhee writes just exactly what he thinks. He says, "If I were writing the ticket, I would say that anyone at all is free to build a cabin on any federal land in the United States that is at least a hundred miles from the nearest town of ten thousand or more—the sole restriction being that you cannot carry in materials for walls or roof or floors." A typically nifty formulation. We could do worse than have McPhee write our laws. In 1980, he enlarged on this view in a letter to Secretary of the Interior Cecil Andrus, whom McPhee had earlier visited in his office in Washington, D.C. On the river people's requirements for subsistence living in that part of the world, McPhee had this to say: "It seems to me that these needs are modest. The cabins are small—five or six would fit in your private office—and they are scattered through the forest and they are biodegradable. The people are small and they are scattered through the forest and they are biodegradable. I feel that the subsistence living they practice is important to us all, that it is not an isolated pocket of nostalgia in a technological world, and that it is as worthy of preservation as any aspect of Alaska."

Echoing the early Park Service planners who were determined to make parks in Alaska different, McPhee told Andrus: "I would like to add that I believe Alaska should be dealt with uniquely, that it would be a mistake to apply many rules there that are universal in the nation as a whole. Customs and practices can be allowed there that would overwhelm a place like New Jersey's pine barrens. In the past four years, people have come and gone in the upper Yukon, but, despite the considerable attention that has been given the region, the population has not increased. The latitude is in charge, and Alaska screens its own."

It didn't work out as McPhee had hoped, though it is said that his book, which came out three years before the passage of ANILCA, had appreciable influence on Congress (portions of it were read into the congressional record). The law did speak to the value of residents living the old-time subsistence lifestyle, and it did provide for the continuance of subsistence activities within park lands in Alaska. But because of the way the law was implemented, the way the regulations were drafted, subsistence is regarded less as a value than as a nuisance.

The empirical result is clear enough. Asking around, I have come up with a list of people who lived between the Canadian border and Circle City in the 1970s and 1980s, before the park was established and cabin regulations promulgated. The list is almost certainly incomplete. But I tally more than eighty people, counting the kids, in about thirty-five households. They were spread out along some one hundred seventy miles of Yukon River. In many cases, they were far up a side creek, as far as sixty miles off the Yukon. Today there is not a single person holding a permit to live in a cabin within the entire Yukon-Charley Rivers National Preserve. Resident subsistence activities are now, finally, eliminated from the preserve. That is, they are eliminated from two and a half million acres—an area larger than Delaware and Rhode Island combined. That includes one hundred twenty-five miles of Yukon River, one hundred miles of Charley River, and all of the lower Nation and Kandik Rivers. There are only two permits issued in all of this area that allow the periodic use of a cabin for subsistence purposes—but not for use as a primary residence.

One of the Park Service's chief planners in Alaska, Zorro Bradley, says the agency constitutionally cannot abide subsistence activities. "The Park Service as a whole has a 'no subsistence' attitude. I think that's pretty well recognized. They'd like to get rid of it." Bradley, now retired, was a key man in Alaska overseeing subsistence research. "I suspect that what we'll do is eventually kill it off entirely," says Bradley. "And, as we did in the Southwest, remove the Natives from park land. Today you go to a place like Navajo National Monument, where they excluded all Native peoples, now they hire them as people to come in and demonstrate their cultural activities at the visitor center. They are paid actors."

Bradley was a career Park Service man, but growing up in and around Indian reservations in the Southwest, he saw the Park Service from both sides. "At Wupatki National Monument we had resident Navajo families the Park Service tried for years to move them out of there, even though they had lifetime tenancy status from when the area was established. And I found the Navajo families in there to be darned good neighbors and friends. But they thought of these Indians being in there—to many of the superintendents I served under, it was just anathema to them. And they'd pull all kinds of stuff trying to get them out of there. Same thing at Chaco Canyon. At Grand Canyon. The harassment of the Havasupai Indians by the Park Service just really bothered me."

In the 1960s, Bradley spent time in rural Alaskan villages and saw firsthand the dependency of the rural people on fish and game, including marine mammals. He even stayed in a whale camp on the Arctic coast and watched the Eskimo people hunting whales. "It made me realize very early on that if we ever develop any kind of parks up here, these people would be excluded by—not by written policy or anything like that—but by Park Service attitudes. So I started talking early on about the need for these people to use these resources."

But Bradley has little faith that that will happen. The attitudes and tactics that he saw growing up have a long history, dating back to the world's first national park, established at Yellowstone, Wyoming, in 1872. As Mark David Spence has documented in his book *Dispossessing the Wilderness: Indian Removal and the Making of the National Parks*, Park administrators at Yellowstone thought the presence of Indians scared away tourists, so they drove the Indians off the parklands.

Later, park managers hatched a plan to build an Indian exhibit on Dot Island in Yellowstone Lake peopled with living Indians. Fortunately, this human zoo proposal failed.

At Yosemite National Park, after the Indians were forced out of the valley, they managed to return as hotel workers or to sing and dance and sell baskets. The Park Service used the Indians as tourist bait by staging "Indian Field Days," where the local Ahwahneechee dressed up as the more popularized Plains Indians and competed for prizes in equestrian and basket-making contests. One by one—with relocations and raised rents and new rules and evictions for one cause or another—the Park Service forced the Ahwahneechee out of the valley. In 1969, they burned the last Indian residences in training exercises for firefighters.

In 1895, at Glacier National Park in Montana, Blackfoot Indians confronting incipient starvation agreed to sell to the U.S. government the mountainous territory they regarded as the "backbone of the world." But they did so only with the stipulation that they be allowed to hunt, fish, and collect timber there for their cabins and corrals. Once the land was set aside within the "fixed and carefully policed boundaries of the modern bureaucratic state," writes historian William Cronin, the "original inhabitants were kept out by dint of force, their earlier uses of the land redefined as inappropriate or even illegal. To this day, the Blackfeet continue to be accused of 'poaching' on the lands of Glacier National Park that originally belonged to them and that were ceded by treaty only with the proviso that they be permitted to hunt there." Meanwhile, the Great Northern Railroad lured tourists to the park by hiring Blackfeet to "play Indian" at its depot and at the Glacier Park Hotel.

At Great Smokey Mountains National Park, the Park Service bought out six thousand six hundred private parties—many by using condemnation proceedings. Park managers moved assorted barns and buildings to the Mountain Farm Museum, where costumed interpreters now demonstrate hill-country life at the imitation farmstead. At Buffalo National River in Arkansas, the Park Service condemned and leveled many hundreds of homes; at Ozark Scenic Riverways in Missouri, the Park Service bulldozed the cabins along the river; at Big Bend National Park in Texas, they knocked down the ranchers' cabins. And now they regret it.

At least some of the Park Service employees at Yukon-Charley are prepared for the same thing to happen in their park. The day is not so distant, they say, when all the river people will be gone from the river and the Park Service will put GS-5 summer hires in their cabins. They'll be drama majors from colleges in the States. They'll wear red flannel shirts and spit snoose. They'll hang a few fish so the floaters can see people living the old-time way. And come the first frost, they'll head back to school.

AFTERWORD

―――∞∞∞―――

Ohio

Down on the Cuyahoga River between Cleveland and Akron there is a park called Cuyahoga River Valley National Park. Its superintendent is a man named John Debo. Debo's park suffered through "roughly twenty or twenty-five years of highly unsatisfactory management practice," he says. Then he had an idea. It was to stomp on the brakes, back his park around, point it in the exact opposite direction, and put it in gear. The traffic he now drove his park against included every other park in the entire four hundred twenty-six–unit U.S. National Park System.

The story begins in 1974, when Congress established the Cuyahoga Valley National Recreation Area. It included a pretty stretch of bottomland with twenty-two miles of river coursing through, dotted with picturesque little farms that dated to the early 1800s. Since the 1870s Clevelanders and Akronites had come here in their carriages for a Sunday drive in the country, or for boating excursions on the canal, or for rides on the scenic Valley Railway. Everywhere, the little farms provided a rustic backdrop of croplands and pastures and woodlots. But by the 1970s, things were changing. Small farms were failing and being swallowed up by industrial-scale operations. Creeping urbanization tempted many farmers to sell out to residential developers. When the Park Service took over, it halted the sprawl, and that was a good thing. The park did other good things too, like improving roads and trails, putting in a twenty-mile towpath along the canal, and reestablishing the scenic railroad. But, following usual Park Service practice, managers began attempting to convert the valley back into wilderness. They bought up four hundred residential properties, most of recent vintage, and tore them down. But they also destroyed, either by purposeful demolition or by neglect, historic farmsteads. They knocked down the farmhouses and barns or had them burned by local fire departments for training exercises. Other property they simply boarded up. Fields grew up in weeds, then brush, then trees, cutting off the views. By the 1980s, the Park Service had eliminated most of the residents, and park managers presided over a linear eyesore, devoid of the activity that gave the rural landscape its celebrated character, namely small-scale farming.

The congressman who authored the legislation creating the park, John Seiberling, made it clear to the Park Service that Congress had not intended that the agricultural landscape be obliterated. "So we stopped," says John Debo. "But then it sort of entered this long period of inaction. We weren't destroying these properties, but we also weren't effectively preserving them. They remained boarded up, unoccupied, and even though we weren't actively pursuing demolition, slowly over time that's what happened. You'd come in one morning and, guess what, another barn fell down. It was a kind of management by neglect. And it simply wasn't satisfactory. Farm buildings were falling down around us. You can't help but view these farmsteads, which date back to the early 1800s, as anything but historic resources and scenic resources." In a word, the valley was losing the rural landscape that the park was supposed to protect.

Debo says the situation became intolerable. "I became convinced that we had to do something, and we had to do something very different." He finally realized that the reason the area was attractive enough to warrant the creation of a park in the first place was because of the farming activity. People working the land had created and maintained a patchwork of lovely scenery and structures: row crops and orchards, pastures and woodlots, barns and farmhouses, and tractors working the fields. He could not possibly maintain hundreds of buildings over miles of landscape as components of an outdoor museum. The only practical way to reestablish the countryside landscape was to reestablish a working agricultural community. What he needed was exactly what park managers everywhere abhor: people living inside the park.

As he looked for models, he found that elsewhere around the world, especially in Europe, the concept of a national park is different. Sometimes, he says, it involves the idea of a "lived-in landscape." He thought it was possible that the American notion of a park could also incorporate "the idea of national parks as not only places that people visit, but as places where people can live."

Debo launched what he called the Countryside Initiative. The plan was to revitalize thirty to thirty-five old farms within the park. The park that had closed down farming was now in the farming business. It would now lease the farms back to farmers. But because the farmland was now a park, and because the valley had already seen free-market forces result in failing farms and encroaching asphalt and sprawl, there would be carefully drawn-up terms and conditions. Starting with five farms, the Park Service rehabilitated the farmhouses so that they were ready to move into and the barns so that they were ready to use. They cleared old fields that were not too far into succession. Then they redrew the property lines of the parcels around the houses to make them less haphazard and so that they better fit a modern, small-scale, retail farming operation. Small-scale and retail, not agribusiness. And while they were at it, they declared "organic" and "sustainable" farming plans to be more consistent with park values and one basis for the selection of tenants. They wouldn't offer two-year or five-year leases but rather sixty-year leases, with the right to transfer the property, so that tenants would be encouraged to invest in improvements. And then they tried to integrate the next logical component—a market. The plan called for the development of local farmer's markets where farm products could be sold. The park set up a nonprofit corporation to act as its partner, to handle much of the administration, and to collect the rents (including a percentage of the value of the crops). Prospective farmers interested in farming in a national park, and who could live with the idea that there would be some concomitant restrictions, were invited to submit proposals for the first round of farm offerings in 2001.

It was a stunning reversal of policy and, for the Park Service especially, a radical idea all the way around. "I would say that it has received really wonderful critical success. People are moving into the valley to settle into these farmsteads. These are people who want to engage in environmentally sophisticated farming operations, or highly sustainable farming operations, in a manner that is consistent with Park Service stewardship goals for the valley," said Debo. "So it's very different. It's not something that's really been attempted before in any unit of the Park Service." It was "bold and creative thinking," as the director of the National Park Service said in 2004 when she presented Debo with the National Appleman-Judd Award. The award is given annually to a single Park Service employee as the service's highest honor for managing cultural property.

JOHN DEBO WOULD NOT PRESUME to suggest that the concept that has worked so well at his park would necessarily suit another park. But I don't mind pointing out that the extirpation of local people from Yukon-Charley and the destruction of cabins there, willfully and through neglect, presents a reasonably analogous situation. The Cuyahoga story proves that the task of drawing up suitable safeguards, though complex, needn't be "a management nightmare." It can become a model program, an award-winning program. As Debo has shown in a farming context, it is not an impossible undertaking to find ways to allow a few people, suitably scattered, to live in a park landscape. Guided by their knowledge of local ecological conditions and the carrying capacity of the land, and within the limits of sound conservation practices, Yukon-Charley managers might allow people to lease a remote cabin, or to build a new one, and use the surrounding land. Maybe there would be only a dozen allotments in the entire preserve, maybe fewer, meaning a density of roughly one occupied cabin per one-quarter million acres. Huge tracts could be identified, such as one allotment on the entire Nation River and one on the Kandik. One on the upper Charley River, one on the lower. One relatively near to Eagle and one near to Circle. A tenancy duration of five years might be appropriate. As at Cuyahoga, proposals might be solicited where prospective tenants described their qualifications and intentions. But the people selected needn't be only those who want to trap and hunt and sew skin clothes and who require sizable territory. Some might be like Gaetan Beaudet and take from the land the inspiration and the peace that sustain their art, whether woodcarving or writing. Some might come simply for the space to think, to sit by a pond, say, and formulate ideas about self-reliance and simplicity, about rejecting materialism and living close to nature.

There is a wide literature on what wilderness is, what it means, and whether and how people may coexist within it. I have not engaged that discussion directly. But these stories of the river people are their own kind of argument. They suggest that it is a thing of value when frontiersmen and -women are living out in the country—of value to the people themselves, as they grow in courage and competence; of value to the land, as their deep local knowledge informs our stewardship; of value to our culture, as their residency conserves nearly extinct pioneering ideals. For now, the land is lonesome by decree, artificially empty as if, to enshrine the trees, we banished the birds.

ACKNOWLEDGMENTS

THE NARRATIVE IS CENTERED on a particular trip I made on the Yukon River in August 2001. I made six trips on the Yukon that year and another in 2005. Details of these trips are incorporated according to geography, rather than chronology, so not all particulars existed simultaneously.

The National Park Service supported much of my work. Thanks to Cyd Martin, David Shoemaker, Anna Cottle, Mary Alice Kier, Amy Scheibe, Carol Smith, Melissa Root, Sarah Campbell, Kyle O'Neill, Bill Schneider, Melody Webb, Dave Norton, Susan Blalock, John Kooistra, Paul Matheus, Steve Ulvi, Dave Krupa, Fred Andersen, Charlie Campbell, Robert Holbrook, Mary Ann Sweeney, Eileen Devinney, Bob Satler, Coral Conway, Bill Caldwell, Ann Cook, John Thies, Holly Cook, Dawn Skully, John Kostohrys, Marla Statscewich, Karen Brewster, Dick Kocan, John Debo, Torrie Hunter, Tony Grabowski, Helen Slama, David Neufeld, Dave Payer, Chris Florian, Zorro Bradley, Bob Ritchie, Dick Wood, Elva Scott, John Borg, Kevin Fox, Austin Nelson, Greg Birchard, Chris Christensen, Linda Nelson, Theresa Dean, Laurel Tyrell, Ray Bell, Arlene Bell, Knut Kielland, Keith Mueller, Angela Matz, Marsha Henderson, Carl Staples, Doug Becksted, Dave Mills, Tommy Taylor, Mike Taylor, John Taylor, Clinton Taylor, Allejandra Duk-Rodkin, Rene Barendregt, Florence Weber, Oam Leonard and especially Cor Guimond, Tim Gerberding, Mel Besharah, Stan Zuray, Bill Fliris, Chris Ball, Louie Borste, Gaetan Beaudet, Crane Vangel, Sean Milligan, Lynette Roberts, Mike Sager,

Anonymous Trapper, Wayne Hall, Scarlett Hall, Seymour Able, Terry McMullin, Dick Cook, Dave Evans, Sage Patton, Randy Brown, Karen Kallen-Brown, Mark Richards, Lori Richards, Ed Gelvin, Charlie Kidd, Carolyn Kelly, Faye Chamberlain, Richard Smith, Second Anonymous Trapper, and Skip Ambrose.

INDEX

Able, Leif, 69, 71–72, 102

Able, Seymour, 69–72, 74–80, 85, 111, 115, 148–150, 166, 174, 186–187

Adney, Tappan, 38, 135, 220

Ahwahneechee, 235

AIP (Alaska Independence Party), 203–204, 207, 209

air force jets, 182, 196, 226

Alaska Coal and Coke Company, 151

Alaska Commercial Company, 67, 140

Alaska Department of Fish and Game, 50–51, 105–106, 122, 176

Alaska Independence Party. *See* AIP

Alaska National Interest Lands Conservation Act. *See* ANILCA

Alaska Native Claims Settlement Act (ANCSA—1971), 73, 85, 170

Alaska Natives, 73, 135

Alaska Road Commission, 175

Alaska State Historic Preservation Office, 186

Allen, Lilly, 129, 130

Ambrose, Skip, 221–228

American Creek, 68

Ames, Al, 184

Ames cabin, 184

Andersen, Fred, 122

Andrew Creek, 191–192

Andrew Creek Flats, 189

Andrus, Cecil (U.S. Secretary of Interior in 1980), 232

ANILCA (Alaska National Interest Lands Conservation Act, 1980), 75, 94, 106–109, 137, 171–172, 189, 194, 233
  Congress's intent, 137
  and subsistence uses, 173
  Title VIII, 173

Anvik River, 14

Appalachian Mountain Club, 130

argillite, 24, 80

Athabascan (Indian), 31, 49, 74, 82, 122, 162, 230

AU Placer, 200

bald eagle, 56, 143

Ball, Chris, 53

Barendregt, Rene, 24–25

Barnacle Bob Hilliard, 2
Barron, Genezaret, 208
Barrow, Alaska, 79
Bauer, Rudolf, 144, 163–164
Bayless, Joe, 199
bear story (mauling), 213–218
Beaudet, Gaetan, 55–56, 241
Beck, George, 146, 151–152,
    161–162
Beck, Max, 161
Beckloff, Ole, 185, 199
Beech, Fred ("Dirty Fred"),
    165–168, 173–174
Beechman, Bane, 121
Bell, Arlene, 191, 213–214
Bell, John, 15
Bell, Ray, 191, 213
Belle Isle, 67
Belous, Bob, 173
Ben Creek, 189
Bennett, Frank, 201–202, 211
Berail, Phil, 187, 189, 218
Berglund, Evelyn, 164
Bering Sea, 11, 13, 15, 25, 52, 201
Bering Strait, 68
Berton, Pierre, 34, 39, 135
Bertoson, Gordon, 162, 165, 174,
    213, 218
Beshara, Mel, 42–45, 55, 121
Biederman, Bella Roderick (Ed's
    wife), 158
Biederman, Charlie, 161–162, 164,
    176
Biederman, Horace, 161
Biederman, Max Adolphus ("Ed"),
    82, 87, 144, 151–152,
    157–162
Biederman, Nellie, 152
Biederman Bluff, 144, 178

Biederman's camp, 151, 157, 161,
    164, 175–176, 178
Big Bend National Park, 134, 235
Bio Camp, 58–59
Birchard, Greg, 65
black bear, 42, 143, 184, 216
Blackfoot Indians, 235
BLM (Bureau of Land
    Management), 72–75, 78,
    98–101, 131, 148, 156, 172,
    179, 232
Bonanza Creek (originally Rabbit
    Creek), 8
Bonanza Creek (tributary of
    Charley R.), 184
Borg, John, 126
Borste, Ludger ("Louie"), 54
Bouton, James, 40
Bowers, Thomas DeWayne,
    127–128
Bradley, Zorro, 173, 234
Brentlinger, Fred, 200
Brooks Range, 229
Brown, Bill, 173
Brown, Randy, 165–173
Brunn, Charlie (Charles L.),
    127–129
Bryant, C. A. "Bert", 153
Buffalo National River, 235
Bureau of Land Management. See
    BLM
Bureau of Outdoor Recreation, 73

cabins, 150
    and cabin-bound women, 192
    as nuisances, 150
    ownership, 150
    removal, 185
    sanctuaries, 150

Caldwell, Bill, 91, 97–98, 102–105, 107–109, 111, 114, 119
Calico Bluff, 80, 82
Cameron, Robert, 56–58
Campbell, Robert, 14–15
Carmack, George Washington, 7, 9
Carmack, Kate, 7
Cassiar Creek, 27–29, 31
Catham Island, 70
Central, Alaska, 176, 179, 213
Chaco Canyon, 234
Chalkytsik, Alaska, 169
Chamberlain, Faye, 17, 214–218, 244
Charley Creek (Kandik River) band, 124
Charley River, 120, 136, 146, 162, 179–182, 185, 187–188, 228, 233, 241
Charley River Charlie. See Kidd, Charlie
Charley Village, 67, 154, 162
Chena River, 52, 157
Chester Bluff, 180
Chicken, Alaska, 126, 128
Chief Charley, 124, 154, 220
Chilkoot Pass, 34
Chilkoot Trail, 7, 38
chinook salmon. See king salmon
Christensen, Chris, 66
chum salmon, 19, 45, 193
Circle City, Alaska, 12–13, 16, 24, 35, 40, 60, 75, 136, 151, 157–159, 162–164, 168–169, 174–175, 178, 181–182, 187, 192, 199, 213, 215, 218, 221–222, 228–230, 232–233, 241
Clark, Lynette, 209, 228
Coal Creek (Alaska), 136, 195, 197

dredge, 197–198
mining camp, 146, 191
See also dredge (gold operations)
Coal Creek (Yukon), 40
Coghill, Jack, 204
Colben, Dan, 199, 200
Colville River, 15
Coming into the Country, 59, 83, 126, 137
See also, McPhee, John
commercial fishing, 107
Connette, Hank, 218
Cook, Ann (Dick's ex-wife), 92, 99
Cook, Captain James, 14
Cook, Dick, 89–121, 130, 139, 156, 180, 189, 210
Cook, John, 173
Corazza, Rich, 155
Coulter, Bill, 35
Countryside Initiative, 240
Crazy Man Island, 176
critical fire protection, 200
Cronin, William, 235
Cruickshank, Moses, 160
Cuyahoga River Valley National Park, 238

Dawson City, Yukon Territory, 1–2, 4, 6–13, 15–18, 20, 24–28, 30, 35–36, 38–44, 52–55, 86, 91, 121, 136, 140, 195, 207, 210, 214–215, 217–218
Deadwood Creek ("Hog-Um" Creek), 35
Debo, John, 238–241
Delta, Alaska, 70
Department of Environment, Yukon, 41, 44
Department of Fisheries and Oceans (Canada), 53, 58

departure from the mores of
modern society, 135
depopulation of the country,
171–172
Devinney, Eileen, 138, 152
DeWolfe, Percy, 25–30, 54, 69,
159, 220
Diamond Tooth Gertie, 2
dog team, 2, 27–28, 30, 35, 43, 82,
84, 87, 94, 99, 103, 106, 108,
132, 150–151, 157, 161, 174,
180, 190–191, 212, 215
Doyon, Ltd., 170, 172
Dozen Islands, 53
dredge (gold) operations, 197–200
buckets, 197
stacker, 198
trommel, 198
Drews, Max, 91, 93, 101, 109, 189
Drews cabin, 101–105, 111, 119
Duk-Rodkin, Allejandra, 23, 25

Eagle, Alaska, 13, 15, 18, 26–27,
30, 35–36, 40–43, 54, 60–62,
64–71, 75, 84–88, 91–92, 94,
99–100, 102–104, 108–111,
113–117, 119, 121, 123–126,
129–131, 136–137, 139, 142,
151, 153, 155–161, 163–168,
171, 177–178, 185, 190,
193–195, 222, 232, 241
alternative names, 68
regional homicide rate, 126
Eagle Jack, 124
Eagle Milk Kid. See Grinnell,
Willard
Ed Gelvin's A-frame, 180
Edwards, Charlie, 71
Edwards, Cheryl, 71
Eielson Air Force Base, 222

Eldorado Creek (Klondike region),
8
Emmonak, Alaska, 52
endangering public safety, 185
Environmental Conflict in Alaska,
211
Erickson, Oscar, 132
escapement. See salmon
Eureka Creek, 174, 199, 213, 215,
220
Evans, Dave, 125, 129–134,
137–138, 142, 144, 145–147,
152, 162–163, 169, 174, 185,
199
Everett Creek, 185–188
extirpation of local people, 241

Fairbanks, 7, 15, 24, 30, 37, 50,
60, 65–66, 74, 82, 96,
100–101, 109, 111, 114, 123,
127–128, 141, 144–145, 147,
157, 160, 164, 170, 176,
184–185, 190–194, 196, 199,
201–203, 207, 209–210,
212–213, 222–223, 232
Fairbanks Daily News-Miner, 230
Fanning Creek, 26, 54, 55
Fenton, Magistrate Judge Tom, 109
Fifteenmile River, 17, 23–25, 216,
218
geological history, 23–25
Fire Management Plan, 145
Fish boys, Al and Frank, 162
fishing, 212
fishing allocations in Canada, 44
fishwheel, 28, 46–48, 53, 57, 151,
212–214
Fleurant, Sylvain, 53
Flewelling, Frederick Fairweather, 9
Fliris, Bill, 47, 49–53

Fliris, Kathy, 49
Florian, Chris, 221, 227
forest fire of 1991, 228
forest fires, 146, 188
Fort Egbert, 68–69, 111, 195
Fort Reliance, 16–17, 31–32, 40, 67
Fort Selkirk, 41
Fort Yukon (Alaska), 159, 161–162, 184, 229–230
Forty Mile townsite (Yukon), 8, 26, 31–32, 34–40, 56, 86
    etiquette, 34
    unlearned lessons, 39
Fortymile River, 7, 16, 17, 31–33, 40, 126–127, 201
Fortymile site (Alaska), 213, 218
Fourth of July Creek, 141
    mines, 142
Fox, Kevin, 111–114, 117
Franklin, Howard, 32–33

Galena, 59, 122
Gates of the Arctic National Park, 113, 117
Gaudio, "Little John", 165–167
Gelvin, Ed, 178–180, 183
Gerberding, Tim, 40
giant (Pleistocene) beaver (*Castoroides ohioensis*), 42
Glacier National Park, 235
    hotel, 235
Glazunov, Andrei, 13
Glenn Creek, 70, 74, 147–148, 214
gold mining, capital-intensive, 198
Gold Placers, Inc., 195, 197–199
gold rush as mass hysteria, 38
Great Northern Railroad, 235
Great Smokey Mountains National Park, 235

Grinnell, Willard, 132, 144, 147, 162–165, 170, 184
Grizzly bear, 215–218
Gruening, Senator Ernest, 230
Guimond, Agata, 28, 30
Guimond, Cor, 27–30
gulls, 20
Gunderson, Morris, 165
Gundrum, Morris and Silas, 162–163, 165
Gwech'in Indians, 15, 228

Haines, John, 83, 134
Hajec, Pollack Joe (Joseph J.), 126–130, 141
Halfway House, Yukon Territory, 25
Hall, Scarlett, 109–110
Hall, Wayne, 104–105, 109–112, 116, 119–120, 124–125, 129
Han Indian people, 16, 20, 40, 61, 67–68, 87, 143, 155, 167
    language, 162
Hanna Creek, 146, 183
Hard Luck Creek fire, 142
Harper, Arthur, 16, 17, 32, 220
Havasupai Indians, 234
Henderson, Marsha, 111–112
Henderson, Robert, 7–8
Hickel, Walter, 204, 205
historic gravel rule, 196
historic nails rule, 196
historic structure rule, 147
historical archaeology, 138
Holbrook, Robert ("Sterling"), 111–114
Holder, Russ, 51
Honea, Don, 46
Hudson's Bay Company, 14–15, 228

Hunter, Torrie, 41, 44
Huntington, Sidney, 59
Hutchinson, Fred, 32, 33

Ichthyophonus hoferi, 49–53
Iditarod Sled Dog Race, 30, 46, 190
Independence, 40
Indian Field Days, 235
Indian Grave Creek, 163, 166, 170
Ivanov, Aleksey, 13
Ivy City, 40, 136, 142–143

Johnson Gorge, 143, 163, 165–166, 169–170, 174
    Johnson Gorge cabin, 166
Johnson, Albert, 189
Johnson, Sandy, 175, 189, 195
Judge Creek, 162, 166
    Judge Creek cabin, 169
Juneby, Willie, 84, 93, 121

Kaiyuh Flats, 122
Kallen, Karen, 170
Kandik River, 67, 70, 82, 124–125, 130, 132, 137, 143–144, 151, 154–156, 158–159, 162–171, 173–174, 176, 178, 186, 193, 195, 221, 223, 227, 233, 241
    See also Charley Creek; Chief Charley
Kathul Mountain, 149, 151
Kelly, Carolyn, 189–190, 194, 196
Kennicott, Robert, 229
Kidd, Charlie ("Charley River Charlie"), 180–182, 185, 187, 189, 191, 199, 214, 228
Kielland, Knut, 123

king salmon (chinook), 19, 44–45, 49, 51, 53, 58, 86, 105, 122, 159, 175, 193
King, Jim, 231
Klondike region, 1, 6–9, 12, 27, 34–35, 38–40, 54, 68, 135, 201
Klondike River, 8–9
Klondike stampede (1898), 6
Kneeland, Donna, 93
Kocan, Dr. Richard, 51–52
Koontz, David, 152–153
Koyukuk River, 12
Kwikhpak. *See* Yukon River
Kwikhpak, paleo-Yukon River, 25

Lake Bennett, 6
Lake Lindeman, 38
LaRouche, Lyndon, 232
Law of the North, 126
LeBlanc, Louise Profeit, 42
LeFevre, Dr., 147
Liard River, 14
lifeline of transportation, 136
Liken, Louie and Otto, 2
Limestone Hogback Ridge, 71
Lindauer, John, 204
lining canoes upriver, 62
Llewellyn Glacier, 11
Logan Creek, 186
Ludwig, Stefanie, 187

Mackenzie River, 15
Madison, Harry, 32
Mahalic, Dave, 206
mail carriers of the Yukon, 161
mail trail, 121, 123, 175, 189, 195
Malakof, Vassili, 14
malamute (breed of sled dog), 190
management by neglect, 239

Marshall, Alaska, 52

Marshall, Robert, 135

marten (American marten), 84, 92–97, 125, 162–163, 165–166, 174, 214–215

Matthews, Ted, 199

Mayo, Al, 16

McGregor, George, 182, 201

McMullin, Terry, 84–86, 101–104, 130

McPhee, John, 8, 59–60, 83, 89–90, 93–94, 105, 120, 126, 137, 155, 179, 180, 199, 202, 212, 232–233

McQuestin, Jack, 16, 32, 220

Mercier, Francois, 67, 229

military operating areas. *See* MOAs

Millard, Monty, 50

Miller, Arthur, 211

Miller, Frank Charles "Heinie," 87–88, 101, 120–121

Miller's Camp, 87–91, 119, 121, 156, 159

Milligan, Sean, 58, 243

Mills, Dave, 113, 185–186

The Misfits, 211

Mishler, Craig, 42

Mission Creek, 67–69

MOAs (military operating areas), 227–228

Montauk Bluff, 123

Montauk Mountain, 97

Montauk Roadhouse, 123

Moon, Charlie, 218

Moore, George, 190

Moore, Zach (George Moore and Carolyn Kelly's son), 192–194

Moosehide (Indian village), Yukon, 9

Mounties (RCMP), 1–2, 5, 9, 31

Murray, Alexander, 15, 229

Mustelidae (weasel family), 95

Napoleon Creek, 127

Nathaniel, John, 218

Nation Bluff cabin, 130, 131, 132

Nation City, 40, 136, 140–142

Nation River, 40, 70, 82, 91, 93, 103, 124, 126, 129–133, 136, 138, 140–146, 154, 159, 162, 233, 241

  fire of 1999, 145

National Appleman-Judd Award, 241

National Geographic Society, 181

National Historic Mining District, 200

National Park Service, 60, 64, 68, 73–76, 78, 79, 83, 85, 94, 98, 100, 103, 108, 111, 113–115, 117, 122, 129, 132–138, 142, 145–147, 149–153, 155, 156, 170–174, 179, 180–183, 185–188, 189, 193–202, 205, 218, 219, 227, 228, 233–236, 238–241

National Postal Museum (Smithsonian), 161

National Register of Historic Places, 187, 195

Native land claims, Canada, 43

Native people, 8, 44, 45, 68, 73, 93, 121, 122

  exclusion from parks, 234

Native subsistence traditions, 45

Native wisdom, 122

NATO war games, 222–223, 228

Navajo National Monument, 234

Nelson, Austin, 66

Nelson, Chris "Phonograph", 113, 129, 132–133, 138–140, 145–147, 162, 220, 243
New Yorker magazine, 60
Nibaw Zhoh, 67
Nigger Jim, 27
Night Island, 37
Ninth U.S. Circuit Court of Appeals, 206
noise and traffic, 193
Nome, 30, 68, 86, 158–159
North American pioneering, 135
North American Water and Power Alliance (NAWAPA), 232
North Country Challenge, 201
North West Mounted Police, 34
Northern Alaska Environmental Center, 189
Northern Commercial Company, 87–88, 158, 184
Nuklako, Yukon, 16
Nulato, Alaska, 14

O'Leary, Bill, Eddie, George, and Maurice, 157
Ogilvie Mountains, 23–24
Old Man Fanning, 54, 57
old trails, 133, 165
Old Yukon. See Wickersham, Judge James
Olson, Ed, 132, 162
oral history, 42, 68, 82, 87
oral tradition, 82, 230
overflow (water-on-ice hazard), 91, 97, 132, 150, 160, 164
Ozark Scenic Riverways, 134, 235

Palace Grand Theatre, 2
Palm, Johnny, 175
Parker, Harry, 144, 163–164

Pass Creek, 92–93, 99, 101, 103–105, 110–113, 116, 119
Patton, Sage, 129–130, 142
Patty, Dale, 199
Patty, Ernest, 197, 199, 200, 201, 211
Paul, Tony, 84
Payer, Dave, 96, 97, 243
Pelly River, 12
Percy DeWolfe Memorial Mail Race, 30
peregrine falcon, 138, 221–222, 225
  causes of mortality, 225
  monitoring, 224
  monitoring nests, 226
permafrost, 33, 93, 205
permits for everything, 194
Pickerel Slough, 71
The Pit "Beer Parlour" Dawson City, 4
Pollack Joe. *See* Hajec, Pollack Joe (Joseph J.)
pollution by large-scale mining, 199
Poppy Creek, 55
Porcupine River, 12, 15, 164, 229
Potts, Mike, 166, 190
Presley, Elvis ("Tagish Elvis") story, 4–5
programmatic agreement, 186
Prohibition (of alcohol in U.S. 1920–1933), 2, 140
Prudhoe Bay, 73
public use cabins, 188
Pyle, Ernie, 88, 120–21, 160

quaking aspen, *Populus tremuloides*, 23, 123, 203
  aspen leafout and black bears, 123

Rampart, 158, 159, 230
Rampart Dam proposal, 231
Rapids, the, 52
resident permits, 187
Reynolds, Cap, 189
Richard Smith's cabin, 215, 220, 228
Richards, Mark, 99, 101, 103
Richards, Mark and Lori, 177, 178
Ricketts, Larry, 156, 162, 193
right-of-succession disputes, 125
Ritchie, Bob, 136
rivals, word origin, 125
river-bound families, 192
roadhouses, 39, 76, 106, 136, 154, 159
Roberts, Lynette, 60, 61
Rock Creek, 143–147, 162–163
Roman, Walter, 205, 218
Ross, Ken, 211
Rourke, Mike, 16, 25, 53, 54, 67, 176
Royal Canadian Mounted Police (RCMP), 1
    See also Mounties (RCMP)
Russell, Earl David, 127, 128

salmon
    escapement, 51, 59, 105–106
    fry, mortality, 20
    harvest restrictions, 105
    tagging, 57–58
    See also chum salmon; king salmon
Sam Creek, 189, 191, 192, 195
Sarah (sternwheeler), 66, 151, 243
Schneider, Bill, 82
Schwatka, Lt. Frederick, 17, 31, 41, 67, 155, 229
Schwoyer, Ed, 128

secession from the United States, 204
Seiberling, Congressman John (OH), 239
Senate. See Shahnyaati'
Service, Robert, 3, 12
Seventymile, 40, 81, 84–86, 130, 136, 141
Seymour Lake, 148
"Seymour Stick," 115
Shade Creek, 71
Shahnyaati', 228–230
SHPO (state historic preservation office), 187
Sierra Club, 189, 194
Simeone, Bill, 42
Sixtymile River (Yukon), 17, 28
Skookum Jim (Mason), 7, 220
Slaven, Frank, 29, 146, 181, 189, 195–196
Slaven's Roadhouse, 29, 146, 181, 183, 189, 192, 195
smallpox quarantine (1902), 16
Smeagol, 167–170
Smith, Richard, 17, 199, 213–214, 216–219
Snow, Brad, 129–131, 155, 212
Snowy Mountain, 162
social experimentation, 135
Solomon, Paul, 162
sonic boom, 227
Sourtoe Cocktail, 2–3
Spence, Mark David, 234
Squatter Policy in the Yukon (book), 56
St. Barnabas Church, 9, 10
Star City, 40, 86, 136
state historic preservation office. See SHPO
Stefansson, Vilhjalmur, 14

Stevens, Art and Charlie, 93
Stevens, Silas, 87
Stevens, U.S. Senator Ted, 74
Stevenson, Captain Dick, 2
Stewart River, 12
  as they invest landscapes with
    value, 82–83
Stout, Al, 142, 144, 164
Stuck, Hudson, 68, 153–155, 160,
  220
subsistence, 44–45, 74–80, 85, 90,
  94–95, 98, 105–108, 110, 121,
  135–137, 150–151, 171–173,
  189, 212, 232–234
  elimination from parks and
    preserves, 233
  etiquette, 150
  in National Parks, 173
  lifestyle, 44, 75–76, 78, 94, 137,
    172, 233
  living argument, 232
  priority, 107
Summerville, Pete, 144, 162
Sundborg, George, 230–231
Sweeney, Mary Ann, 138, 152
Synge, J. M., 41

Tagish Charley, 7–8
Takhini River, 130–131
Taku River, 14
Tanana, Alaska (village), 11–12,
  46–47, 49, 52, 158–159
Tanana Flats, 223
Tanana River, 11, 13
Tatonduk River, 86–87, 89–93,
  101–104, 108–115, 117–119,
  121, 130, 189
Taylor Highway, 61, 128, 163
Taylor, Jim, 132, 141–243

Taylor, John, Mike and Tommy, 18
territoriality, 124
Teslin River, 12
Thoreau, Henry David, 134, 149
Tintina Trench, 25
Tolovana River, 190
trail routes, 113, 132
trails, 136
Trainor, Jean, 156, 193
trappers, 28, 41, 44, 60, 82, 132,
  147, 150, 156, 159, 162–163,
  165, 212
trapping, 3, 28, 43–44, 47, 61, 64,
  71, 74, 84, 93–94, 97–98, 125,
  127, 130, 133–134, 141, 145,
  150–151, 164–166, 174–175,
  184, 190, 193, 212, 214–215
Tr'ondek Gwech'in, 9, 19, 40, 44,
  55
Tr'ondek Gwech'in village, 9
Tr'ondek River, 9
Twelve-Mile (former Han Indian
  village), 20
Twelvemile River, 17
Twenty-Two Mile Roadhouse, 160
Tyrrell, Laurel, 176

U.S. Army, 39, 68, 230
  Corps of Engineers, 230
U.S. Fish and Wildlife Service,
  47–50, 73, 96, 108, 170, 222,
  227–228, 231
U.S. Forest Service, 73
U.S. National Park System, 238. See
  also National Park Service
U.S. Postal Service, 161
U.S. Supreme Court, 206
Ulvi, Dana, 61, 62
Ulvi, Steve, 60–64, 125, 166, 186

Underwood, Tevis, 47–48
University of Alaska, 82, 100, 123,
    136, 144, 170, 203

Van Bibber, Dan, 132
Vangel, Crane, 58
Vogler, Doris, 206, 210
Vogler, Joe, 201–211
von Wrangel, Ferdinand. See
    Wrangel, Baron Ferdinand von

Waldron, Jan, 70–72, 74, 148–149,
    166, 191
Waller, Sarge, 130, 155–156, 162,
    186
Waller's cabin, 156, 167
Wal-Mart, 211
war games, 221–224
warplanes,
    A–10 Warthogs, 222
    C–130s, 221, 224
    Jaguars, 222
    Toranados, 222
Washington Creek, 141, 146,
    151–152
    Roadhouse, 152
Webb, Melody, 67, 134, 142, 144,
    151–152, 158, 172–174, 184,
    188, 201
Webber Creek, 205–206
Welch, Jack and Kate, 200–201
West, Manfried ("Fred"), 207, 209
White, Sam, 141
White Pass and Yukon Railway,
    123, 197
White River, 11–12
Whitehorse, 5, 15–16, 27, 30, 52,
    130, 196–197, 206, 218

Wickersham, Judge James,
    123–124, 153–54, 161, 175
    Old Yukon (memoir), 124
Wild and Scenic Rivers designation,
    223
wildfire. See forest fires
Windfall Mountain, 121
Wolfe, Ernest, 199–200
Wood Islands, 87, 121
Woodchopper Canyon, 200
Woodchopper Creek, 202, 224
Woodchopper Roadhouse, 201
Woodchopper Smith, 200
The World Turned Upside Down
    (NPS report), 199
World War I, 140, 200
Worldwatch Institute, 211
Wrangel, Baron Ferdinand von, 13
Wrangell-St. Elias Mountains, 11,
    25

Yellowstone National Park, 234
Yosemite National Park, 235
Youcon. See Yukon River
Young, Congressman Don (AK), 74
Yukon Flats, 12, 24, 229–232
Yukon News, 4–5
Yukon Order of Pioneers, 2
Yukon Queen, 2, 5, 18, 20–21, 36
Yukon Quest Sled Dog Race,
    29–30, 176, 196
Yukon River
    geography, 10, 12–15
    geological history, 23
    geology, hydrology, 25
    origins, 10–11
    salmon run, 46
    steamboats (1867–1955), 6

Yukon River Commercial Fishing
    Association, 19
Yukon River Drainage Fishermen's
    Association, 50
Yukon Territory, 1, 4, 14, 30,
    55–56, 130, 196, 210, 215,
    220
Yukon: The Last Frontier, 144

Yukon-Charley Rivers National
    Preserve, 75, 80, 82, 85, 98,
    113, 137, 145, 171–172, 186,
    188, 194, 199, 206, 219, 223,
    227–228, 232–233, 236, 241
Yu-kun-ah. See Yukon River

Zagoskin, L. A., 14
Zuray, Stan, 46, 48–49